"A rose
—Ger...

. . . is a rose . . .

Speaking the language of roses:

Pink for simplicity and happy love; red for passion and desire; white for innocence and purity; yellow for jealousy and perfect achievement.

I have none of the tolerance rose devotees need for pampering and fussing. I have less patience with the chemicals rosarians seem to require to produce perfect, pest-free blossoms. Kate tells me there's a local belief that planting roses with a lump of fat or salt pork will . . . do what?—make them plumper, of course.

"Don't laugh," Kate says, "My mother planted them with goose grease. And she had wonderful roses, over by the barn and the well house."

They're still there. I know. I've pruned them. Their old stalks are so tough, I needed a saw.

There are roses in France, planted in the Middle Ages, still— *still*—going strong.

My roses are stock and proven varieties, hardy Max Graf, Spring Gold, Austrian Copper, rugosas.

By any name, they smell as sweet.

Jennifer Heath was born in Australia, raised in Latin America, and has lived and gardened the world over. Heath is the author of the novel *A House White with Sorrow* and the nonfiction books *Black Velvet: The Art We Love to Hate* and *On the Edge of Dream: The Women of Celtic Myth and Legend* (available in a Plume edition). She lives in Colorado.

The Echoing Green

The Garden in Myth and Memory

Jennifer Heath

A PLUME BOOK

PLUME
Published by the Penguin Group
Penguin Putnam Inc., 375 Hudson Street, New York, New York 10014, U.S.A.
Penguin Books Ltd, 27 Wrights Lane, London W8 5TZ, England
Penguin Books Australia Ltd, Ringwood, Victoria, Australia
Penguin Books Canada Ltd, 10 Alcorn Avenue, Toronto, Ontario, Canada M4V 3B2
Penguin Books (N.Z.) Ltd, 182–190 Wairau Road, Auckland 10, New Zealand

Penguin Books Ltd, Registered Offices: Harmondsworth, Middlesex, England

First published by Plume, a member of Penguin Putnam Inc.

First Printing, March, 2000
1 3 5 7 9 10 8 6 4 2

Ⓟ REGISTERED TRADEMARK—MARCA REGISTRADA

LIBRARY OF CONGRESS CATALOGING-IN-PUBLICATION DATA:

Heath, Jennifer
    The echoing green : gardens in myth and memory / Jennifer Heath.
        p.   cm.
    Includes bibliographical references (p. 248).
    ISBN 0-452-28166-0
    1. Gardening—Anecdotes.   2. Gardens—Anecdotes.   3. Gardeners—Anecdotes.
    4. Heath, Jennifer..   I. Title.
SB455.H46   2000
635—dc21   99-047574

Printed in the United States of America
Set in Bembo
Designed by Eve L. Kirch

For these, who are my teachers and friends:
Rickie Solinger, Nancy Robertson, Marda Kirn,
Jeanie Weiffenbach, Norene Berry, Lucy Lippard,
Susan Edwards, and Dennis Robertson

for Clara Redmond,
who tried without much success to teach me to
"stop and smell the roses,"

and in loving memory of
Eloise Wilson and Bernice Wright

... there never was a world for her
Except the one she sang and, singing, made.

—Wallace Stevens, "The Idea of Order at Key West"

CONTENTS

PREFACE

I love to get my hands and feet in the dirt, but if it were not for mythology, folklore, and fairy tales I wonder if I would garden at all, at least with the kind of fanaticism and fantasy I apply to it.

This book is an exploration of how and why I step into the garden and stay there, some days from dawn to dusk. One of the most vital "whys" is the attachment I've had all my life to story and sacred text.

This book is also an examination of those things, past and present, that make the garden a divine and interesting place. Thus, it's written in an associative style, part memoir, part family anecdotes, part gardening history, past cosmology—a mosaic of inquiries about where the garden *comes from* and what makes gardens sacred, historically, mythologically, and within the soul of the individual gardener. In this case, I am that individual gardener, but readers I hope will absorb this book from their own points of view.

The garden is soil and seed, water and work, and it is also ritual. Many of the world's gardens are designed around legends and myths, spiritual and sometimes political. Some, such as Japanese gardens in the Shinto tradition, are linked to the founding of a faith. Loosely speaking, my garden is, too.

I wrote this book as a means of thinking about how I, with thirty years of gardening experience, fit into *that* big picture. A big picture, such as history, is collaged of large and small details and relationships, just like a garden.

The Earth, it's often said, is a garden, and gardening affirms that Nature is bountiful. This book is constructed of cultural memory, ancient to recent. Cultural memories—unearthed as cosmology, mythology, history, and personal experience—are every gardener's lineage. It's intriguing that we can each call on many worlds of gardens past and bring that much choice into our contemporary space, then make these ideas truly our own.

Cultural memory is quickly disappearing under the weight of television, shopping malls, and wanton destruction of Nature. Yet whether we realize it or not, each time we plant a seed, we are rebelling against materialism and the loss of Soul. We are preserving and nurturing an undogmatic, universal energy and Presence, honoring that which is truly divine—Nature. A little bit with every seed.

Seed by seed, we join "The Ecchoing Green," which the English poet William Blake so eloquently named in *Songs of Innocence*, a vision of life seen through childlike, trusting, natural eyes. It is one of his first "illuminated paintings," created in 1789.

> *The Sun does arise,*
> *And make happy the skies.*
> *The merry bells ring*
> *To welcome the Spring.*
> *The sky-lark and thrush,*
> *The birds of the bush,*
> *Sing louder around,*
> *To the bells chearful sound.*
> *While our sports shall be seen*
> *On the Ecchoing Green.*

Green is our salvation. In green we find playfulness, clarity, honesty, beauty, and freedom, key ingredients toward discovering the essential Self. Even as this Paradise called Earth is paved, even as we crowd into asphalt jungles, it is the green—in parks or in planters on windowsills—that anchors us. Deprived of it, we grow bitter and cynical, the Self withers and takes everything else down with it. The Self can flourish only in a larger—green—context.

When horticulture began, gardeners and farmers were interchangeable, synonymous. References in Egyptian papyri are made, for example, to *gardens* of barley. In modern China, fields are called "gardens." They are manageable; they are not monocultures. "Gardening is the noblest of callings," wrote the Roman poet Horace, himself a gardener/farmer.

Even after gardening was established, early horticultural societies continued hunting and gathering for a long time. As horticulture turned to agriculture—a larger, more single-minded endeavor—a new politics of power took shape. Yet beliefs, rites, and celebrations—from Yule logs to scarecrows, from corn funerals to fertility festivals—remained common to both, in some places right into the middle of the twentieth century. Today's agribusiness not only depletes the soil, pollutes the air and is hazardous to every living thing, it steals our cultural memories. It silences the green; it replaces innocence with ignorance.

Even the word *green* has been coopted, as with "green advertising," which exploits our increasing concerns about the ecology. Gardening can address these concerns and the problem. We can't and never will have control over Nature—it's past time to give up that notion—but having assertion over the garden helps us reconcile what we believe to be our helplessness in the face of Nature—the source of our violence against Nature.

Thousands of gardeners have taken on the tasks of stewardship, preserving untainted, as well as ancient and rare seeds otherwise lost to development, monoculture, and genetic tampering. The statistics are frightening and more is lost daily. These gardeners constitute a growing movement—whose activities, information sharing, and seed exchange programs can be found, among other places, on the Internet—but much, much more is needed if we are to save fast-disappearing plant life on Earth.

This book is about place. Its diverse elements are probes, sometimes tentative, into how gardens inform our sense of space and belonging on the Earth.

I grew up moving from country to country on an average of every three years. Wherever we lived became instantly and truly *home,* and home was always centered around the garden. As I wrote this book, I realized how thoroughly our daily lives, the domestic details within the house and family rituals, depended on the garden. Gardens provide and illuminate our place now, our place past and future, our place in the cosmos.

My garden is my personal paradise—something every gardener feels. It presents me here and now with all the gifts promised in Paradise. It also reflects my itinerant heart and mind. Here, I've developed a sense of place that is *many* places, real and imagined.

This book is also about art: the garden as a time-honored art form. Art for me *is* a place. Like most gardeners, I'm a highly visual person. This is no surprise, since my eyeballs have been crammed with fabulous sights since I was a child. I studied art and in my day job I work as an art and theater critic for newspapers, so that I'm constantly exposed to artists and their processes. As a gardener, I'm inspired by dancers, dramatists, poets, and performance and visual artists, particularly those who make "ephemeral," Earth-, or ecology-based work. It's as if those artists not only give me permission to manifest outlandish ideas in my garden, but they have taught me ways I can do so, as well. From the beginning, horticulture and the arts have been entwined.

(I refer in this book to "gardeners" and "gardenists." In my mind, the gardener performs more or less intuitively, artistically. The gardenist uses more calculated, formal methods, is perhaps more material and "scientific.")

Nature poetry has existed both outside and within the garden since writing was invented. Alphabets were once considered sacred, the words they formed like flowers or fruit. I've peppered this book with old and new poems and some prose about Nature, as well as ancient prayers and incantations. Various nursery rhymes here began life as word charms to raise and command the spirits of the garden, the soul of the green. Where no sources are cited, the poet, rhymer or originator of the verse has disappeared into the anonymity of oral tradition.

*   *   *

A friend once noted that there are "garden people" and there are "plant people." Combine these two qualities—both can be *cultivated*—and you've got those amazing miracle workers such as Tasha Tudor, Lauren Springer, and Thalasa Cruso, whose instructive books are gardening bibles.

I fall headlong into the first category. I am "garden people." While I love plants, it's the lore of plants, the staging of plants, the mythological environment I create that motivate me. I am too restless, too absentminded, too unspecific to be "plant people." Though there are a hundred or more different kinds of plants thriving (or struggling) in my garden, I still confuse "pistils" with "stamens" and must consult a dictionary every time these words come up.

True plant people possess a kind of solid contentment, concentration, wisdom, and vision that I can't claim. This statement would seem to contradict the profound joy and spiritual satisfaction I get from my garden, but there's really no conflict. This is one place and one activity where I can transcend my grasping desire to find "happiness," an illusive and sometime thing at best, never guaranteed for long. It is not that I don't carefully study what each plant needs to survive and prosper; it is merely that I have no head for botany.

The women gardeners of the late nineteenth and early twentieth centuries—among them Gertrude Jekyll, Vita Sackville-West, Ellen Wilmott, Frances Hope, Beatrix Farrand, and even Beatrix Potter—produced the first gardening literature I read from my mother and grandmother's shelves.

Although I've not inherited the mantles of these women gardeners (I'm a fabler, not a professional gardening writer), I did inherit their books. Their gardens, like mine, were their domains, where they found a natural tableau in which to express all their imaginings and artistic impulses, as well as their considerable scientific and technical skills. In their writings and their garden designs, the mythological references that were then popular abound—usually classical Greek myth and fairy lore, often expressed in heated romantic terms. Some were "plant people," some were "garden people." All thought not only about landscape design, planting, pruning, and so on, but about the poetry and meaning of gardens.

All believed in the application of their labor for a higher purpose, and I do, too. But as I've become a more confident gardener, I've given myself carte blanche to be utterly idiosyncratic and eccentric. The styles, preferences, and aesthetics of these marvelous women hold less and less interest for me. Their aesthetics were, of course, informed by their place (usually England or the American Northeast) and their time.

At some point—having established my domain—my gardening concerns veered away from these influences. Instead, I now seek primal models. My own no-holds-barred imagination is also my guide. And I look for inspiration to the gardens I grew up with in the so-called Third World. My cultural memory resides less on the lavish grounds of Sackville-West's Sissinghurst Castle, Ferrand's Dumbarton Oaks or in Jekyll's genteel suburban gardens, than in the marigold fields and cemeteries of Mexico, the potato beds of Inishmore, or the Altiplano and the ancient palace gardens of the emirs of Central Asia.

The garden's shape is created by the gardener's memories, background, necessities, and worldview. In many of the world's cosmologies, human life or essential aspects of human societies begin in a garden. What makes the garden sacred is determined ultimately in the heart of the gardener and realized in loam, sand, clay, manure, and compost; in scent, texture, and color; in flowers, vegetables, and trees; among the wild creatures who inhabit or visit the garden; and in the garden's relationship to the wilderness. In some faiths, the garden is our reward after death. Gardens are perpetual realms of art and spirit, cyclical weavings in which space and time are warp and weft.

Is it any wonder, then, that there are now approximately 77 million gardeners in the United States alone?

All human beings have, I think, an abiding need to work with our hands—I don't mean typing at a keyboard or making the same fitting on a production line eight hours a day. No labor is really "humble," in the demeaning, servile sense of the word, unless the worker is tyrannized by profiteers. But the hands bring humility—

and liberation—by way of creativity, modesty, respect, and simplicity.

Hands, unlike the mind, are conduits of the soul. Hands are generative. The mind turns back endlessly on itself, too frequently perverted by ambition, analysis, lists, vanity, trivialities, *wants*. Hands respond primarily to *need*.

The hand is among the most significant and ubiquitous images in human iconography. Its gestures have infinite meanings. In Mesoamerica, the image of an open hand signifies magnetism, attracting higher powers into ourselves. The same principle is at work in religious services where hands are uplifted, spread wide, waving in ecstasy. In ancient Egypt, images of the disembodied hand meant, among other things, charity and planting.

Working with our hands is an unconditional invitation to the divine; it unburdens the spirit and offers immeasurable satisfaction. Perhaps this—and the green that echoes in memory and in our unconscious—is why we're experiencing an unprecedented reawakened passion for gardens. Why the post–World War II American longing for a suburban "estate"—"a man's home is his castle"—symbolized by acres of chemically maintained Kentucky bluegrass (on prime growing land or precious wilderness), is slowly giving way to trees and to flower, vegetable, and herb gardens. Why residents of suburbs and cities are creating water, sculpture and mural, xeric, and wildflower gardens. Why pots of petunias and ivy flood apartment balconies. Why battalions of neighbors attempt to reclaim strips of land between buildings in slums, not as parks, but as gardens, where there is familiarity, chores are ongoing, hands producing food and grace, triumph, in the midst of pollution and poverty.

Those gardens, of course, feed the soul of a community . . . which brings us inevitably back to a sense of place. Community gardens worldwide are increasingly threatened. We have witnessed this recently in New York City, where more than a hundred community gardens have been under the gun, and gardens are bulldozed daily from Bangladesh to Buenos Aires to make way for factories or housing projects. Community gardens upset the status quo and the—very little—space they use, particularly in cities, infringes on the pursuits of capitalism.

The recent gardening explosion mirrors our search for a renewal of the sacred in Nature, a yearning for wonder, the fanciful and fantastic beyond our mortality, as well as the visceral necessities, like working with our hands.

This book will give you little or no instruction about gardening techniques, plans, or designs. You might glean a few useful tricks or ideas, but my methods are idiosyncratic. I recommend you get a second opinion. What works in my yard may not work in others. Gardening seems to be a remembered activity for me. I have no formal training. I've learned new things by reading gardening history, but especially by word of mouth. It is time spent digging, planting, watering, fertilizing, and composting, time spent *in* dirt and among leaves and petals, seeds and sprouts that has led me this far. Even my failures are fascinating, edifying, and beautiful, never really *failures* at all.

In 1752, the Georgian calendar, the "New Style," replaced the Julian and eleven days were dropped from the year. The traditional garden calendar is still usually based on the "Old Style." For the most part, this book honors the Old Style and is divided into four seasons, then split into months within each season. I begin with Winter, a natural new year for most horticultural people. In November, gardens in the northern hemisphere die, and the process of rest and regeneration begins anew. Winter is a time of reflection, ideas, dreaming, and magic creeping around in the shadows and begging to be examined before being let into the light of spring to grow. Spring is dazzling, beguiling, enchanting. The heart is revitalized, sings and zings in merry May, lusty and fertile. Yet there are years when I am most charmed by August, the time of reaping and harvest, a month strong on *love*—mother love, Earth love, spiritual love.

It will make no difference what region or zone you live in, for this book ranges from ancient Egypt to modern Mexico, skims above and below the equator with stopovers in the tropics or the Arctic. Most of the personal gardening experiences described here—culled from my journal—take place, however, in Colorado, where I've now lived the longest and built the most extensive garden. Gardeners unfamiliar with the vicissitudes of the Colorado climate may be surprised by the timing of certain blooms, fruits and vegetables. Some plants that are invasive in humid climates behave modestly here, while plants which apparently comport themselves well elsewhere become aggressive trespassers in this environment. It's said that in Colorado we have all the seasons and that they often occur on the same day. What's more, they don't necessarily happen in the conventional seasonal order! The variations can be confusing. For example, peaches from the Western Slope of Colorado begin showing up in the markets toward the end of July, but mine don't ripen till late August or early September. Everything seems to depend on location. Within my garden there are at least two microclimates, where seasonal changes take place as much as a month apart.

This book is about the garden as healer and holy. About the garden as it unifies us with time and place, unifies Earth with the divine. The garden won't cure every ill, but taken in all its aspects it can go far toward making us healthy in spirit, mind, and body. It is not a panacea, but it comes close.

Prologue:

A Tour

Each spring and summer morning, I roll out of bed and head first for my bedroom window. There I have a full view of my crowded garden. I rub the sleep out of my eyes, blink, and survey the yard, as if I were looking at an Asian scroll painting in which every wonderful detail comes alive with equal value in equal proportion.

I'm hardly the mistress of all I survey. Each morning there's inevitably havoc wreaked by raccoons in the night: stones overturned, food floating in the pond, a set of beads I left on the patio table now hanging from a tree branch.

I stumble downstairs, step out the back door, and head for the pond, clutching coffee, papers, and books. I cross the patio, inhale deeply at the culinary herb garden. I mince onto the dewy grass path in bare feet, touch the apple tree for luck, then duck under the clothesline. I stop to inspect the poppy-tansy-rose garden and consider what's sprouted or needs special attention today. At last, I'm warming my toes on the pond's sandstone verandah, where I salute the goldfish—and the waterlilies if they're blooming.

I settle at a table in the little pavilion we named the Fiesta Dinner Theatre and try to work awhile. Once I allow myself to begin the transcendent tasks of gardening, it's almost impossible to stop.

From this vine-covered hideaway tucked into one end of the old red shed, I glance up and over a planter of petunias or geraniums, through a drapery of grape, clematis, and morning glories to yet another curtain of silverlace vine. In late summer, these clouds of tiny white blooms are slathered high up the telephone pole in the alley, a doily foreground to my view of the Rocky Mountains.

At night, we sit on a bench at the pond's opening, listening to the "waterfall" splatter and splash from a bamboo pipe. Here is the Moon Garden. This year, a datura shoots pungent fragrance into the dark, while its white trumpet flowers mirror moonlight.

In the morning, the datura naps. The rising sun washes the cottage garden outside the Dinner Theatre, illuminating larkspur, love-lies-bleeding, cosmos, feverfew, coneflower, roses, yarrow, daisies . . .

I'm restless now and coffeed up. I secure my books and papers against breezes, meander into the glorious strangle of cottage garden blooms along a stone and plank path to the vegetable bed, which this years hosts squash, tomato, marigold, and parsley. A tall ceramic vase, glazed with calligraphic bamboo designs, long-ago broken and glued, upholds a rotary sprinkler, part of the Rube Goldberg "system" I've jury-rigged with hoses threaded throughout the yard.

If it's late May or early June, when irises are the dominant beauty front and back, the flower patch just to the side of the vegetables effervesces with fleshy poppies and Chinese and "Sarah Bernhardt" peonies, like red and pink cannonballs. There's no such thing as "enough" when it comes to iris, poppies, or peonies.

If it's later in the season, this flower bed will have transformed to clumped or spikey blooms—the yellows of goldenrod, gaillardia, and mums.

Anything goes in the central vegetable bed, including flowers. It was dug smack into the middle of the lawn, obliterating the last expanse of Kentucky bluegrass, and is bounded by sea lavender, lunaria, Russian sage, scabiosa, and speedwell. Irises and Provence lavender are good guardians of corners that are always in danger of mashing by feet or wheelbarrows.

Thin gladiolus blades push through the soil, strays I missed when I transplanted, divided the bulbs, and moved them to a bed where they could be staked to bedposts, metal head- and footboards I scavenged long ago.

Across the lawn path is another raised garden, skirted with purple alyssum, where I favor low-lying vegetables, salad greens or ful-some cabbages, as well as basil and cilantro.

In May, during the great bird migrations, if I wake early enough, I take myself, my coffee, and my books to the tea house in our En-chanted Garden, where I watch for warblers or flycatchers darting around the pear tree, the grapes, the columbine, sweet woodruff, and Kate's Pond. There are two ways to enter the Enchanted Garden, but my favorite route is through the bower of plum trees that make up the Faux Forest. If there's been rain, the forest floor hosts tawny mushrooms.

On either side of my house are turn-of-the-century homes like mine, converted to accommodate tenants, usually students. (Ours may be the only remaining single-family house on the block.) This turns out to be fortunate. The landlords have been decidedly absent and there are no neighboring gardeners to fuss at my transgressions and my trespassing.

On the east, the landlord planted too many pine trees too close and neglected to water them. All but one are dead. Their carcasses support the Enchanted Garden grapevines. We are separated mainly by my plum trees. Until recently, I'd never met anyone in that house, nor ever so much as laid eyes on its owner. Occasional property managers disappeared by the end of lawn-mowing season.

To the west, the landlords allowed the garden to turn to dust. But it is in this west-side house that Susie Next Door lives (so dubbed, because that's how she identifies herself on the telephone). When Susie moved in, her vivid energy transformed the neighborhood.

By June, all evidence of the yellow and orange Emperor tulips fronting the Faux Forest have disappeared under a spreading carpet of violets. Lately, my morning meanderings take me straight past that glade, past a border of rue, garden sage, comfrey, coral bells, peony, and lavender, to the new rock gardens, terraced hillock, and fern-and-hosta berm. I stare at the expanse, trying to decide whether to add a curved, shredded bark trail to echo the one in the Enchanted Garden and whether blue flax might be a sparkling, airy addition to the feathery ferns and complement to the broad hosta leaves.

From here, I'm led past more irises, climbing roses, honeysuckle, a rowan tree, and Austrian and mugho pines to the cool, sheltered front yard hedged with Persian lilacs and Mongolian apricots. Here is the scented medicinal herb garden with dog and apothecary roses and field lilies amid carpets of ivy and vinca cut through by paths that proceed to a knee-high flagstone wall drowned in succulents.

Between the sidewalk and the street, I've planted my only truly "xeric" garden. In spring, it presents astonishing variations of green sprouting from silver groundcover. But by late summer, this "water-wise" garden is scraggly. Gardening with plants native to this arid climate presents a continuous, often frustrating challenge to me and now I sit awhile on the front steps considering what to plant—or remove—in order to maintain its beauty through the hot, dry late summer months.

The front yard is more formal than the rest of the garden, less needful of my attention. Nonetheless, it's such a cacophony of greenery, it's erased the house numbers as if we had no address but sprang magically out of the ground. The excessive growth absorbs traffic noise. When I'm ready to breakfast, I often do so on the porch, where Canadian hemlock, old-fashioned lilac, and a mock orange dart over the porch railing. Ivy creeps onto the porch floor. This is the closest I've yet got to a space that is simultaneously indoors and out, a garden room, where we're sheltered from the elements, yet thoroughly embraced by vegetation.

I complete my morning circle along the cobbled path in the corridor between Susie's and my houses; under crab apples, which in heavy bloom recall the Japanese cherry blossom festivals of my childhood; through the gate to the shady fern and plumbago garden, where I adjust the willful woodbine climbing the fence.

I retrieve my books and my coffee cup, cross the yard with big strides, and plunge back through the climbing roses into the house. In no time, I'm out of my nightgown and into my gritty gardening gear.

The garden I traverse for inspection each morning is a map of my mind and a topography of my "gypsy" upbringing.

My father was an American diplomat. My grandparents were immigrants to the United States from Ireland and Denmark, and I have relatives, as well as close, extended family around the world.

Readers will encounter some of my (over)population of aunts and uncles, including my mother's brothers, O'Shea, O'Malley, O'Conor, and O'Hara. The Oh's, as we called them. My grandmother's Irish chauvinism came up short when she had girls to name. My mother was called Genevieve and her twin was Augusta. Emmaline died before I was born.

All families have a few sour pickles, but mostly, I adored my aunts and uncles. My Aunt Kate was always closest to me, my best friend from childhood.

I, too, am an immigrant—behind the beat—having settled in the United States only after I was grown. When I was a child, we visited the States periodically on home leave, and one year we lived in a rental house in Washington, D.C., while my father did something mysterious and possibly sinister at the State Department.

I was born in Australia and grew up in Japan, Bolivia, Colombia, India, Afghanistan, Spain, and Switzerland, where my parents sent me during a particularly difficult period of my adolescence. At the chateau-style girls' boarding school in Montreux, I learned two things about the garden: how to climb the high, thorn-covered wall to brief freedom and trysts with my boyfriends and where to hide with the other girls to sneak a smoke.

Wherever we lived, we had all the fancy amenities of diplomatic life in the 1950s and '60s, including a gardener. (The whiplash between living abroad and living in the States was known as "going from mink to sink.")

My mother wouldn't have been caught dead in the kitchen interfering with the cook, but she was glued to the gardener. At dawn, she stumbled into the yard in rags and tatters, wearing a wide, shedding straw hat she'd got in Japan, and worked side by side with the gardener, often infuriating him, but also laughing and chatting.

Shortly before noon, she reemerged, dressed to the nines in Chanel and pillbox, ready for luncheon and other official functions. From that magic moment on, she was no longer our gardener's dirt-smeared field hand, but a princess. A Cinderella.

Gardening was my mother's art form as it is mine. I don't know, however, that she actually thought of it as an art. Yet it was one of the few activities in her subsumed life that she had for herself alone.

She was not humble about much, but about the garden she was modest and eager to listen and learn. No doubt gardening provided a kind of therapy for her, as it does for us all. And I believe, though she would never have said so, that gardening for my mother was a spiritual practice.

My family participated enthusiastically and as fully as seemed appropriate in the native customs and holidays of the countries where we lived, but my mother, a lover of ritual and theater, also went to great lengths to preserve—and embellish upon—the traditions with which she'd been reared. Doing so, she linked our tiny traveling troupe to a larger world of ancestors we might otherwise have known little about and to family we rarely saw, but to whom she hoped we'd be tied by these rites. Without that bond, we were in danger of becoming psychically unanchored.

Ours were not for the most part religious celebrations. Rather, our family rituals were associated with the garden, the gardening calendar, and the cycle of birth, growth, and death that is so immediately apparent in the garden.

Instead of pounding religion into my head, my mother taught me, primarily by example, to garden. How to do it and more important, to love doing it. Out of gardening came faith and devotion and a fundamental belief in Nature as the divine.

My mother was a cross between a farmer-gardener and a gentle-woman-gardener. The "shanty Irish" people she came from planted practical culinary gardens. But my mother loved beauty . . . and she was ambitious to rise in the world and "make a good impression."

In my Irish family, awareness of garden lore was essential to success. You had to know not only when and how to plant something, but whether it attracted spirits, was auspicious or unfortunate, as well as its history in the context of folklore, magic, and everyday cooking and medicinal uses.

I have always had some version of a garden, even when I was very small. In the years when I first left home all I had were barred windows in flats in New York, Washington, and Boston. I yearned for something green, longed for some territory where I could, without inhibition, create my own outdoor world and traverse it with bare feet. My solution was to "squat." I blithely took over bare spots in apartment complex courtyards, weeded or planted in existing, institutional beds, dug around and tossed seeds in empty lots or planted, in secret corners, little trees I snagged from acquaintances or got at Arbor Day giveaways. Today, friends and many others labor to reclaim burned-out city lots as gardens or to save community gardens in danger of obliteration from developers or soulless politicians.

When I was a city gardener, I hung as many planters as I could fit over grimy windows, and pushed shelves full of plants against the glass. I installed grow lights and heaters. Once, on the advice of an electrician from Tennessee, I planted tomatoes upside down in hanging pots and actually got a fruit or two, before the whole rigamarole got so heavy it crashed, taking a chunk of ceiling with it. I've got friends who can grow anything anywhere, and though they may hunger for a bit of real land, they have managed to transform balconies into gardens and apartments into greenhouses. Most of my efforts, I'm afraid, were, as they say, "the triumph of hope over experience." Indoors, my green thumb shrivels.

My first grown-up, full-out garden was on a farm in central Pennsylvania. The politics I had embraced living abroad seemed to be manifest in the hippie movement, and I dived right in. After a few years of urban activism, I went "back to the land" . . . acres and acres of land I had no idea what to do with and no gardener. I had been coddled by people who did all the hard, physical work for us, so for a time I was brought up short.

On the farm, there were cows, chickens, goats, and pigs; an orchard; and almost a full acre of vegetable garden. It was tough going. Yet it was a splendid time and I was earnest and very young with two very young children, one of whom I often carried on my back as I labored. Oh, if only our gardeners in Kabul or Tokyo or Bogotá had seen me then! I had become a faux *campesina*.

I rototilled and weeded and milked and chopped wood and carried water, canned, and even learned to quilt. I built rickety trellises for hundreds of tomato plants, beans, and peas, and experimented with Ruth Stout-ish ideas such as growing potatoes under piles of newspapers. There were still scraps of the *Philadelphia Inquirer* floating around the grounds and in the stream when we left for Colorado for a "real" job. That is, a job that came with a *real* paycheck.

In Boulder, we moved into this house. Twenty-year-old photos bear witness to the parched, yellow, and hard-packed yard. I often broke down trying to break ground.

But a few years after we moved here, we divorced and I became the primary support of my two kids. The garden became moot as well as mute. I had no spare moments.

In my first years of single motherhood, my pal Jimmy and I put together a landscaping business we called Green Goddess Yard Dressing. Seasonal work comprised mainly of raking gravel, mowing lawns, and laying sod, work that had to be supplemented in winter with waitressing and freelance reporting until I landed a full-time job on a newspaper. Looking back from middle age, I can hardly believe that Jimmy and I actually performed such daring feats as climbing cottonwood trees to prune them barefoot with chainsaws. Where did I get such foolish courage? (In fact, our leathery soles, cleated with calluses, probably saved us from falling.) I had, after all, always wanted to be a pirate.

There was no time for my own garden, but I taught my kids the absolute essentials, such as how to find fairy rings and make poppy and hollyhock dolls, although there was no time to plant poppies or hollyhocks. My parents visited often and planted them for me, then worried that I'd let the flowers die. Luckily, you can't kill a poppy or a hollyhock.

I remarried. My children grew up and went their ways. Suddenly, with frantic energy and enthusiasm, I made up for lost time. I'd once stood with my mother in Jordan looking in awe—and some horror—at Israel. We stood on hot desert sand—where what little water there was had been siphoned away—and gazed at a green and fertile field, which stopped at a ditch with a barbed-wire fence and a sign: Welcome to Israel—HALT!

Israeli-Palestinian politics notwithstanding, I never lost that picture. I decided that I, too, could turn my desert into a lush paradise.

WINTER

November

SEASON'S THRESHOLD

I have news for you:
the sea runs high, the stag bells;
the bracken's red, shriveled, and shapeless.
The wild goose cries.
Cold seizes her wings.
Season of ice, high wind, low sun.
Summer has gone.
This is my news.

—Irish, ninth century, author unknown

Snow on November Eve

Snipping twigs. Tidying up before the Halloween storm.

I picked the three pumpkins and a pair of cabbages somehow overlooked in last week's gathering. The Russian kale, though it'll be tough and only suitable for a soup or two, can hold out against the coming cold—at least a little while. I planted cosmos with the kale this year. Blue-green leaves with lavender stripes against the tissue-pink blooms. Wide, rumpled foliage in stunning contrast to feathery leaves. Now the tall cosmos stands are tangled and withering, stalks hardening to sticks.

The collards are long gone, boiled into stew with black-eyed peas.

The veil between the worlds is visible. The echo of death is everywhere this morning. The lighthearted atmosphere of the garden has become, not gloomy or solemn, but honest in its admission of mortality, its need to disappear and rest. Death is never so obvious as in the waning garden.

Tonight, the dead, the ancestors, ghosts and demons, spirits and fairies will let loose upon the world and roam the garden. Clumped seeds hang from the hollyhocks, so heavy they drag the ground. The seeds sliced perfectly within the flat, round pod are another miracle of cosmic mathematics, Earth geometry.

The autumn gilt of the rabbitbrush has lost its vibrancy. Chrysanthemums, gaillardia and rudbeckia, a yellow rose, one ivory foxglove, and an odd marigold or two were fueled by Indian summer and have braved chilly October nights, but this, surely, is their last day. I pick a ragtag, farewell bouquet for the dinner table.

The flat leaves of the glade violets are yellowed; the creeping phlox between the path stones is blackened by chill.

Tiny ice floes in the big pond. Goldfish pile into a tight, sunny corner. The water irises droop like broken umbrellas. Within the week the pond will be frozen. I refresh it, then toss a log in the water to create an airhole for oxygen so the fish will survive the winter.

I remember on November Eve we sat around the table—my mother, my brother, and me—rolling balls of flour, water, and millet seeds. Into each ball we pressed a message to a deceased relative on tightly folded paper:

"Dear Grandpa, hope you're doing well, wherever you are, I'm fine"; "Dear Granny, please don't let Senator Joe McCarthy find out Daddy was a Young Socialist in college" (that one dictated to me by my mother); "Dear Uncle O'Conor, you were funny, my favorite uncle next to Tío Yomi. Why did you die? That was silly of you. We miss you. Mama says I can have your watch someday"; "Dear Tooth Fairy, I forgot to thank you for the quarter you left me" (to my brother, all fairies looked alike).

At twilight, we three dashed into the garden, scrambled around the trees, and balanced the seed balls in the boughs, sort of the obverse of the Easter egg hunt. The dead, my mother told us, would send their messengers, the crows and ravens, to carry our greetings to the departed.

*   *   *

The ancient Celts called Halloween *samhain,* the last harvest and the new year. Christianity supplanted *samhain,* as well as the ancient Roman Egyptian harvest/new year customs and replaced them with All Hallows Eve, All Saints Day, and All Souls Day. These are the days to remember our ancestors, whose lives depended on their relationship with the Earth, a relationship that evoked ritual and ceremony at each arc in the horticultural calendar.

Gardens began around 8000 B.C.E., when the first gathered seeds were planted in an organized, protected fashion to provide a steady food supply and as a defense against Nature's apparent whims. In the garden, the randomness of death can be contained, controlled by the gardener's art. Ceremonies ensured the largesse of the seeded land.

In Mexico, these are Days of the Dead. In India, the Festival of Deepawali. In Finland, the Feast of Kauri was celebrated, when ancestors' ghosts were invited into the house and a sheep slaughtered. In Lithuania, the spirits were entertained with scraps of food called "death gifts" tossed under the table at dinner.

November is one of four liminal months, with February, May, and August—threshold months containing both seasons, during which seasonal activities and tasks are split. Most agrarian cultures celebrated more than one new year, based on harvest and planting times. The sun's progress into solstices and equinoxes, fixed astronomical phenomena, the rutting of animals and the ripened crop, and the waxing and waning of the moon determined the calendar. When I was a child in Japan, we celebrated Big New Year in winter and Little New Year at midsummer.

I sit on the back steps, rolling seed balls around strips of paper with the names of those who've gone. There are more dead every year. A raven skims into my yard. I shiver.

To see a crow or raven on November Eve can be an omen of impending disaster. To the ancient Celts, crows and ravens—distinguishable for the wedge in the raven's tail—were foretellers of doom, of death, and of war and loss in battle. The Mórrígan, Triple Goddess of Destruction, frequently appeared as a screaming flock of "scald" crows.

In the Babylonian tale of the Flood, which predates the Biblical story of Noah, it was a raven who, on the seventh day, found dry land. The Norse god Odin was accompanied by two ravens, and two ravens guided Alexander the Great across the desert. The raven is almost universally a trickster in the mythology of Native Americans of the Pacific Northwest. To many peoples, ravens are the dead reborn.

To me, they're familiars. No matter where we lived, there they were, scavengers thriving on detritus—whether flesh or french fries—and reassuring because they were travelers, too. They seemed to journey along with our family, birds I could always recognize, whose history is elegant and powerful.

Carrion crows are white with black hoods. Jackdaws have silver eyes. The rook has a bare white face. They're all cousins to jays, magpies, and nutcrackers, all corvids, fearless and sociable. When I was eight, my Tío Luis introduced me to a raven named Carlos who could talk—"*¡buenos dias, guapa!*" he croaked and nicked my hand for an offering.

The scarecrows that gardeners invent have personalities as various as the birds themselves: straw mannequins dressed in Oshkosh overalls and bandannas, wooden clackers, wind chimes or flashing silver banners, tin cans, flags, trashcan lids, or a dead bird hung from a stick in the plot or in the field as a warning. And there are human bird scarers, who spend all day throwing stones, flapping arms, shouting, shaking rattles, shooting slingshots.

In ancient Greece, wooden effigies of the ugly, twisted deity Priapus were used by kitchen gardeners and vineyard keepers to scare birds. Priapus, God of Gardens, had grossly oversized genitals, carried a club for protection and a sickle to encourage a good harvest.

In Japan, farmers burned the scarecrow at the harvest as an offering to the spirit god of the fields.

Garden figures of St. Francis of Assisi have the opposite effect and are meant to attract birds.

My scarecrows come from the "White Nightgown Lineage." All my life, I've worn white cotton nightgowns. At some point, I began saving my old, torn gowns and transforming them into cinder-lasses and princesses, window and wall hangings (frocks have been a fairly constant medium for contemporary female sculptors). I soak them in plaster or gesso and affix them to or wrap them around objects typically and not-so-typically associated with woman's work: spindles and weaving sticks, musical instruments, spoons, wreaths, toys, chair backs, brooms, baskets.

One was dipped in mortar, sealed to a "throne" (a metal folding chair), and set near the Faux Forest, as our Gray Guardian of the Wood.

Each year, an irreparable nightgown becomes our scarecrow, "scaredress" or "scaregown," headless (not necessarily hatless), draped over an armature made of an old porch column and staked in the center vegetable garden.

The raven lands on the scaregown's outstretched arm, rasps, jumps into the denuded, turned bed, then flies off. I tell myself this visitation portends nothing.

As gardens change form and move in rhythm with time, they naturally evoke ritual. The simple act of planting a seed, bulb, rhizome, or root is in itself a ceremony. The harvest is a celebration and a wake.

Our Halloween seed-ball ritual and other family "games," as my mother called them, were embellishments of customs practiced by our ancestors. Traditions, like stories, shift and modify through the generations.

Our family rites were also inspired by my mother's rampant imagination. Like most devoted gardeners, she had an elaborate sense of theater. Gardeners love dramatic flourish in lines, texture, and color and arrange plants for the most extravagant show, which plays the lead in the drama. Equally important are the subtleties— anything from groundcover to gravel—which perhaps no one else would notice, but are the transitions and improvisations, the "jazz" of the garden.

Gardeners enjoy variation and rhythm. And gardening is collaborative, like theater or music—the arts to which it's most often compared. For the gardener, the partnership is with Nature, a dialogue requiring intimate and urgent involvement. Gardening can be contemplative, but it's never passive.

Gardening is an art form that embraces all the other arts. Nature is the mother of the arts and dance was the first of these. Dance and the "theater" of the gardening art have interacted from the day the first seed was planted with intention. Dance rituals occur again and again to assure fertility.

Long before there were gardens, there was dance, binding clans in hand-clasped choral rounds, loosening repression and thus illness as well, and through ecstasy, opening the gates that divide this world and the Other, allowing access to mystic realms. Soles drum the Earth, speaking to her bones; words and tunes interlace with her breath. Exhilaration that dissolves the barriers between body and soul and frees the Self of its weight. Dance—and such practices as yoga and the Chinese martial art of T'ai Chi—mimic movement from Nature. The Sufi poet Rumi (1207–1273) wrote:

> *Whoever knows the power of dance,*
> *dwells in God.*

When humans settled and made gardens, they danced to them. In Oaxaca, Mexico, I have seen the annual *danza de las jardineras,* dance of the gardeners, when male dancers in red silk dresses wore arched garlands atop their heads and swirled in circles like the seasons.

My mother had a dance floor built in the backyard every summer. Under moon and stars, amid green trees and flowers, fragrances and breezes, whether we were conscious of it or not, we foxtrotted and jitterbugged *to* the garden. These were ballroom, not primal ritual dances; nevertheless, our bodies were in synch with the garden's spirit. My mother despaired of teaching my brother to samba. My father and I glided back and forth in a mock tango, and we all waltzed.

To dance, sing, tell stories, make poems, paintings, objects, and ceremonies dedicated to (not necessarily about) Nature maintains the equilibrium. Imagination, our voices, the skills of our hands, the receptiveness of our bodies, the nimbleness of our feet—these are the gifts we exchange for Nature's generosity. The artist, including the gardener, becomes the carrier of the power of growth or death and is thus intensely connected to the Earth, the source.

In almost every faith throughout the ages, there are deities of dance, music, poetry, visual art. These are associated with deities of the elements, plants, and gardens. Art and horticulture—and early agriculture—are interconnected, mutual inspirations. Safe enclosures, later the Medieval *hortus conclusus,* helped focus and nurture creativity. When migratory humans settled, there was time and space to develop the arts as extensions of the gods. One of these art forms was garden making. The primary materials are plants, earth, stones, and water. These produce color, texture, shape, movement, and sound.

And every gardener I know sings, hums, or talks quietly in a kind of free verse to the plants and soil, chanting with the work, conversing with the dirt, greeting the ladybugs, praising the sprouts, cursing the grasshoppers.

The mountains we can see from our yard have vanished behind storm clouds. I glance at the sky, keeping track of the weather, while twisting primitive stick figures, male and female, out of grasses and the last chrysanthemums.

Once upon a time, the last cuttings of the field were woven by the community's most skillful artist into a "kern" or "corn" dolly, which represented the Earth Mother and was given a place of honor at the harvest feast, where toasts, poems and songs were made to her. (The word *corn* comes from *kern,* which simply means grain.)

When seeding recommences, the dolly, who waited patiently for spring in enforced idleness with gardeners and farmers, was placed in a furrow and plowed back into the ground. Mine will be saved in a shoebox on the shelf with my gardening journal and "planted" on May Day.

Puppets, poppets, scarecrows, effigies of the human figure as deities have been vital to human ritual from the first. They're not replacements for a god, not divine substitutes, but messengers to higher powers and manifestations of the Presence, in human form. In the garden they are fructifiers.

Images of the gods Pan and Priapus in ancient Greece were flogged when gardens were unproductive and food was scarce. Sluggish or lazy in-dwelling spirits of fertility and prosperity were shaken from their dormancy—or complacency. According to artist/santero Carlos Santistevan, among some Mexicans and Mexican Americans, when a saint ignores prayers, he or she risks punishment. The saint is warned beforehand that the shrine will be dismantled and the figure buried in the ground or stuffed into a drawer. In this way, too, the talisman has a chance to recoup its spent powers.

On November Eve, the Celts opened the graves and did not leave their homes while the dead crossed the thin frontier between this world and the Other. If the living met the dead, they'd perish. Or the Tuatha Dé Danann, the fairy people of the Goddess Danu, might pluck a mortal soul away to Tír na n'Óg, as in this story whose fragments, recorded by, among others, W. Y. Evans-Wentz, I pieced together. It is very like a version told to me when I was a child, along with other ghost stories on Halloween.

> *Headless riders cloaked in crimson gallop across gray skies. Fairies go to war this night, and when the frozen lichen thaws, the blood of their battles can be seen on the rock.*
>
> *The warrior Nera dares step out on* samhain, *in answer to his chieftain's challenge, to sling the corpse of a hanged man across his back.*
>
> *The scarlet-clad gentry swoop upon him. They ride red steeds and each of the host has a headful of shocking red hair. They force Nera into a strange house, force him to give the dead man drink. In his great thirst, the corpse swallows and gulps, drinks and drinks, but the last mouthful he spits at the faces of the people in that house and they, too, die.*
>
> *Then Nera returns the corpse, hangs him again on the gallows and follows the Tuatha Dé Danann into a cave, for fairy mounds are always open on* samhain. *And Nera remains in Tír na n'Óg and takes a fairy wife . . .*

Withered leaves clinging to branches clap and clatter in the breeze like April rain. The wind picks up. Snow clouds close in. The low sun gleams on the straw covering the root vegetables—carrots, beets, turnips—protected under this stringy gold I've piled a foot and a half high.

Some gardeners dislike the practice of mulching the root vegetables through winter for fear they'll rot in the ground. In Colorado, the snow until mid-March is usually light and dry. In the months to come, we'll stomp through it, separate the straw, feel for weary foliage with gloved fingers. Pull, and the vegetables pop easily from the soft soil. The scent of that dirt is a distant sigh of spring.

In Ohio, my Aunt Kate's house, built in 1832, has a storm cellar that doubles as a root cellar. She was born in this house ninety years ago and lives there yet.

When I was a kid, visiting with my parents on home leave, I loved to frighten myself sneaking into Kate's cellar, into cool, damp air that smelled of must and apples from hardening cider. In the old days, a man was hired to help Kate's mother Celinda with the harvest. Everything was stored, canned, pickled, dried, smoked. Celinda had only to pass through a chilly pantry, like a railroad car built of logs off the kitchen, with shelves and shelves of canned goods and a fruit gallery or loft. Three brief steps outside and she wrenched open the lean-to cellar doors, lit her lantern, and descended to collect dinner fixings.

The pewter sunlight, what's left of it, pushes through the bare boughs onto glistening evergreens. If the weather-lorists are to be believed, we have a long winter ahead.

"It's a great life if you don't weaken," my paternal grandmother (and apparently everyone else's) used to say. I hear myself repeating it aloud to my garden.

By noon, the sky is entirely gray. I can smell the turkey farm twenty miles east, a certain sign of snow. I never doubt it will snow on November Eve. Snow fulfills the Halloween magic.

Deep cold must be closing in: I haven't seen any signs of raccoons—the urban backyard bear—for days. My husband says he saw one just last night sauntering over the skylight in our bedroom, crashing through the branches of an overhanging tree.

Shadows in the garden are swallowed across the afternoon. The thin veil between the worlds flutters in slow, quiet sheets, like the tag end of a torn feather quilt.

Each morning, year-round, the blue jays—pealing like electronic alarm clocks—circle our house demanding their breakfast of peanuts, which they hide and I find sprouting in odd places. Now they're quiet, their gang warfare on hold. If the snow stops tomorrow, they'll be back with the starlings to peck at the seed balls we've left on the trees. Unless the squirrels get them first. Who consumes our paper notes to the ancestors? Those disappear, too.

No visible sunset yet, only snow clouds illuminate the dark sky. Three houses away, an elm, undistinguished in summer, takes on a spectral role for winter, a focal point, winter's mother lode. When the sun is behind it, I squint and imagine headless riders, Jabberwocks, giants, and the White Night Mare perched in its skeletal branches.

Tonight, we celebrate November Eve with a tureen of roasted root vegetables. Onions, potatoes, turnips, rutabagas, carrots with peppers, garlic, and the last of the rosemary doused in sherry. Rosemary doesn't survive the winter here, and I've abandoned efforts to pot it for the kitchen. In an old house like mine—a 1905 general development home—windows were kept to a minimum for heat in winter, shade in summer. It's never quite warm enough for herbs to thrive in my kitchen, which was designed to be heated by a wood or coal stove and has no furnace duct. I keep a basil plant there anyway and pamper it, for basil indoors blesses the house. It sits in a heavy torpor all winter, with just enough blessing to keep us going, but not enough foliage for pasta. I pick basil from the garden throughout the summer for salad and pesto. I freeze it in icetrays for soup, and dry some, too, but it loses most of its bite.

A side of barley and butter, green tomato pie, a dessert of persimmons. At my Irish grandmother's house, Halloween dessert was always blackberries.

"Stuff yourselves," she said. "After this night, you must not eat berries. The fairies pass over them tonight and anyone who eats them from November Day on will be struck by deadly illness."

"The devil spits on 'em," my great auntie Mil added.

The fairies, we knew, had also immigrated to America and were up to their old tricks, undaunted, in California.

*   *   *

Not all gardeners grow vegetables, though most seem to dedicate at least some space to foodstuffs. Some city gardeners—apartment dwellers—load pots and planters with all manner of edibles and herbs, although root vegetables, which require lots of area and depth, are usually too demanding.

One friend installed pots of squash and pumpkins—and moon flowers!—beside a sunny window in her cramped condominium. The vines curled up curtain rods and trellises she nailed to her living and dining room walls, pumpkins knocked knickknacks off the shelves, zucchini hung like great green globs and summer squash like yellow giants' tears flopped over paintings and books.

Food accompanies every celebration and ritual worldwide, the more so when the rite includes fasting. The Rice Festival in Japan celebrates the moment when the rice god Inari, sometimes depicted as a fox, returns to her cold mountain. She was the animal I loved best. She had infinite supernatural powers. Her vision was limitless, she could hear near and far. She could hear my secrets and share them. In November, she took away the rice and stored it in her mountain until spring.

Harvest festivals are the hardiest feasts: not only do we revel in the abundance, but without supermarkets, this was the time to stoke up and fatten up before winter and the dwindling of fresh supplies. "Meat 'n' potatoes and two veg," was my grandmother's formula for a decent supper. Grab it when you can get it, for tomorrow there may be famine, as there was when she came out of Ireland as an infant, with her mother and sister Milicent, a skinny two-year-old on rickety legs.

I remember everything important about my granny. I remember her dumpling body and the big, hard muscles in her upper arms. My head fit right between her breasts and rested on the cameo she always wore, which I have now. Her eyes were round and blue and slightly rheumy. I remember her dark clothes; the dresses that reached her ankles; her dark, salty hair pulled into a tight bun. A few loose, coarse curls. The squared Irish chin on a face that was once beautiful had tripled and jiggled like Jell-O when she sang to me in her high tremolo.

*   *   *

Our house tonight is lit by jack-o'-lanterns. An eerie light, goblins sneering their sneery grins at us from the porch, in the front hall, in the living room, and on the dining table.

The house looks wonderfully weird, like a wild patch of ignis fatuus, the phosphorescent light in marshes from which the terms "will-o'-the-wisp," "foxfire," and "jack-o'-lantern" come. The will-o'-the-wisp illuminated visions of spirit women dressed in white, running across swampy ground, radiant beings large and dazzling in human form ascending from the glow, pixies dancing in circles, phantom funerals, or corpse candles that forecast a death.

In the countries where I was reared, there were harvest festivals, but there was no Halloween. Except for the year we lived in the States, when I was ten or eleven, I'd never experienced "trick or treat"—an American tradition from Britain and Ireland. We didn't eat pumpkins when I was a child, except on visits to Kate, who baked rich pies with bourbon and whipping cream.

We didn't have jack-o'-lanterns, either. Pumpkins are a North American native. In rural Ireland and Britain, the custom was to carve a turnip or rutabaga lantern, put a candle in it and string it to a pole. Children roamed the streets frightening people with the monster-face lamps, which were also hung from gateposts to scare away evil spirits. In Scotland, they're called "neep lanterns" and set along the streets and roads to light the way for "guisers."

My kids and I carve ours from the pumpkins the raccoons have taste-tested. The challenge is to create the face around the bite marks. They invariably have round mouths and no chins, making them appear jollier than we'd wish.

The ritual lighting of candles, lanterns, torches, or bonfires guides the spirits, proclaims victory over the sun, or entices the sun's return.

At harvest new year, the ancient Egyptians lit lamps for the dead so they could find their way back. At Celtic *samhain*, bonfires were laid on the hills and all the hearths doused, but each house was bright and cozy with many lamps. In the morning, when the dead had moved on, the households relit their hearths from the communal fires. Such dousing and relighting from a central blaze is customary in many places, an emblem of community solidarity, symbolizing the power of the living over the dead and a fresh start.

> *This is the night o' Halloween*
> *When all the witches can be seen.*
> *Some are black and some are green,*
> *And some the color o' the turkey bean.*

In old rural Britain, children wandered the streets chanting verses or calling, "Please help the guisers"—boys and girls disguised in old clothes (girls favored dressing up as boys), faces blackened with soot. Door to door they danced, "guising" in groups of three or four— singing, dancing, and reciting poems for handouts of pennies.

At our house in Colorado, as everywhere across the United States, "things that go bump in the night" take the form of giggling children in masks and costumes, crying "Trick or treat!" The doorbell rings again and again through supper and we take turns answering it.

It's pretty tame compared with country traditions, when mischief makers customarily removed garden gates to let loose the fairies who reside in the flower and vegetable plots, the trees and shrubbery. Removing the garden gates is doubtless a throwback to the ancient Celtic *samhain* practice of opening the graves and fairy mounds.

The kids who come to our door mostly wear store-bought costumes. Parents wait watchfully on the sidewalk for the little ones. A brief "ooh!" and "who are *you?!*" gasped in mock astonishment, candy tossed in the bag, and they're gone. A far cry from the origins of this holiday that marked the closing of summer and a new year, challenged death and evil and vented the dark psyche of the entire community (not to speak of venting the children's naughtiness without stuffing them full of sugar). Like the garden, children act as mediums between this world and the Other, fears and prejudices of adults not yet barnacled to their souls.

We come only to sleep, only to dream.
It is not true, it is not true that we come to live on this
　　Earth.
We become as spring weeds,
We grow green and open the petals of our hearts.
Our body is a plant in flower.
It gives flowers and it dies away.

　　　　　—Nezahualcoyotl, poet king of Texcoco, Mexico,
　　　　　　　thirteenth century

Sun and Blue Skies on November Day

The snow left a clean, shiny blanket on the garden and hides its messy remains. Not a cloud overhead. Halloween passed with no ghoulish disasters, no ghostly hauntings, despite the raven visitation.

I broadcast seeds collected from my flower beds onto the snowy field in the yard Susie Next Door is cultivating. Hollyhock, bachelor buttons, asters, feverfew, wild monarda, cosmos, larkspur and poppies housed in their hard shells. I've performed this wildflower ritual for years, attempting to make silk purses from some very scruffy sows' ears. By now, I should get some sort of Lady Bird Johnson award, although the technique I use is labeled the "shotgun approach" by experts.

The patch of tromped-upon dirt between street and sidewalk in front of my house—named the "hellstrip" by gardener Lauren Springer in her book, *The Undaunted Garden*—was beautified this way, and so were areas on the alley, out back behind my fences and shed. A friend and I spread seeds in a field outside her newly renovated study. White sheep graze behind a fence, beyond what is gradually becoming a flower-radiant meadow. The vegetation nearest the fence has been munched to the roots.

The birds will thin the seeds. The rest will sink slowly into wet ground and the fissures left by frost, finding their own right depth. By midsummer, the floral residents of the wild garden will stake their territories, determine for themselves which thrives and which must wait their chance. Two or three winters of seed broadcasting and Susie's yard will become a tapestry of blooms throughout the season. It's a handy solution for an eighth of an acre that no one will take much care of when and if Susie Next Door moves away.

The few marigolds that survived the Indian summer are forlorn and bowed low by the snow. Throughout autumn, I picked them to dry in a basket. In spring, I'll open the whole dried flower and plant the waiting seeds.

These Mexican natives are called African or Aztec marigolds and don't survive the Colorado winters. The calendula, or Mediterranean pot marigold, reseeds itself outrageously in my garden. It's a fortuitous flower, which, when steeped for a few weeks in almond or olive oil, helps ease sunburn, among other uses.

The Aztecs called the marigold "twenty flower," *cempoalxóchitl.* Priests mixed the leaves with tobacco to smoke for prophetic visions. When the Spaniards took seeds back to Spain, the plants prospered and spread all the way to North Africa, where they were "rediscovered" and named *Flos africanus.* The *Tagetes lucida* variety of marigold was called *yyauhtli* in Nahuatl, and was used by Aztec physicians to cure hiccups.

A girl who puts marigold petals in her shoes will understand birdsong.

Last week, the trucks came up from Mexico loaded with marigolds, like parade floats. They steamed into towns and neighborhoods, blossoms flying, leaving tangerine trails along the streets. I've seen the fields where they're grown—more vibrant and eye-shattering than even the sunflower farms of South Dakota or the south of France.

The flowers are sold to Mexican Americans for *El Día de los Muertos,* the Day of the Dead. Its origins are the Aztec harvest rites absorbed by All Saints and All Souls days introduced by Catholic priests during the Spanish conquest. Everywhere there are marigolds, cockscomb, candles, and special dishes of *mole,* corn, tortillas and merriment. Honoring the dead with a three-day party celebrates those who are alive now, as well as those who lived before, by acknowledging the relationship.

*   *   *

A respite between snows, a melt that lasts two or three days. The props that kept the delphiniums from sprawling with the weight of blooms, the gladiola stakes, the poppy "prisons," the bare brown stalks, the dun-colored beds give the garden a vagrant look, exposed and vulnerable, but never sad.

There is no real holiday in the gardener's year, even when the frost is set hard against digging. There are tasks, big and little, planning, mapping, reading, and the compost to turn. The garden catalogues—trimmed for Christmas—don't stop coming.

Soon it will be Thanksgiving, the only national agricultural holiday in the United States, gained at the cost of Native American sacred land, an unappetizing fact of which most Americans are finally becoming poignantly aware. Yet thanks to indigenous people's sacrifices, there is at least one day on which we are duty-bound to consider gratitude for our "amber waves of grain" (even as they are being industrialized by factory farms), one day when we are asked to be conscious of our families, friends, and communities.

In Bolivia, my mother raised turkeys in our backyard, convinced that if she only fed them the right delicacies, mixed with wine, they'd be tender for Thanksgiving dinner. She refused to accept that the altitude, 12,000 Andean feet in La Paz, was what really made them so tough and stringy.

The garden sage will still be green and pungent enough to use in turkey stuffing with oysters and walnuts. Meantime, I make what we call "English pesto," grinding the sage in the food processor with walnuts, goat cheese, garlic, and olive oil, then freezing buckets of it for winter. And dried garden sage makes a wonderfully invigorating tea. Oregano, which grows voraciously, also makes a good "Greek pesto" with feta cheese, almonds, and cumin.

I shake the frost from the sage and cut tender twigs with kitchen scissors. Serene silence. Misty hours. The fastness of winter. Under this snow lies all possibility.

December

... the hearth which is dark and smoldering
may glow again.
The torch which is quenched
may blaze anew ...

—Ancient Babylonian hearth blessing

An Arctic Freeze Closes In

An eerie stillness. The chunk-chunking of my ax is the only
sound. Dusk descends midafternoon. The world is suspended, as if
this were the time before time. When at last it snows, there will be
at least a sense of life beginning.

But it's too cold to snow. The clouds are frozen and constipated.

The woodstove blazes. Our house, my children tell me, is like a
fudge sundae: hot on top, cold on the bottom. In this weather, it's
cold upstairs and down.

There are pie plates over chimney holes that held wood or coal
stoves. Our gas furnace, originally built for coal, looks like a 1930s
B-movie spaceship. As the freeze intensifies, I light the oven at dusk
and keep it on till bedtime. I'm pleased that I neglected until last
year to cut down three of the trash elms that sprout like dandelions
next to the house. The ancient Romans claimed the shade of the
elm was nourishing to any plant that grew beneath it. I'm skeptical.

Hinges squeak on the family trunk, oak lined with cedar. I pull out the alpaca bedspreads from Bolivia, Kate's homespun blankets, and quilts made by my paternal grandmother's mother and aunts: Roxana, Eunice, and Carrie, my great-grandmother, who died young of diphtheria. Roxana and Eunice never married, but were consigned to live at home with their possessive mother, caring for their motherless niece and nephew. Their spare moments were spent quilting and pottering over sweet peas and tea roses.

Eunice's picture hangs in our kitchen in an ornate frame. She's our "kitchen witch," the guardian angel of the hearth.

I've repeatedly mended these century-old quilts. There's breath in old objects. Until the latter half of the twentieth century, ordinary people in our culture respected the essential magic residing in used and worn things. Old homes under renovation are frequently found to have talismans stuck in the rafters, floors, or walls. These carry the substance of the past and the heart and soul of the person who owned it. Recycled objects have *meaning*.

Discarded tables and chairs become our garden furniture. Found pieces of fences and bedsteads act as barriers and lattices in the flower and vegetable beds. Stakes and ornaments were household objects or are Dumpster finds. Wrought-iron gates or decorative ironwork in the garden have an age-old reputation for protection. An old piece of ornately curled iron hanging on the shed catches morning glories. A mattress spring serves as a trellis for silverlace vine by the pond. Another mattress spring—a remnant from a friend's art installation—has been cut in half and arched to make a rose arbor.

When we lived in Pennsylvania, we hiked the hills and along abandoned railroad tracks, I collecting old iron plough points, junked farm implements, railroad spikes, nails, and a myriad of unidentifiable objects. I suspend some from fruit trees like the Pennsylvania Germans; others, eaten by rust and transformed into weird, wonderful new shapes, hang on an outside wall of the house. A manhole cover leans against trees in the Faux Forest, covered with ivy. My dulled woodchopping wedges are retired to a row between the path and a bed of yellow geums.

A shoe or a tool or household item made of iron is commonly

placed in the hole dug for planting a tree. I include them with the "Grandma White" method of tree planting, outlined in Rodale's *The Complete Book of Composting.*

The shoe's rotting leather and the salts from human sweat do, in fact, gradually nourish the tree; the rusting iron does, in fact, provide minerals; and the mystical power vibrating from them lends fecundity and sympathy, strengthening the bond between human activity and Nature. Iron is said to change the color of certain plants, such as hydrangea from pink to blue.

Pre-Christian Nordic peoples believed iron was thrown to Earth by the god Thor, ruler of thunder and thunderbolts, who rumbled across the sky in his goat-drawn wagon. Thus iron becomes a link between Heaven and Earth, a masculine aspect, symbolic of the Sun.

Mjolnir or "hammer of Thor," long, crooked iron braces where house and wall bisect, indicate that crucial moment when house and garden connect as equally significant halves that make a home.

Quilts and alpacas at bedtime. I toss sheets over my three indoor plants, those stalwart survivors waiting patiently to get outdoors again. Sleep is cozy. In the morning, it's hard to get out of bed. The windows are iced. Outside the conifers are frosty, shimmering with spiderwebs like Christmas tinsel.

The pampas grass plumes stand high and stiff, white torches near mounds of blue fescue. The vinca along the front walk is peppered with icy dew, and crunches like broken glass. The splayed oxblood branches of the shrub dogwood, which I feared would be awkward near the shed, disappear against its barn red.

Such a freeze is more likely to come in January, but lately, weather patterns are weird, whether from the greenhouse effect or Nature's enigmatic behavior, which takes us by surprise despite meteorologists' best calculations. I hate to go outside in this weather. When I do, I look up more often than down. The Earth is gray-brown, the sky frigid blue. The stars are crisp and ostentatious. The Chinese called the glitzy Milky Way the heavenly River Han, attended by Chu Pa Chiai, the pig fairy. Mother Ganges in India is thought to be a continuation of the Milky Way.

Stars are the seeds of Heaven. We plant by them, guided by the

Pleiades or Sirius. My grandmother said winter stars are astral milk. She put saucers of actual milk on the back stoop for the fairies, who lapped up the magic white gleam reflected by the chilly stars. The neighborhood cats drank the rest, "but it makes them sick," my grandmother said blithely. The poor cats' plight didn't faze her.

The hearth confirms our identity with the house, with shelter and safety, as the garden confirms our identity with *home.*

The hearth is the altar of the house, and according to the old folk, must be kept spotless. As the heart is the center of the Self, the seat of emotion, the vessel of the soul, so the hearth is the heart of the home, the gathering place. To Chinese and Hindu sages, the vital heartbeat was the expression of the entire universe, the tempo of eternity. The hearth is where the family's rhythms harmonize.

When the land is fallow, the work of spinning, weaving, quilting, artmaking, studying, repairing tools and mending of all sorts goes on here, beside the embers. As the heart beats in pace with poetry, song, color, and dance, so the hearth's glow emits stories, inventions, and comforts. The word *earth* is neatly embedded in the h-earth.

And when it's time to celebrate a new moment on the winter garden calendar, the hearth is the locus from which rituals and festivals such as the Yule evolve. In Latin, the hearth fire is *focus.*

We've lost the integration of hearth, house, and garden, and too many of us are lonely, yearning for a sense of place that attention to the calendar, rituals of seasons, and care for the simple art of the ordinary might solve. "The secret of happiness," said William Morris, a founder of the nineteenth-century Arts and Crafts movement, "lies in taking a genuine interest in all the details of daily life and elevating them to art."

For the Ainu people of Northern Japan, the hearth fire is a goddess resident in the home. And every Chinese household kept a small niche in the wall above the stove that held incense and the image of a god. At the new year, the image was burned and the stove god traveled to heaven on the smoke to report on the family and determine its future.

Burn ashwood green
'Tis fire for a queen.

Green ash—from an autumn snow that half cracked the tree—is among the wood we burn this year. In old England, to burn applewood was sacrilege. To destroy this ancient symbol of plenty might bring a home to ruin, a fate we hope to avoid, though we use apple prunings for kindling.

The Yule log ("clog" or "block," as it is variously called in England) in its oldest, pre-Christian form, however, may have been holy applewood. Because its heat and the length of the log's burning time was essential to keep the Sun on its path "upward," the oak—sacred to Celts and their Druids (possibly from the Celtic *Duir,* meaning oak)—would have been more favorable.

The custom of burning a Yule log was held by the English, French, Germans, and Southern Slavs. According to Walter W. Skeat's *A Concise Etymological Dictionary of the English Language, yule* comes from the Middle English and Anglo-Saxon words for *feast.* The origin of the word is disputed, Skeat tells us, then fairly shrieks from the page: "The attempt to connect this word with *wheel* is futile."

Nevertheless, the Yule log is one of the great European symbols of the wheel of the year, the circling of stars toward the Sun's demise and glorious reawakening.

When the log was brought into the house, it was festooned with ribbons and bows and strewn with peas, bread, and wine. In the Scottish Highlands, the Yule log was carved into the image of an old woman, the *Cailleach Nollaich,* the "auld" Christmas wife. Like the kern dolly, its remains were an important talisman. In some places it was customary to weave them into the last sheaves cut at harvest, or to put the charred ember in the garden at planting time.

Wash your hands, or else the fire
Will not tend to your desire.
Unwashed hands, you maidens know,
Dead the fire, although you blow.

The tale of Cinderella appeals deeply to me, among other reasons because it's centered around the hearth. And—the shoe motif notwithstanding—it is to my mind an archetypal garden story. All the ash girl's fortune originates in the garden. The French heirloom pumpkin is said to be the model for Cinderella's coach in later retellings.

"Cinderella" is one of the best-known stories in the world. More than seven hundred versions have been collected. A Scottish variant is perhaps the most agrarian: Rashin Coatie's benefactor, her "fairy godmother," is a little red calf.

In nearly every permutation, there is Cinderella's relationship with the hearth. She is the "cinder-fool," who remains faithful to her mother's memory beside the hearth, the girl's body close to her mother's heat, her heart coupled with the heart of the mother, interchangeably Cinderella's birth mother and Mother Earth. Her stepmother forces Cinderella to work in the kitchen, day and night, tormenting her by tossing peas and lentils into the ashes for the girl to pick and sort.

When I misbehaved, my mother railed and ranted, making me, or my brother, responsible for all the ills in the world. My father—who read to us each night by the fireplace—preferred sending me to sort things, to *focus*. I was to clean my desk or closet, weed a flower bed, polish my mother's silver, or write an essay about my transgression and its larger meaning to my life, our family, and so on.

In the ashes, Cinderella discovers patience, she recovers herself and triumphs. All lives come down to sorting. Sorting seeds, separating the wheat from the chaff. Working in the garden—where we must appraise, sift, discern, eliminate, add, arrange, and sometimes simply let go—allows us the opportunity to ponder and absorb each day's events, one day at a time, and deliberate the past so it can inform the future. Hearth and garden serve many of the same functions: they *focus,* bringing peace where there's disorder and warmth to the heart.

Old wives, when they're not reading tea leaves, read the hearth ashes to divine the future, and it is in the hearth that Cinderella finds hers.

Although she is marginalized in her own mother's house, the

hearth and garden are nonetheless Cinderella's cradle, her abode. As an ash-lass, she is ragged and filthy. As a "princess," a woman who can really stoke a fire, she's cleaned up and dolled up with the goods of the garden, empowered by the spirit of the garden, her fairy godmother. The garden is the paradise of Cinderella's autonomous Self—as it is mine—offering fulfillment and balance and providing choices.

Stargazer lilies perfume the house. Their scent mingles with pine, elm, apple, and oak burning in the stove, and the paperwhite narcissus and amaryllis I've started all around the house despite the cold.

"Stop pouting!" my mother scolded when I was downhearted. "Do something for others and keep busy!"

"And for God's sake always keep fresh flowers in the house!"

Each time I leave, I return with roses, the flower among thorns. Flower of holiness, maternity, bliss.

My son announces that between the paperwhites, amaryllis, long-lasting stargazers, and now these bouquets, we resemble a funeral home.

Roses fulfill a profound requirement for me, especially around Christmas, when the intensity of our relationships increases and the absence of family members who've passed on becomes most acute.

In her book, *Your Essential Nature,* Nita Morrow Hill describes the essential oil of rose as speaking to "the relationship we have with ourselves, our bodies, our friends, our lovers and the world . . . to wholeness and the longing to join and make whole. . . . Rose relates to completeness in the world and the universe. Rose is comforter. It holds people close to you emotionally."

The oil of rose is said to ease postnatal depression, which is how I feel when the holiday is over and everyone's returned to their own lives. In times of personal crisis, I crave the scent of roses. The summer my father died, I stumbled through my days, constantly on the verge of tears, weaving impulsively into anyone's yard, cupping my hands around a rose and inhaling hard. A snoutful of rose is nothing if not the manifestation of love and love remembered.

Roses are nostalgia for places I've called home, my hearths. Homesickness for our garden in Afghanistan, where rose bushes and hollyhocks stood proudly against the high, white stuccoed compound wall. After the 1979 Soviet invasion, the terrible, constant bombing, thousands of leftover land mines, and the internecine wars since the Soviets left in 1989, could there be much left of ours or any other of the gorgeous gardens of Kabul?

But in happier times, when we were fifteen, my best friend Nadia taught me to color my hair with red rose petals in the Egyptian fashion. Her black hair glinted burgundy as if washed with wine. In Persian, the words for *flower* and *rose* are the same: *gul,* which may derive from an ancient Babylonian goddess, Gula, "the great physician," who could cure as well as inflict disease and who lived in a garden at the center of the world.

Roses may come closer than any other plant to representing the ideal human life, as gardens themselves represent the ideal human life*style.*

Roses at Christmas honor the Virgin Mary's miraculous accomplishment. (The lily, her other flower, signifies purity.) Some say Christmas roses will only bloom if planted near the front door, to welcome Christ into the house.

There were rose bushes in the yard when I moved to this house twenty years ago, badly neglected between owners, yet blooming . . . sort of. I transplanted them as they became shaded by the trees and most have recovered their rosy assertiveness.

The damask and "Alfred Dumas" roses, I suspect, were planted by the first owner of this house, Miss Susan Hicks, a chiropractor, one of few women in any kind of medical profession at the time. Miss Hicks worked at home as I do. I often speculate about which room might have been her office—was it the same one as my study?

Just as a new homeowner is advised to let a season go by in the garden to discover what's there before plunging in to landscape, so should we try to uncover the histories of our houses and their residents, as well as the history of the land on which we're living. Who was the farmer who may have sold off this parcel for your house and/or the development it occupies? What did he grow? What is the geology? The original vegetation? These questions can also inform the gardener about the content of the soil and other factors.

Who might have been the primal residents on the land where you live? What animals—wild and domesticated? Which birds and insects? If gardening offers us a sense of place, it's good to learn to know that place intimately and share that knowledge with our community. History and neighbors help shape and confirm where we are and seal our devotion to the environment.

In Colorado, in what was virtually the frontier in 1905, Miss Hicks must have anticipated the arrival of her rose orders from the East Coast with breathless excitement.

The grandiflora roses—developed in the 1950s—were probably planted by the Candelaria family, who moved to this house in the early 1940s, after Miss Hicks passed away. I transplanted a large, thickly foliaged "Mme. Hardy" from the bed I use for vegetables, but before I did, a man who'd brought his children here for Señora Candelaria to baby-sit, told me that she'd had a large backyard grotto, which housed the Virgin of Guadalupe, and another in the foyer. The yard grotto sat squarely in front of the "Mme. Hardy" rose bush, which continues to blossom with amazing pizzazz.

The Virgin of Guadalupe appeared in Mexico on December 9, 1531, to the Aztec Juan Diego on the Tepeyac Hill where Spanish Archbishop Juan de Zumárrago had destroyed the sanctuary of Tonantzin, the Aztec Mother Goddess of Corn and Flowers. As her token, the Virgin caused Castillian roses to grow where only cacti had flourished and Juan Diego to present them to the bishop.

Nuestra Señora de Guadalupe traveled from Spain to become the patroness of all the Americas, top to bottom. She cures epidemics, stops pestilence and floods, and in the many battles against oppressors, she stands on the side of the people. Surrounded by roses, blood red and celestial white.

The Candelarias left their spiritual imprint on this house. I recently realized that figures of the Guadalupe occupy every room and are nestled in numerous nooks and crannies around the garden. Today, a blue-and-gold plaster figurine of the moonlike Virgin of San Juan sits under the "Mme. Hardy."

The grandiflora has been transplanted and with spikey gray

grasses, lightens the scene around a suffocatingly huge juniper bush (a long-ago Dumpster find) near the back door.

> I am a tree in a covert . . .
> When the trees were enchanted,
> There was hope for the trees.
> —"Battle of the Trees," *Book of Taliesin*

The Faux Forest

The holiday closes in. Frantic days of shopping, wrapping, cooking, exhaustion, resentment at the season for intimidating us to "buy-buy-buy," regardless of the original significance of this crucial, dark time of year.

Despite objections from my kids, I substitute a large poinsettia—a spurge sacred to the Aztecs—for a Christmas tree. I'm uncomfortable with commercial trees. Would tree farming be necessary if we were more conscientious and discriminating about our wants?

I'd prefer to have live trees, but my yard is full. I had a live mugho pine in honor of my dad the Christmas after he died, and ten years later a live blue spruce for my mother, each chosen for their resemblances to my parents' personalities. Last year, I broke down, unable to resist a potted Italian rock pine, beatific with blue lights and three glassine cherubs handed down from my Irish grandmother. I planted the rock pine in the silver garden in the hellstrip, that miserable spot between the sidewalk and the street. And there it died, maybe from exhaust fumes, perhaps from lack of water.

When they retired to Virginia, my folks had live trees every Christmas. Their house was set smack in the middle of a large, patchy swath of woods. What had been a ragtag conglomeration of scrawny beeches along a desiccated stream near an outcrop of the Potomac River was transformed—with Christmas trees and my mother's assiduous planting of hardwoods, azaleas, and rhododendrons—into a rich and glorious parcel of forest.

We buried my father's ashes there, in a grove of dogwoods.

The live Christmas trees were necessarily small, decorated minimally, and taken outside quickly before they withered. Today, as I ad-

mire the enormity of the mugho pine and the speed with which the
blue spruce has grown, I'm suddenly aware of how many years it's
been since my parents died. A continuing sorrow. And a mortality
alert.

Of the sacred trees, the evergreen pine ranks high as a symbol of
everlasting life. In Egyptian art, a pine is often depicted between the
dead and rising Osiris, and pine cones appear on his monuments.
The pine was sacred to Attis, vegetation god lover of the Phrygian
Nature goddess, Cybele. It was on a pine that Attis was castrated,
died, and was resurrected.

The Corinthians were enjoined to worship the pine "equally
with the god" Dionysus, who in some images carries a wand tipped
with a pine cone. Among certain African clans, evergreens are cut by
unmarried men who rock the holy tree and sing lullabies to it. In
the Celtic *Book of Taliesin*'s "Battle of the Trees," the pine is described
as courtly. It was considered a "chieftain tree" by the Celts, who used
its timber to make puncheons.

Many cultures have a World Tree, a powerful axis binding the
Earth to the cosmos and through which immortality is bestowed. In
India, a fourth or fifth generation of the Bodhi Tree, *Ficus religiosa,*
where the Buddha sat for forty-nine days and experienced his awakening, is still preserved at Mahabodi Temple in Bodhgaya. Yggs-
drasill, the World Ash Tree upon which the Norse god Odin hung,
questing for wisdom, continues working its magic in, among other
places, the twelfth trump of the Tarot, the Hanged Man.

In Greece, the World Tree was the olive. In Mesoamerica, it was
the ceiba, which held aloft the four corners of Heaven.

The blue spruce I bought for the first Christmas after my
mother's passing is the centerpiece—the World Tree—of the Faux
Forest, which began life years earlier as three or four plums, neatly
arranged in a row against the rusted east-side chicken-wire fence.
As our personal World Tree, it seems to draw the whole garden
toward it.

Tree worship was once common around the globe. The earliest
worship in Egypt may have been of the tree goddess, who lived in
the dense sycamore groves. Trees were divine and each had a soul.
Where trees scarcely grow—or are clear cut—poles often substitute:

elaborately carved totem poles or poles hung with banners, ribbons, or prayer flags, perhaps metaphors for the leaves and boughs that mediate between Heaven and Earth. At ancient festivals, worshipers danced around trees to honor them, sing them into being, telegraphed with pounding feet, messages of love and obeisance.

I wanted a sacred grove. I gave the four plums carte blanche and they took it. These hardy, self-pollinating Stanleys got so thick they stopped blooming or producing fruit. They provided a seasonal screen from the east-side renters, who came and went with the frequency of campers. The unkempt yard of that stately old house sometimes looked like a used car lot, at other times a kennel.

Creating a sacred grove where none existed seemed a tad irreverent, until I read that in Mesopotamia and Greece, cypress tress—like pines, symbols of eternity and immortality—were imported then planted in clumps. If the ancients could pull a sacred grove out of a hat, so could I.

Sacred groves have been composed of olive, cedar, poplar, sycamore, pine, almost any tree at all, so why not plums? Oak worship, practiced by the Celts, led to the great French cathedral at Chartres, built on the site of the sacred oak grove. Throughout Europe, the process of conversion from paganism to Christianity included the destruction of holy trees. Yet in England, folk visit the Major Oak in Sherwood Forest, which offered sanctuary (an important function of churches during the warring Middle Ages) to Robin Hood, the Anglo-Saxon Green Man-cum-John Dillinger of his day.

Sacred groves—and consider the number of towns whose names include the word *grove*—are also found in the United States, sites for revivals, camp meetings, places of soul-stirring religious experience, many coopted from Native Americans who revered the groves before the settlers took their land. Comfort apparently being next to godliness, the newcomers usually cut surrounding trees to make benches for worshipers! Throughout Christianity, it has not been natural but human action that sanctifies a place.

Trees are shelter for body and soul, yet their longevity and strength seem also to threaten our notions of ourselves as masterful and masters of the Earth. Long ago, all Europe was covered with thick forests, as was much of North America. Greece, Italy, and Ireland, among others, were wooded, but logged for ships, buildings, and pastures, then overgrazed for centuries.

I'm sometimes surprised that, having spent most of my life in the Andes, Hindu Kush, and Rocky Mountains, my garden does not reflect those climates' spacious aridity. I love visiting sparse and stony terrain, where the air is thin, the plants huddled low, the rock formations enchanted, and where there is a mysterious ethereal quality, closeness to the sky.

But my heart and imagination reside mostly in the woodlands. When I think of our various gardens, my memory alights fondly on my parents' Virginia woods and on those beyond our house in Yokohama—another faux forest.

As soon as I let the plums go, they exploded into a snarled mass. I thinned, using a Japanese technique that reverses perspective to give a sense of depth and space in cramped areas. In fact, the forest is only six or seven feet at its deepest. Within it, I took advantage of the rampant violets to create a glade, which opens the forest out into the rest of the garden. I added primroses (long since trampled by the violets), Grecian wildflowers, snowdrops, white crocuses, purple dwarf iris, and other spring surprises scattered on the forest floor.

My ten-year-old daughter and I built a fairy ring in the forest's "deepest deep," and within that, grape hyacinths, dormant for who knows how many years, sprang back to life. I added hardy cyclamen to the ring's edge with Jack-in-the-Pulpit, which lasted only two seasons in this dry climate. We placed two, foot-high storytelling stones, like stools, within the fairy ring, where we sat together and caught up with the day or told each other tales, much as my father and I had on the rocks beside the stream at our Yokohama house.

When the plums leaf out, the silvery spruce peeks through the green like the White Lady rising in foxfire or from wells in the tales my grandmother told. In winter, when the plums are bare, the spruce, like any World Tree, holds forth promise.

The Faux Forest is a microcosm of diminutive disasters and incredible joys. Like everything else in the garden, it evolves both with my help and on its own. I use little supplement, and instead allow fallen leaves and rotting branches to nourish it.

Swept up in Xmas, dustball that I am!
And sold to Solstice—stuck in a solar turn.
Somehow the pause allows both flow and dam
Sim'ltaneously, like the like of ice and burn. . . .

I believe the sun has not gone away to death
But wheeled again, causing a silver breath.
                   —Jack Collom, *Dog Sonnets*

Bless the Light

It is said by Muslims that Allah creates the light anew every day.

If the Sun shines through apple boughs on the Winter Solstice, there will be a fine blossoming in spring. The magpie pecking at my compost heap makes a kind of Rorschach blot-and-line drawing, a haiku of green-black markings shining iridescent against the snow that's finally fallen.

The Winter Solstice is another of the gardener's new years. On this day, the Sun plunges into the darkest dark to begin the long climb toward summer. The world seems dead and dreary; all action is underground. This is the time—time-honored—for introspection, a natural opportunity to look into ourselves; to acknowledge the unseen, the denied, the hidden, the masked; to dredge it and if need be, dispense with it. Just as seeds cannot germinate until they've spent time under moist ground, we need the darkness to examine and revitalize our souls. Although we tend not to visit our gardens now, it's a good time to do so. The garden reminds us—and gives us faith—that what's gone will return.

Among the Greeks, Egyptians, Aztecs, and Mayans, the solstice marked a five-day period outside the calendar. The Aztecs and Mayans regarded these days as unlucky, dedicated to no god (unlike every other "named" day in the complex Mesoamerican calendar) and therefore vacant, inauspicious, and unfit for any activities, religious or civil. No gardening, housekeeping, judicial, or spiritual transactions took place. The entire society descended into darkness to await renewal.

Around the globe it was necessary—as the light retreated on the Winter Solstice (whether in December or in June below the equator)—to confront demons and evil spirits, then drive them out to ensure fertility. Again and again, throughout the horticultural calendar, fertility—the greatest concern to all living beings—is summoned and action taken to assure it.

Some cultures expelled evil from the community by sacrificing a solstitial scapegoat—animal, human, or effigy. In the Highlands, the decrepit old year was burned in the form of a straw dummy—another "auld wife," like the Yule.

With Christianity, burning the "hag" to make way for a new beginning was transformed into the custom of torturing and burning witches—with Jews, the Medieval scapegoats of choice—during the critical days between Christmas and Epiphany, as well as at the commencement of Summer in May. As in the killing of the Green Knight at Yuletide in the Medieval poem "Sir Gawain and the Green Knight," the old year is beheaded to make room for the new.

In India, Winter Solstice is greeted with raucous noisemaking against devils. In France, bells were jangled and pots and pans pounded to rout out evil. The banging of pots and pans by the Mothers of the Disappeared in modern Argentina, who have marched in Buenos Aires' Plaza de Mayo, since 1983, seems an apt contemporary correlation. The din not only draws attention to the demands of these *abuelas* that the whereabouts of their missing children and grandchildren be revealed, but is an exorcism of the demon death squads, who terrorized the nation.

Solstice practices also include driving in the good. In Austria's Tyrol, in France, Germany, Belgium, and New Caledonia, it was common to beat the fruit trees to make them grow.

On the seventh day of Sukkoth, the Jewish Feast of Ingathering, folk struck the ground with willow sticks. The *Talmud* tells us that

> *Every blade of grass has its prescribed destiny and for each there is an angel in heaven who beats it and says "grow!"*

Heliolatry is extant in our modern Euroculture. When we aren't playing, basking, or working in the Sun, we yearn for it. Garden supply catalogues offer gizmos that capitalize on our unconscious, continuing Sun worship and our forgotten belief in magic of and for the garden: Sol Invictus, the unconquerable Sun, made of clay or cast-iron; bas-relief clay Bacchus medallions; Green Man or Woman statuary; glass gazing balls; sundials; fairy figures and plaques carved with aphorisms are advertised as beneficial to the gardener's art. If we believe in their effectiveness, then they indeed have power.

In our perilous era, we are like Icarus about to burn. The shredding ozone layer brings us too close to the Sun. Our refusal at this time of year to look inward deprives us of an essential tool in our collective and individual growth.

Light begets light. Bonfires and torches were lit to attract the Sun, to guide it on its journey toward the sky's zenith and midwife it through rebirth. In Denmark, my relatives celebrated St. Lucy's Day on December 16 with churchgoing, parties, pastries, and glögg—mulled wine intensified with aquavit, sugar, and fruit. Young girls, called *lussibruden,* Lucy Brides, wear crowns of candles. St. Lucy could, like Christ, restore sight to the blind. That is, she could restore light.

On the outer isles of Barra, in Scotland, a hymn is recited to the Sun each morning:

> *The eye of the great God,*
> *The eye of the God of glory,*
> *The eye of the King of hosts,*
> *The eye of the King of the living.*

On the Winter Solstice, my mother hauled out the costume trunk and we dressed up and had a family party. This was really just a sop to keep us distracted. She was actually preparing, with unbridled enthusiasm and almost all her concentration, for Christmas.

Christmas was her favorite holiday. Within a week after Epiphany, she started planning for the next year. She hid gifts around the house all year long. On Christmas mornings, a cloud passed over her face as we opened our booty, a cloud we understood meant she'd forgotten something and could not remember what. We knew we'd have to keep a sharp eye out at the Easter egg hunt.

The customary family dress-up party on Winter Solstice may have been related to "Fool Days" or "Daft Days," remaindered from the ancient Roman Saturnalia. With the appearance of Christianity, the commemorations of Saturn, god of sowing and husbandry, who taught the people to till the ground and to make laws, were integrated into Twelve-Day celebrations.

In some parts of Europe, it's believed that the weather on each day of the twelve is a token of what to expect in the corresponding month of the coming year.

In England, the Solstice is the feast day of St. Thomas, when the St. Thomas onion was planted. It grew in size and pungency in relation to the Sun and was harvested on the Summer Solstice. These days, the shallot has replaced the St. Thomas onion as the solstitial allium.

On each of the Twelve Days of Christmas my parents gave us a tiny gift—and we them—except on Christmas Day, when we were loaded with presents from the U.S. relatives, who pitied us for having to live without American goods. Bless them, they really thought us deprived. The comic books, model airplanes, Matchbox cars, Ginny dolls, baby dolls, Butterfingers, puzzles, and games spilled from package after package. This way our aunties and uncles hoped to preserve our culture, though we had almost no experience, let alone memories of anything much American—and little need for such embarrassment of riches. The presents were piled under tall, terribly skinny, oxygen-starved Christmas trees. There was once a gangly behemoth that fit nowhere except the front hallway and soared past the second-story landing, where my father climbed a ladder to get the angel on top.

Like most non-Indian families in Bolivia, we had an elaborate nativity scene bought in the *mercado*. Ten-inch figures made of papier mâché and painted in thick, vibrant colors stood in a wooden barn around the baby Jesus, who lay on real hay. There were the Three Kings, a shepherd boy, horses, a cow, llamas, and golden cherubs, with one "den mother angel," as my mother called her. It was my job to arrange this creche in front of the fireplace, which was cold, because it was Summer Solstice below the equator. The house was filled with flowers and poinsettias bought in the market, trucked in to La Paz from the tropical Yungas region.

In December, the crops have recently been planted, the corn, potatoes, yams, rice, beans, quinoa, and peanuts. The llamas have given birth and the babies frolic like cartoon lambs. The Aymara farmers and the poor have little time for holiday cheer beyond church, and the dances with which each turn on the calendar, each event is greeted. Among Andean natives, dance *is* prayer.

On the Altiplano at Christmas, groups of city children—like the Highland guisers at Halloween—dress in costume and play drums and other instruments on the street for gifts of food and money. We waited for the *villancicos* by our garden gate. I wanted badly to join them, but we were never allowed.

At *la nochebuena,* Christmas Eve, I stir the oyster stew traditional in our family. I make it with canned oysters, like the ones Kate mailed to my mother along with bayberry candles and cans of cranberry sauce, or "crane-berry relish" as early Massachusetts Cape Codders called it, for cranes were first spotted by settlers feasting on the berry.

A *flan* bakes in the oven, the windows steam. I rub a peephole with my dishcloth and look out at the pale, grizzled garden. The journey back into the green can be long and arduous, grievous and studded with stillbirth and death, even as it is reflective, refreshing, and felicitous.

Juncos hop about the grass and branches. I call my husband to the window to greet these little hooded harbingers of snow. The freeze is about to break.

January

From nothing the begetting
From nothing the increase
From nothing the abundance
　—Origins chant of the Maori, New Zealand

The Blizzard Swells and Roils

We shovel the sidewalk five times a day. The task is backbreaking. Drifts accumulate fast. All this means moisture, and every flake seems precious as we heave shovelfuls off the cement and onto the garden.

The blizzard pounds at the windows and shakes the doors. The cats cringe in the corners. Humbled, we lower our heads when we step outside.

Nights are white as noon. The tops of houses have disappeared. No sky, no ground. A white so white, it bears no contrasts and few variations. Everything is saturated, the lines between known and unknown are blurred. The storm is unfathomable as creation.

The gardening life reveals many secrets about endings and beginnings and our existence in between. From December's descent into dark (and the blankness that comes after revels and shopping sprees), Chaos arises, battles of gods and elements, the primordial stew out of which order and disorder separate while Being and not-being unify. This is the unity we call "holy." Across the months, we reel along Nature's rhythms from infinite to finite and back again.

This blizzard, indeed all of January, with its massive, dramatic weather, seems like the first creation, reenacted year after year, Chaos marking the first bubbles of beginning:

From China: *"In the beginning there was Chaos. Out of it, pure light built the sky . . ."*

From ancient Greece: *"Before the ocean, or Earth, or Heaven, Nature was all alike, a shapelessness, Chaos, all ruse and lumpy matter . . ."*

From the Tungus of Siberia: *"God sent fire into the primordial ocean. In time the fire vanquished the power of water and burned part of the ocean . . ."*

From Japan: *"When Chaos began to condense, but force and form were not yet manifest, and nothing was named, who could know its shape? . . ."*

The Hindu Rig Veda questions the origins of all things long before material life was so much as a gleam in the creators' eyes. Buddhism speaks of the universe, like the days of the year, expanding, contracting, dissolving, then reevolving, again and again, forever. All existence depends on this marvelous, indescribable cycle.

> *The Tao, the way, stands alone,*
> *never changes . . .*
> *Mother of the World . . .*
> *The way that can be named*
> *is not constant.*

Out of Chaos, the diverse divine adventures, the forces of Nature gradually sort themselves into mountain, ocean, valley, river. Tree, herb, shrub, grass, grain. Fish, peccary, cricket, deer, human, wolf, bird. All are part and parcel of the same Earth, none more or less.

The process of creation is accomplished many ways. Life springs from the limbs and blood of a dead god. It ascends from a god's vomit or from the semen of a masturbating god. It is conceived by the copulation of masculine and feminine, and Father Sun mating with Mother Earth. It crawls—a snake, a dragon, a worm, a spider—up from underground. It emerges from an egg at the bottom of the sea, a seed under the ground. It is trial and error, everlasting improvisation.

Creation accomplished, never complete. Chaos goes on, creating, re-creating. The weather will change and again change; the elements persevere as warriors in the great primeval battle. Wind combats rain, ocean combats shore. Evolution, ongoing modulation and alteration, the sacred is never static, obeys no rules.

With the creation, flora and fauna establish themselves and discover the systems by which they can survive. First attempts are the subject of folklore worldwide—how the bear lost its tail, how the bird got wings, how mountains were formed, how corn came to the people. In all these tales, and in actuality, each one's life is woven with and dependent upon the others.

In most cosmologies, there are maelstroms and long, embattled preludes before a common creation. But, as Barbara Sproul notes in *Primal Myths*, some creation stories focus solely on a particular event, the origin of specific things. In the Judeo-Christian and African Ngombe origin myths, for instance, human beings are shaped by a god who situates them on an existing Earth. The mortals' appearance on Earth introduces or motivates evil and other qualities that come of being human.

There are no people on Earth. People live in the sky with Akongo. They are happy. Everyone except Mbokomu. Mbokomu complains. She makes everyone crazy. One day, Akongo puts the woman in a basket with her son and daughter and lowers them to Earth.

Mbokomu is happy. She plants a garden. The garden thrives. Then Mbokomu worries. "Who will care for this garden when we die?" she asks herself.

She asks her son. He shrugs.

"You must have children," Mbokomu tells him.

"Impossible," he replies. "There is no one here but us."

"You must take your sister and have children by her. If you do not, our work is lost," Mbokomu says.

Brother marries Sister. She becomes pregnant.

One day, she encounters a creature, who looks like a man covered

*over with hair. She is frightened, but he is kind. He becomes her
friend. She shaves him with her husband-brother's razor. She sees he
is Ebenga, the Beginner. He bewitches her. He bewitches the child.
The child brings evil and sorrow into the world.*

*Brother and Sister have many more children. There are new
families. New gardens. But evil and sorrow continue and are always
with us.*

In the Ngombe tale, there is acceptance that evil is a part of our
legacy. In the Judeo-Christian stories of the fall, the Earth is no
longer a pure and pleasurable place, but one of hardship, toil, and
poison. Yet having ejected Adam and Eve from Eden, so the doc-
trines tell us, God prepared them for a better place, redemption in
Paradise.

This Colorado blizzard seems to describe the cosmic dance, the
universe in flux moving toward an eventual miracle of birth, the
trickle of a stream that grows into a river, an infant sliding out from
between its mother's legs, a sapling.

In Paradise, gems spring from the ground, trees blossom and fruit
simultaneously, birdsong constantly fills the air. The water in pools
and burbling streams is always fresh and sweet.

Paradise is a garden. The garden is a sanctuary *of* Nature against
Nature's terrifying power.

Paradise is an enclosure. The word comes from the Persian, *pairi-
daeza,* meaning *park.* Paradise is the walled garden, safe from the
wilderness that frightens us. In the Middle Ages, "paradise" came to
mean the Church itself, Nature diminished in the equation. Almost
from the beginning, we required security, like the Garden of Eden,
perfect and self-contained.

The garden emphasizes the contrast between the outside world
and the inner. Gardens are sacred spaces juxtaposed against the hub-
bub and profanity of our daily lives, re-creations of the abodes of
gods or Shambhala, peaceable, lost city of dreams. We visit the garden to remind ourselves of higher realms, loftier states of being, as
when we visit church, temple, or synagogue. We work in the garden
in order to immerse our souls in the great labor of creation, in order

that our spirits, through our bodies, our hands and feet, can embrace soil, root, leaf, loam, flower, bark—all that is present. To garden is to be conscious of ourselves as connected with the primal, which is eternal. To remind ourselves of our place on Earth, in the cosmos, and in the eye of the divine. To move in sync with NOW, and therefore grasp and live in harmony with ALWAYS.

The garden can only mimic that divinity and act as accessible holy ground, which we can attend to and visit daily to remind us of vaster powers. In the garden, it is possible to cultivate, in shelter, a sense of place on the Earth. With our labors—reaping, weeding, watering, and harvesting—with ritual, rites of seasons, the building of community around the garden, and with stories, it is possible to renew a greater sense of place within Nature.

Leave a garden alone for a few weeks and it will begin to quicken, if not back to indigenous Nature, back to some natural state of its own.

The actual, and therefore nonmaterial, spiritual world lies beyond these walls. It is in wilderness, in sensuous, generous magnitude, in tides and volcanoes, passion and vitality, that perfection— "god"— exists. Even in creeds where the gods are named, and prayers are intimate, there is mystery beyond and above them: Nature, the "unspeakable name," the "hidden face." The garden is representative, a temple, a refuge, where we commune with the mysteries. A place within a place, as Nature is god behind the gods.

For eons, prophets have withdrawn "to the voice that cries in the wilderness," as in Isaiah. Among the many wild men, saints, and hermits of Ireland, the twelfth-century recluse Suibne recited:

> . . . *Though you think sweet*
> *your students' gentle talk in yonder church,*
> *sweeter, I think, the splendid talking*
> *of the wolves in Glenn mBolcáin . . .*

In countless mythological and historical legends, "revolution" begins in the wilderness. The rebel flees into wilderness—into the divine—and returns to civilization to claim righteousness and justice.

To raze the Earth is to do battle against Nature and presume ourselves gods. But even gods can't win. What the myths teach us is that mere gods have no final authority over the forces of Chaos.

In Islam, which originated in the desert, the Qur'an describes Heaven, or *janat,* as a garden.

> *In the Name of Allah, the Beneficent, the Merciful: In gardens of bliss . . . a numerous company from among the first. On thrones decorated, they recline, partaking fruits such as they choose and the flesh of fowl such as they desire. How happy the companions of the right hand! Amid thornless lote-trees and banana trees. Extended shade and water flowing constantly.* (Surah LVI)

And—as in the New Testament of the Bible—gardens appear in nearly every major religious drama to describe abundance, fertility, renewal, and rebirth:

> *Now in the place where he was crucified, there was a garden.* (John 19:41)

For many primal peoples, Paradise, "Eden" *was* the wilderness, the entire, unbound natural world. The ancient Celts, enthusiastically maintaining their animal natures, could transform into wild beasts. What "civilized" pleasure gardens exist in pre-Christian Celtic mythology belong to the *sidhe,* the fairy clans, whose homes were elaborate, luxurious affairs complete with jeweled orchards situated in the Otherworld: The Lands of Eternal Youth or Ever-Summer, the Fortunate Isles, Avalon, the Blessed Isles. In early Celtic Christianity, despite church doctrine that eschewed Nature, the worshippers, saints, and mystics were still attached to pre-Christian Nature worship and thus found the Presence all around them.

I used to believe that, because my mother was an excellent, devoted gardener, I'd inherited my green thumb from my Irish grandmother. But a visit to the West of Ireland suggested this might not be so.

Although it is at last becoming prosperous, the Republic of Ireland appears to have little or no landscaping and gardening heritage—except on estates established by the English. This is no surprise, considering Ireland's history of oppression by the British. Poor and hungry folk haven't much time for pleasure gardens.

Even Saint Fiacre, the alleged Irish patron of gardens, left Ireland to practice horticulture in France. Yet it was an Irishman, William Robinson, whose ideas most inspired the contemporary garden. In the late nineteenth century, Robinson proposed the "wild garden," in contrast to the punctilious Victorian landscape design then in vogue. Nature, he realized—and lamented—was considered threatening to most people, and was also jeopardized by bad taste.

His was an informal, naturalistic approach. He wanted each gardener to "create his own private, personal wilderness." Robinson believed in mingling native and exotic plants, set massed bulbs into long grasses and utilized low-growing alpine species in rock gardens. He was surely inspired by Ireland's wild splendor and maybe especially the sensuous, untamed landscape of its West.

Needless to say, Robinson's ideas kicked up fierce controversy. It wasn't until a woman, Gertrude Jekyll, came along that the warring factions were reconciled. Working with architect Edwin Lutyens, she shaped a compromise and began rethinking Robinson's wild garden. She maintained many of his notions, such as the use of native plants, but set them into formal geometric frameworks, with herbaceous borders, complementary color, large masses of single color—a concept later used by Vita Sackville-West—and drifts of contrasting textures planted against walls. Jekyll's poor eyesight prevented her from realizing her dream of becoming a painter. Through landscaping, she may have had a far larger aesthetic and cultural influence.

As I drove along Ireland's west coast—through the town of Ballybunion, through County Clare and the towns of Ballyvaughan, Galway, Connemara, Sligo, and Donegal—nearly every garden I saw seemed silly and artificial, exactly like the absurd formal lawns, parterres, fountains, and yard art that people who live in the majestic mountains near Boulder often build.

Why gild the lily within a paradise of natural, intricately carved rock, cut randomly by streams and freshets? What could possibly improve upon Ireland's striations of mosses and wildflowers, flag iris, wild fuchsia, and rhododendron? Why would anyone living here bother with an ornamental garden?

As I oscillated along skinny country roads past herds of sheep, wagons, and bicyclists, stone walls, and rocky pastures, it occurred to me that while my grandmother was indeed devoted to growing things, hers was a subsistence garden, only a step or two upmarket from the cabbage scratch-patch kitchen yards kept by those "back home." Those who were lucky, that is.

She had rose bushes and other common ornamentals in California, where her family at last owned land away from the Hunger and poverty, and she took great pride in them. But most of her efforts went into the culinary garden.

This wilderness is the animated domain of the *sidhe,* where the Fianna and Fionn mac Cumhall wandered, where any rock or bush might be an entrance into Tír na n'Óg, the Land of Eternal Youth, the Otherworld. Here, I realized that it was not my green thumb I inherited from my grandmother. It was the fantasy and mythology and inspiration for the *story* of gardens, tales existing and yet to be invented, that were her legacy to me.

Gardens and myths are companions, twin visions that touch the same desire for transcendence. Gardening and storytelling are both acts of love, veneration, and imagination. Gardens are populated by magic of the practical kind, by gods, devas, fairies, and Pan, who help them thrive or destroy them to punish mortal folly. Vegetables converse, shrubs dance, beanstalks lead boys to riches. Maidens turn into flowers and frogs into princes. Foundlings are nurtured in gardens, true love is kindled in gardens.

One of the tragedies of immigration is the loss of customs—and the diminishment of identity—through assimilation. Traditions, like gardens, maintain a sense of place. In the so-called melting pot of the United States, although original languages are boiled away with much else, there are signs of origins in holiday rituals, cuisine, and gardening techniques and designs.

My late mother-in-law's home in Bellefonte, Pennsylvania— where her family was the first from Italy to settle at the turn of the twentieth century—had Italian terraced gardens climbing a steep hill, each level lined with rock walls. The garden produced grapes for wine (and champagne for Nonna's digestion), cilantro, tomatoes, basil, salad greens, spinach, zucchini, and lush flowers. It was one of the prettiest gardens I've ever seen, and in Bellefonte, it was exotic.

> I made for thee groves and arbors of date trees,
> lakes full of lotus flowers, *isi* flowers, *dedmet* flowers,
> the flowers of every land,
> myrrh and sweet and fragrant woods
> for thy beautiful face.
> > —Inscription in the Temple of Amun-Ramses III,
> > 1198–1166 B.C.E., Egypt

Ritual Fulfills Myth

Western gardens began in the Mediterranean basin, where nomadic communities first settled and plants were first grown as crops. Garden enclosures held back harsh winds and mercurial weather. The earliest gardens were functional and laid out in practical rows for irrigation. Shade and fruit trees blocked the relentless heat.

Many gardeners continue—with great decorative success—to mix vegetables and herbs with ornamentals.

It couldn't have been long before plants for food and medicine were understood also to be beautiful, partaking of all beauty's possibilities—including harmony, truthfulness, and originality—then sown and embellished in such a way as to make the garden pleasurable as well as useful, a model for paradise in the Otherworld. It could not have been long before the act of making a garden became a ritual itself.

With increasing trade routes and especially the expansion of the Persian Empire in the sixth century B.C.E., more and more decorative and utilitarian plants were introduced and exchanged. The first known importer of plants was Egypt's Queen Hatshepsut (1501 B.C.E.), who sent five ships to the land of Punt (thought to be Somalia) to obtain myrrh trees for her own mortuary temple in Thebes.

The first known written description of a garden was by Amten,

governor of Egypt's northern delta district (c.2500–2576 B.C.E.).
Egyptians planted flowers and trees "for the majesty of the gods."

Gardens were—and are—sanctuaries, and they were—and are—
also shrines, another kind of place within a place. In Japan, the Jingu
Shrines at Ise were originally virgin forest conserved for the Shinto
Sun goddess Amaterasu. It has, of course, been lightly developed
with lovely meditation and tea houses, bridges, and *torii* gates. We
can't resist tampering, making our mark, reminding the gods that
we're here, and mighty, too. Nevertheless, the pilgrims who visit
Jingu, as I did, come away feeling purified and blessed.

Examples of garden shrines abound everywhere from arranged
stones to elaborately landscaped parks, Edenic recreations, such as
cemeteries and botanic gardens. A spiritual architecture, like nesting
dolls, comes into play. Fountains, mausoleums, niches, and reliquaries: throughout history, people have built their gardens with and
around art forms as sacred spaces.

Within the garden as shrine, personal shrines were—and are—
built. Every gardener I know reserves some portion of the garden
for absolute holy space, a homegrown "chapel." It may or may not
have idols or objects—bells, fountains, altars, cairns, statuary—or
be constructed from building materials. It might simply be a pot
of petunias or a straggly vine, planted with special, private intent
or perceived as having divine value, by the curve of its stem, the
color of its blossom, the cut of its leaves, its taste or scent, its ability to heal.

Or less likely these days, it may be a section of uncultivated
ground, a respected bed of weeds: Pan's acre.

From the very beginning, plants have been grown as religious offerings and for their spiritual symbolism and magical qualities.
Everywhere, flower, herb, tree and vegetable offerings are made to
the divine, whether as formal, ritual acts or spontaneous displays of
love and devotion. They could be the intricate flower mandalas such
as those which women painstakingly create for the Onam Festival
of Kerala, India, to welcome the annual return of an ancient king.
They could be bouquets of wildflowers placed along a hiking trail
in West Virginia.

Ancient Egyptians had such reverence for natural beauty that they considered flowers, garlands, bouquets, and gardens the most precious propitiations. Where treasure might have been lavished on Tutankh-Amun (1362–1253 B.C.E.), three wreaths were instead discovered in his tomb, one made of the leaves of olive, willow, and wild cherry, another of lotus and cornflower blossoms, and the third from bittersweet berries and mandrake fruit.

One friend has filled an antique traveling trunk in her garden with pansies. I often think this cunning, boxed display is her precious and personal shrine, yet any number of places in her lovely, meticulously cared-for garden could serve that purpose.

Another friend—whose entire environment is oozing with marvelous imagery from every conceivable culture—salvaged a three-ton grotto complete with Virgin from certain destruction. What a celebration and procession that day! Neighbors gathered to watch as the cement structure, inlaid with glass, shells, and stones, was transported down the alley from its first garden to my friend's, lifted over the high fence and set in a quiet area, apart from the vegetable garden, the patio, and flower beds. The green, open space around the grotto is the only *un*cluttered place in her plush, snug home.

For me, the day itself and whatever's on my mind define the shrine. Some days my shrine is the pond, some days the bird baths, some days the anthills, some days the Enchanted Garden, some days the bed where squash grows, some days the various herb parterres, the Faux Forest or a particularly splendid stone.

I am constantly creating shrines and reliquaries, most of them temporary and organic. I love to watch those things that I put in the garden integrate, as plants grow around them, as rain and snow sinks them, as moss consumes them, as groundcovers or vines change their configurations, shaping new striations and textures.

I watch with satisfaction while paint peels, plaster pits, wood weathers, iron rusts, things move gradually back into the Earth. Yet I also observe this dissolution with vague regret, not wanting the thing to disappear, but also unwilling to protect it from the elements. That self-imposed sadness or nostalgia, I suspect, is simply another way to connect emotionally with the garden, as premeditated as any tearjerker. Rituals work like that, spinning us into high emotional states to shake up our souls, transport us, and drive away our complacency for a brief, essential time.

Why do we add decorative objects to a garden? Hardscaping, as it's called, seems redundant.

Yard art can be souvenirs, mementos to document a significant event. Because we infuse meaning into objects—idolatry on some level—we include them in the garden to uplift us, to provoke memory or evoke myths or dreams. Most are acquired without conscious intent or any agenda other than some indescribable need for spiritual or aesthetic enhancement. In Paradise we hope to be surrounded by all that's familiar and comforting. The adornments I put in my garden may have been hanging around the house, the cellar, or the shed until one day they present themselves as something that belongs in the garden, much as, Paul Shepard notes in *The Meaning of Gardens*, an animal appeared to primal hunters only when it was ready. And these objects, Shepard says, are inevitably "little gifts to the eye and the mind realized when they are used to make an environment."

My taste in garden statuary often runs to religious iconography, as the plaster Virgins of Guadalupe scattered about attest. Sheela-na-gig, Kali Ma, Hanuman, Saint Francis, and others are also smothered under excessive foliage, disguised by leaves and blooms, usually only clearly visible in winter. I have a collection as well of playful ceramic mermaids, birds, and garden pottery made by local artists.

In the interest of kitsch—for just plain fun, i.e., kitsch for kitsch's sake—I have round about, on the front porch and in the Fiesta Dinner Theatre, "planters of ill-repute," with plastic flowers or pink flamingos. I love *rasquache,* as Mexican Americans call their particular brand of vulgar ornamentation.

The object acts as a conduit between me, the gardener, and Earth, a kind of telegraph wire or divining rod, transmitting messages, which resonate but can't—and mustn't—be translated into words. Gardening as an act of spiritual expression lends itself, like artmaking, wholly to intuition, though gardenists have long striven to make it not so by compulsively controlling it. Nevertheless, either way, whenever we add objects to the garden, we are, I'm afraid, actively "culturizing" Nature.

I flatter myself that my various garden "designs" and projects occasionally resemble the work of "ephemeral" artists, such as Michele Stuart, Mary Beth Edelson, Kathy Herbert, Charles Simonds, Patricia McKenna, and Ana Mendieta, to name just a few, whose interaction with Nature and Earth I admire profoundly. They have temporarily altered natural environments by carving the Earth lightly, trenching, building forms in the woods, in canyons, in parks or burned-out pockets of cities, on beaches or deserts, marking, inventing, or converting topographies with sticks or stones, clay, hay, plants, or bones. They identify with the history of the land from its primal beginnings to its relationship with human beings.

(I like to believe, as well, that by recycling old things, such as furniture, nightgowns, and iron tools, into the garden, I'm more or less allying myself with the new breed of so-called "garbage artists.")

In her extraordinary book, *Overlay: Contemporary Art and the Art of Prehistory*, Lucy R. Lippard writes that the motivation, which began in the late 1970s—and continues today—toward making art created on and sensitive to a site in Nature "seems to have been a reaction against disengaged art objects that can be moved from place to place, but rarely 'belong' to any place. The word *ecology* was coined by Ellen Swallow Richards from the Greek word for home, and much 'ecological art' reflects a related need to 'return.' At the same time, our social restlessness demands a sense of movement. This gives rise to impermanence as a sculptural strategy well suited to natural environments, allowing many different objects to enjoy a brief but relatively unobtrusive public existence."

And so it is with gardening: fluid, constantly changing, and complete nonetheless, because the act of gardening brings us home.

The differences between the artists I've named and me are many. To begin with, their intention is art making, mine is gardening. I consider gardening an art form. I don't consider myself an artist. The declared artist has far more responsibilities than I want or can shoulder. Observing the work of these ephemeral artists has given me permission to manifest my ideas in my garden and suggested ways I can do so.

. . . this is that enchanted ground
where all who loiter slumber sound.

Here is the sea, here is the sand,
Here is the simple shepherd's land,
Here are the fairy hollyhocks,
And there are Ali Baba's rocks.

I never outgrew Robert Louis Stevenson's *A Child's Garden of Verses.* I never want to.

When I was a child, I built pirate coves, towns, fairylands, Hobbit houses, Persian palaces and Arab camps, Camelots, castles, forests, fjords, beaches, ponds, and lakes under trees and in ditches, arroyos, and flower beds, with sticks, stones, wasp nests and paper, flower petals, leaves, toys, and household implements. I shaped tiny bricks from mud and constructed all kinds of "primal" civilizations—somewhat like Simond's "Little People" settlements, which I saw as an adult and immediately identified with. Once, I tried to build the entire city of ancient Rome and had to be pulled kicking and screaming off my brother when he stomped on my coliseum.

As an adult, I'm self-conscious about play. The fantasies are all there, the desire to construct ritualized, idealized dwellings is intact; but these have become more abstract, stratified with the complexities of my garden and the labyrinthine requirements of adulthood. A child's world is flat as a table, ready to be occupied again and again, each occupation fledgling and unhackneyed.

Yet I still stack stones, probably with "villages" in the back of my mind, sealing them with clay, planting the clay with hens-and-chicks or various sedum. I plant pussytoes around jagged rocks, as if they were the cliffed wilds of the coasts of Ireland or Spain, or caves where the Otherworld could be encountered. I glance at certain striations in the land, among the plants, the way they arch and twist, the blend of colors, and see in them all kinds of exotic places and tales.

Down here, eyes on the ground, I build my ideal, peaceful worlds, my private utopias. Each mini-landscape in my garden was created—largely unconsciously—as the manifestation of stories I've read or written, fantasies I've nursed, my dreams and epiphanies. In the midst of writing, I bolt outdoors to clear my brain and *become* the stories I'm inventing. They take shape in the garden as fictional scenery.

When I return to the keyboard, something fresh has been hatched.

These garden environments aren't necessarily evident to others. The plants grow, the landscape changes, the story shifts direction. The scene continues to be gorgeous, but it has taken up its own narrative.

Some gardens are made entirely of objects. Around the world there are fabulous "gardens of revelation," as John Beardsley calls them in his book *Gardens of Revelation: Environments by Visionary Artists*. These folk art landscapes are similar in purpose to Babylon's Hanging Gardens or the Taj Mahal (both built, incidentally, by husbands in honor of their wives): from Simon Rodia's famous Watts Tower in Los Angeles to "Carhenge" in Nebraska to Nek Chand Saini's rock garden of carved and mosaic Buddhas and Boddhisattvas in Chadigarh, India.

The garden is universally a metaphor for all that's sacred in Nature. It is the ground, so to speak, where civilization and Nature meet. From the first seed planted, the garden has stood as a temple, whether formed of tiles, discarded automobiles and recycled bottles, oaks, elderberries, moss, sweet peas and penstemon, or bricks, tires, concrete animals, and potted plants. It is a habitation where, consciously or not, we communicate with whatever we perceive to be divine; a place, as Beardsley writes, of personal inquiry, moral assertion, peace, and contemplation. The public and private functions and aesthetics of gardens have changed repeatedly across the centuries, and vary with the gardener, yet the garden ethos remains the same: love, care, attention.

On Denver's Federal Boulevard, there is a plain brick house, whose front yard is entirely paved with a concrete red, white, and blue American flag, that seems insistent on the precedence of nation over Nature. Certainly some people are antagonistic toward Nature, asserting too much control or too much concrete. Yet for most gardeners, the act of creating a garden is sacred, however the sacred is perceived and personally interpreted. No matter how humble or plain the yard, regardless of how laden with sculpture or gewgaws, the contemporary garden remains the same paradise to its creator as it was for the ancient Egyptians, Hebrews, Sumerians, Aztec, or Chinese.

The Tower of Babylon was a garden that reached from Earth toward the cosmos to touch the gods. Nebuchadnezzar II (c. 600 B.C.E.) built this tall tribute to the divine, based on an earlier ziggurat form, in colorfully glazed brick terraces that coiled up, up, up toward the heavens. The terraces were fed by the Euphrates and planted with trees and every flower and herb then known to gardeners. Like the spires of a cathedral, the Hanging Gardens was an upside-down root, piercing the firmament, or like a lightning rod, a medium pulling the divine Earthward. And at the top stood the shrine of the fertility god who personified the all-important vegetal forces of the universe.

In 1976, artist Alan Saret created *Ghosthouse*, a ziggurat-like tower in Artpark in Lewiston, New York. Like the ancient tower, "*Ghosthouse* was intended," Lippard writes, "as an ethereal emblem of a life 'where technology bows to the spirit of the natural world from which it derives its materials and inspiration.'"

Archaic Greeks did not build pleasure gardens as such. They set their temples and theaters in natural landscape, amid fantastic vistas, surrounded by myrtle, lilies, honeysuckle, and ivy. This was Arcadia, the wild playground of gods, where they acted out their dramas with each other and with mortals. Elysium, the Land of the Dead, was situated below the Earth, where shades dwelled in perfect happiness.

Still another friend lives in a cabin on 100 acres of untrammeled Rocky Mountain wilderness, just below tundra. This alone is her garden, untouched in the very "heart of god." Walking about the land, I've run across stones painted with god's eyes and other magic symbols, which she's laid here and there to mark the places she feels closest to.

*   *   *

Unable to let go of the outdoors, we bring the garden inside, with birds, potted plants, landscape paintings, glass rooms, and greenhouses or—as were common in Pompeii, Crete, Egypt, and Mayan Yucatan—with murals of garden scenes that anchor indoors to out. Rather than house-with-garden, rich Egyptians had gardens with houses in them. Kiosks or pavilions were built around the pool, the central feature of Persian gardens, where indoor and outdoor spaces were so artfully merged, the division between them was nearly invisible.

Even in Afghanistan, perched high in the chilly Hindu Kush, every privileged home had a glass room—or *gulkhana,* flower place—where potted roses, marigolds, or geraniums grew year-round. I furnished our *gulkhana* with an overstuffed chair and a lamp, and there, among the blooms in porous turquoise pots from the village of Istalif, I read all night.

For the plant-loving, city apartment dweller, windows and balconies become the home's most vital aspect.

> The Song resounds back from our Creator with joy,
> And we of the Earth repeat it to our Creator.
> When yellow light appears,
> The joyful echo repeats and repeats,
> Sounds and resounds for times to come.
> —Hopi *Song of Creation*

Sap Rising in My Bones

"It will be a January when I die," a friend says, peering gloomily outside. "I hate January."

But some discreet seasonal transition is taking place, I can feel it, though the world outside looks the same. For the country folk of Europe, January signified the moment just before spring, when it was once again necessary to ensure the vigor and energy of the land, a time to induce the first rebirth, by wassailing—or hailing the trees—an old custom that corresponds to the ancient Egyptian January "Ascent of Sap" Festival.

Wassail the trees that they may bear
many a plum and many a pear.
For more or less fruits they will bring
as we do give them wassailing.

In most areas of rural Britain, the job of wassailing fell to the farmer and his helpers, who went out in the night to the orchards armed with noisemakers—or guns, a nineteenth-century innovation—and ale or hard cider to awaken the trees. Chants were chanted, shotguns fired into the boughs, and the trees were flogged to bring up the sap.

In some villages, wassailing was more elaborate and included everyone. There was dancing, food, and merriment, bowls filled with a concoction called "lamb's wool," hot ale mixed with roasted apples, toast, nutmeg, sugar, and eggs. Cake was fed to the tree and the robins, the spirits of the tree. Sometimes an Advent Box, a creche, was placed under the fruit trees along with little gifts for the tree. In Italy, folk processed through the orchards, singing and making a din that would startle the fig, almond, olive, or orange trees into abundance.

My great fear is that a sudden warm spell—which, in Colorado, could come fast at any moment—will fool the trees into blossoming too soon.

"Snow fattens the land," my mother used to say. "It's 'poor man's mulch.' A good, tough winter will brisken you kids up."

To that end, she sent us out to clear the bamboo arched and sweeping the ground. Up we climbed, laughing, screaming, and bouncing, until WHOOSH! the snow let go and the bamboo flung us like bungee jumpers, up and off, followed by a soft miniavalanche.

The month is nearly over. The snow drives on and on.

SPRING

February

> boil igneous rock for millions of years
> let stand until cool
> when vast inland seas subside
> uplift red sandstone, crimp edges
> grind soil with glaciers
> boil off glaciers
> decorate with trees, evergreen and deciduous
> then add large mammals, fish and birds . . .
> —John Wright, "Boulder Valley Surprise,"
> *United States of Poetry*

A Liminal Month

Slowly, slowly, pacing the garden, head down, my eyes scan for color.

Spring has begun her cautious flirtation with winter. Snowdrops are the first shy coquettes to appear, followed by miniature irises, such a dark, disappearing purple that searching for them is like a mushroom hunt.

In February, we teeter at the seasonal gate. And standing there is Brigit, Triple Muse. Celtic Threefold Mother of poetry, healing, and smithcraft.

My garden teeters among several micro-climates, most evident now and through the Summer Solstice, when the Sun is highest. The front gardens are a week or two behind the sunnier back and still snow-packed.

I gaze at the backyard from my second-story bedroom window and spot dots of crocus and glimmers of periwinkle. Phlox planted between rocks and near the warm foundation are returning to life, shedding their winter black, readying themselves for the blooms to come. Violets unfold from milder ground on the west and in the glade under the Faux Forest. Impressionist splashes of white and lavender against brown strokes of soil in mottled light. The kind of light that drove Monet to plant a garden at Giverney in France and then replant it repeatedly in his paintings.

Susie Next Door, an intrepid weeder, throws up her hands at the dandelions spreading like an oil spill across her rented yard, then digs in.

Dandelion is the Flower of Brigit, *bearnan Bride,* "little notched of Bride." Its uses range far beyond its reputation as a weed. When I dig them, I'll dry the roots for teas and dress a salad with the new leaves, one of the richest sources of vitamin A (dandelion is also called wild endive). When weeding is harvest, the job seems less tedious. Soon, too, a big stand of lamb's quarters will colonize my yarrow bed. Lamb's quarters are wonderful steamed with rice. If only I could think how to make use of bindweed!

Dandelion spring tonic is said to purify the blood, cure heart disease, cleanse the liver, ease rheumatism, and ward Old Woman Winter from the bones. The *dente de lion*—lion's tooth, the white, incisor-like taproot—has been used for centuries by herbalists to treat diabetes, cure anemia, and as a diuretic, which explains why the plant is also called *pissenlit,* or piss-a-bed. A folk wine is made from dandelion stems and blossoms. Mine turned out to be dandelion syrup.

Blowing on the dandelion seed head fulfills wishes, tells the time, calls spirits, or answers questions about the future.

This is a dangerous, tempting time, when the craving for outdoors is almost overwhelming. The mailbox is stuffed with catalogues exciting the hungry gardener with promises of coming delights. I've vowed this year I'll support our local nurseries and peruse the impossibly pretty pictures strictly for ideas. But the nurseries aren't geared yet for the outdoor flower planting season.

Unable to resist, I order four lavender and yucca plants for a bed I've long imagined (a mistake, it turns out: better to buy xeric plants propagated in the appropriate climate). I also order fern and hosta for a shady terraced garden on the east side, where I dumped dirt from digging the pond. I've supplemented and nourished this mound for four years, fluffing the clay with compost, manure, worms, and leaf mold.

Occasionally, I wish I were more organized. I can maintain a vision for a short period, but eventually I lose track and the first fancy is crowded out by another. I make maps, but in the end my plans and topographies don't amount to much. At least I *do* remember to rotate my crops, and almost always recall where I planted which vegetables the previous season.

Before this garden became a jungle, masking many eccentricities, I frequently forgot from year to year where I'd planted bulbs. Tulips twisted hideously out of the ground, fused like mutants, one on top of another. A single daffodil waved in the center of a parterre like the deserted flag of a retreating army. A fête of pink, purple, blue, red, and white hyacinths appeared where I'd thought each grouping would be a mass of single color. Yet my disorderliness also pays off. The windflowers, snowdrops, snow glories, star drifts, and buttercups naturalize more readily and never shock, but are sweet gifts like those discovered under your pillow.

The older I get, the more whimsical. The older the garden gets, the more it guides me and makes clear its health and aesthetic requirements. Season by season, we—my garden and me—work with increasing synchronicity and symbiosis, become increasingly unified, as if it's crept inside my body and is growing there, too. (More than once, I've been possessed by a funny image of my eventual self as a composting Green Woman, like the figures carved into Medieval cathedral walls, "Jenny-in-the-Green," with vines and leaves winding out of every orifice!)

I am the womb of every holt;
I am the blaze of every hill;
I am the queen of all hives;
I am the shield for every head;
I am the vault of every hope.

—*Song of Amergin,* variation from
Leabhar Gabhála Éireann, twelfth century

Imbolc: Lactation of the Ewes

February 1. Brigit's feast day. The goddess returns from the underworld at *imbolc,* an ancient festival of purification and rejoicing, while the giddy month fluctuates between winter and spring. A Scottish charm still recited to Brigit in this century was meant to heal a burn, yet its leaping invocation from fire to frost also characterizes this mercurial time.

Three ladies came from the East,
One with fire and two with frost.
Out with thee fire!
In with thee frost!

Goddess and saint share the same attributes. Blessing newborns and fire and water, Brigit brings life to the dead of winter and mediates the month's travails as it labors toward the Vernal Equinox. In her Christian aspect as Saint Bride of Ireland, Scotland, and England, she is known as the "Midwife of Christ." When a Highland woman was in labor, the midwife stood at the doorstep (called the *fad-buinn* or sole-sod), clutching the jambs with her hands, beseeching the help of the goddess-saint.

While the Greek Demeter—Corn and Barley Goddess—was thought to protect mothers, her daughter, Persephone—Kore the Maiden, She of the First Fruit—was guardian of midwives. Persephone was also Queen of the Underworld, as always, life and death in one package. Throughout history, the midwife deity has been associated with spring and worshiped more reverently than any other.

In Ireland, a protective charm in the form of a straw rope with crosses on it, a Brigit's Girdle, was worn on *imbolc.* The word means

"surrounding the belly," and the belt encouraged fertility. Brigit sur-
rounds and midwives the garden, nurses it as the plants labor and crown.

> *Every early and late, every dark, every light.*
> *I am shielded.*
> *Brigit my comrade-woman, my maker of song,*
> *Brigit my helping-woman, Brigit my guide.*

On February 1, or thereabouts when it's convenient, I meet with
like-minded friends, anywhere from five to fifteen women who feel
the need to mark the passage of time and seasons with some event.
No matter if it's just a dinner or tea party, we seek ways as a community to make the yearly calendar—and everyday life—more
meaningful.

Not all of us have children and partners. Not all of us are close
to our immediate families. We could hardly be labeled a "club."
None of us is willing to make any formal group/time commitment.
We're all ferociously busy, independent, and idiosyncratic.

Nevertheless, we long for the continuity that such gatherings
offer. Getting together for coffee and bagels early on a particular
morning to note it with some formality constitutes a ritual, so far as
we're concerned.

And if there's sometimes a certain self-consciousness in our gatherings, we try, at least, not to be melodramatic or artificial, but to
sincerely and simply express sentiments that will remind us of our
place in Nature. And *always* in the spirit of fun. I, for one, am unin-
terested in solemnity and spiral dances.

Each of us wants to increase the degree of intensity with which
we regard Nature, our joy in being. Surviving, soul intact, in a culture that dreads Nature is difficult. Joy, without Nature, is hard to
come by.

Like many women of her time, my paternal grandmother be-
longed to a garden club. They researched, composed, and read papers to one another about the life and origins of flowers. They held
sales and plant exchanges and ran the show on Arbor Day. I inherited my grandmother's garden club papers, dry, disinterested essays. I
never once saw her working in her garden. She seemed completely

satisfied with a few cobwebby shrubs, a big apple tree, and a neighbor kid to mow and rake.

My Aunt Kate, on the other hand, bent and crippled by painful arthritis at ninety, plants impatiens and geraniums every spring and remembers with profound pleasure when the side yard, now lawn and woods on at least a half acre, was abundant with vegetables *and* a clay tennis court.

We Brigit-chums exchange plants and seeds, offer advice and tell stories about the garden. We have in common our love of gardens, chronology, history, and myth. Our common ground *is* the ground. We meet on *imbolc*—and other times on the horticultural calendar—in one or another's yard, each contributing a milky food, cheese, cheesecakes, puddings, and, at one notable feast, a sinfully delicious Mexican *tres leches,* "three milks," fruit dowsed and simmered in milk, cream, and wine.

Imbolc celebrates the birth of lambs. One year, in a particularly ceremonial mood, we sprinkled milk on our flower and vegetable beds, reminiscent of an old custom in many societies of feeding mother's milk to the Earth to nourish her. Some farmers allow the first milk of the cow, sheep, or goat to fall on the ground. Each *imbolc,* I step outside in the cold morning and pour half-and-half on the garden before pouring it into my coffee.

In Hindu mythology, to milk the Cow of Plenty, rather than butchering her for meat, brings forth the plants, the nourishing vegetation, cultivation, grain, and the strength of the people.

What would a group of contemporary urban/suburban gardeners want with an ancient celebration primarily honoring the needs of herdsmen and their flocks?

Both prehistoric and Christian Brigit preside over art, poetry, and beauty. It is said that Brigit invented whistling and when her son died, she invented keening and the extemporaneous poetry that ascends from wailing women. Some of the most famous Irish verses have issued from women in mourning.

In India, Saraswati corresponds to Brigit as goddess of speech, learning, and the arts. She, too, is celebrated as the cold winter is ending, at the festival of Vasant Panchami. Like Brigit, Saraswati is a threefold goddess: her sisters are Parvati, goddess of righteousness;

and Lakshmi, goddess of beauty, fortune, and prosperity, who rose from the Ocean of Milk (and is honored in autumn at the Deepawali festival). As straw dolls are made for Brigit, so clay figurines of the goddess Saraswati are taken out in processions and immersed in rivers or water tanks. Like Brigit, Saraswati attends all waters. She is the spirit of the River Saraswati.

Saraswati is called Mother of the Vedas. As poetic muse, Brigit inspires the *Song of Amergin* and the "I am" form, in which the singer subsumes all being. The god Krishna manifests similarly in the Hindu *Bhagavad-Gita*:

> *. . . I am the whirlwind and the moon among the planets,*
> *I am the thunderbolt and the sacred fig tree,*
> *I am a lion among beasts, an eagle among birds,*
> *I am victory, I am effort, I am passion*
> *I am the cow of plenty . . .*

"I *am* what is around me," wrote the poet Wallace Stevens. The "I am" poetic impulse identifies us with Nature and seals us to the land. We all *are* where we live. There is reciprocity between person and place: *I am*. We (almost) become those aspects of Nature with which we interact. We are defined by how we interact with Nature: *I am* my ecology.

Biodiversity = a distinct *I am*. Excitation = *I am*. Awe = *I am*. Love = *I am*. Veneration for Earth = *I am*. Art making (for Nature is the Mother of the Arts) = *I am*. Gardening = *I am*.

Our culture is becoming sadly jaded. We have, as many have noted, lost our sense of awe. Especially our awe of Nature. And there is nothing to replace it. When awe is gone, fundamentalism and material greed rush to fill the void. We require some fuel to drive our souls, something we look toward for fulfillment. For me, this is primarily my family, my home, and my garden. They fill me with awe.

All spiritual epiphanies take place in the natural world. In a cave (Mohammed), under the Bo Tree (Buddha), in the wilderness (Christ), on a mountain (Moses), in fjords (Inuit), on lakes (Iroquois), in rivers (Hindu), and so forth, throughout the landscape: *I am*. The spiritual is not a single floating, diaphanous idea or dogma.

It is found in lived experience. Lived experience—*I am*—begins in place.

Place gives us a foundation, a dwelling, a safe harbor. Even nomadic peoples carve paths along which they migrate (rarely just wandering) and within that terrain they identify sacred places. The sounds their footfalls make on the desert, steppes, or high grazing country is *I am*.

Washing dishes, watering petunias, scrubbing the kitchen floor, repairing a gate, changing a tire, pulling weeds, filling bird feeders, filing papers, playing with children and friends, digging a parterre, fertilizing tomatoes, the daily tasks and pleasures are *I am*. The visionary is woven out of the ordinary. Where everyday and the divine encounter each other, there is *I am*.

Susie Next Door devotes hours and hours to weeding and planting, digging and beautifying a yard she does not "own." Yet doing so, she establishes place for herself and for its own sake. She establishes belonging. Someday, she may leave it, but she will have left behind her labor, love, and art and take with her the spirit, partnership, and experience of transcendent ecstasy that only the land can provide. *I am.*

Poets have always used some version of the "I am" form to evoke a bond between human beings and Earth's elements and creatures. The poet Walt Whitman invoked the magic "I am" in all his works, without employing the ancient form. He understood that attachment of place to self is directly related to stories about the place.

And the twelfth-century German mystic Hildegard of Bingen weaves herself with place and God:

> *I sparkle the waters,*
> *I burn in the sun, and the moon, and the stars,*
> *With wisdom I order all rightly . . .*
> *I adorn all the Earth,*
> *I am the breeze that nurtures all things green . . .*
> *I am the rain coming from the dew*
> *That causes the grasses to laugh with the joy of life.*
> *I call forth tears, the aroma of holy work.*
> *I am the yearning for good.*

I am works another way, too. Alphabets, writing, and poetry were once considered life forms, as sentient as any vine. Egyptian hieroglyphs, Norse runes, Celtic ogham, the cuneiform of Mesopotamia, Japanese *kanji,* Chinese ideograms—nearly all the early forms of writing were committed to Nature. The use of words continues today with such public projects as Shiah Aberjani's exquisite poetry garden at California's Lanier Foundation. Poet/sculptor Ian Hamilton Finlay's *Little Sparta* contains blocks like gravemarkers carved with words hidden among the green or columns sunk into water in his own continually evolving garden in Scotland.

My Poetry Garden started with the words *I am,* chipped roughly with a chisel out of a stone resembling a short, fat obelisk. Unlike the impulsive object placement in other parts of my garden, the Poetry Garden is quite deliberate. Here, I've begun placing brick and shards of concrete on which letters and words are stamped, surrounded by flowers in colors of cadmium, sulfur, and magenta: calendula, Dusty Miller, white irises, gladioluses and "Raspberry Queen" Oriental poppies.

The bed also features a vanity license plate found on a country road, and other bits and pieces of objects with words or fragments of words. The idea is to puzzle these into nonsensical verses that can be read from various angles. Depending on the point of view, and with the addition of new words, the "exquisite corpse" changes. A friend in Brooklyn has found bricks with words like *rose* or *empire* for the concrete poetry gardens he builds in empty lots. These read like chants. The words in my garden read QV OAT LIPTAK JENNY'S RITE LIPTAK PAT. 2 I AM LIPTAK CO NATIVE LIPTAK. I have every hope of expanding its vocabulary.

The day after *imbolc* is Candlemas, which celebrates the purification of the Virgin Mary and the presentation of the infant Jesus at the temple. In Mexico, seeds are blessed on this day.

> *If Candlemas is fair and clear*
> *There'll be two winters in the year.*

Throughout the Northern Hemisphere, it is believed that the weather of the year's first quarter—counting January—determines the harvest. A severe winter destroys insect pests, particularly if the ground has been turned after the last frost and left lumpy. And frost-hard soil retains nutrients. In parts of England, frost is called "God's plough," for it breaks up the dirt.

Heavy, wet February and March snows will trim trees of their weaker branches, a boon, though no one looks forward to cleaning up the mess.

> . . . Universal Pan,
> Knit with the Graces and the Hours in dance,
> Led on th' Eternal Spring.
> —*Paradise Lost,* Book IV, John Milton, 1667

The Whirling Month

So called, for February brings the winds that will dominate early March.

My cold fingers warm with the work of cleaning trash that's drifted in from winter—before the March winds bring it back again—raking, replanting loosened bits of creeping veronica, succulents, and phlox. Asters are everywhere, spread from cottony seed-heads that fly like dandelion puffs. I begin the task of weeding them from unwanted places, a job that will continue through the season.

We wake to occasional rosy dawns and syncopations of chickadees, English sparrows, and house finches ("little bird of Bride songs"). Not full-throated, but in this fitful "brown month," their tunes are gracious respites from winter's disquietude. The male finches' caps are taking on a vivid mating flush. The calls grow more energetic daily as the birds glance past the house from feeder to feeder. The feeders empty fast. Seeds have disappeared into the soil and are scarce.

The blue jays' excited rattles and yells never abate through winter. Their cerulean plumage against the snow and fog cheered me through the cold. Now they're suspiciously quiet, except for a low, mechanical call reminiscent of electronic alarm clocks. A flicker, who drops by at the beginning and end of each gardening season, has returned. He's a quiet, beefy, industrious loner, kindly aerating what little lawn I tolerate as he drills the grass for ants.

One by one, robins are skating into town, the surest sign of spring.

The last paperwhites from the Christmas season have finally quit blooming indoors. I plant the dormant bulbs. Their inner clocks are completely confused. If they don't freeze, in a few seasons they come around and bloom with the daffodils, but never again so vigorously.

The juncos (in five varieties!) still visit, plump, pretty reminders that the snows haven't yet ended. Caution is required until the official frost-free date of May 15. February, March, and April are the least predictable months, though the weather in Colorado is never really reliable. Some years, a succession of warmish February days make it possible to successfully transplant seedlings (especially larkspur, which thrives in cold), perennials, and even small shrubs.

Pan stretches and awakens. He was the only one of the Olympian pantheon who chose to live on Earth and the only Greek god to die. In early times, his demise came as he fertilized the soil and the creatures—a temporary, or "little death," a *petit mort,* as the French describe orgasm.

He stands for Nature intact and uncontaminated by human interference. The Romans called him Faunus, the goat-god who always danced for joy. The Egyptians called him Mendes and in Palestine, he was Azazel the sin-eater, sent out to wander in the desert on the Day of Atonement, carrying with him the wrongs and woes of the people. In Islam, Azazel is a *jinn* or demon. It's not surprising that the goat became a symbol for the Christian devil.

The enactment of a formal and ritualized cleansing no longer exists in our society, except in religious communities. Instead, the concept of the scapegoat—"scape" being a variant of "escape"—has been perverted into generalized blame and promotion of fear, hatred and alienation that makes anyone who is Other a whipping boy for our ills. Nature herself has become the scapegoat, shouldering ever-heavier, filthier burdens, the sin-eater.

Pan is made of every element. His horns are the rays of sun and moon. His skin is pocked like the sky with stars. His face is stained with vermilion and the blood-red juice of elderberries. He is hairy, clothed like the shaggy mountains, like the loam and mulch of fallen leaves and bark on the Earth's surface. He is filthy. He rose from the dirt and rolls in it. He smells sweet, like wet soil, and sour from the dried excrement clinging to his furry haunches. His feet are hooves, solid and steady on rock and hills, light as wings.

He guards the flocks, the fields, and beehives. He helps the hunters find their quarry and loves his naps. He dances and laughs and laughs and laughs.

He couples with wood and mountain nymphs, with grotto and sea and tree nymphs, with Echo, Eupheme, and all of Dionysus' Maenads. He rollicks with the beautiful boy Daphnis, who breaks his heart. On May Eve, he transforms his coarse black goatish pelt into the white, curled fleece of a ram. Selene rides on his soft back and lets him do whatever he likes with her.

He chases sex wherever its odor reaches him. But chaste Pitys turns to a fir-tree to escape him. He wears her branch as a crown.

He pursues chaste Syrinx, who runs from him to the river.

He capers behind her, laughing, laughing. She dives into a thick stand of cattails and horsetails and thistles and tadpoles nesting at their roots. He reaches the place where she leapt, but she has disappeared.

Pan strokes his beard and steps into the swampy riverbed. He looks for the maiden, he sniffs the reeds. He cannot tell one from the other and does not notice the slight, terrified tremor of the reed she has just become.

He inspects the shore for her footprint. He grasps the reed that grows closest to the delicate dents from her button toes, the smear of her sprinting heel. He pulls the reed and then another nearby, until he clutches seven in his hand.

He kisses them, as if one might be darling Syrinx. His breath whistles through the hollow stems, so he kisses them again.

The whistle through the reeds intrigues him. He forgets Syrinx and wanders distracted from the river, blowing into the reeds, one after another, then all together, then blowing a scale up and down. He calls on the bees to give him wax. He seals the reeds and makes a pipe. The pipe makes seven notes and seven tones and these are the harmony of Earth. He laughs and plays his pipe all the days long.

When there is danger, Pan the Goat-God pipes the Panic. The
shrill terror spreads fear and sets the animals stampeding against the
enemies of Arcadia.

Before Zeus and his fellow Olympians were spawned, Pan was
the only god, ruler of Arcadia. He is said to be the son of Penelope
and *all* the many suitors who courted her as she waited out the
decades for her adventuring husband Odysseus to return.

Or he is said to have been hatched from the egg of a woodpecker, whose knocking on oak portends rain. His name is taken to
mean "All" and "everything"—but derived from *paein,* "to pasture,"
or *pa-on* "grazer." He gives us such words as *pan*acea/cure-all and
*pan*demonium/clamor, and the Latinate names for bread: the Spanish *pan,* the French *pain.* In ancient Greece, the *panegyreis* were rustic rites and communal feasts.

He is *numen,* creative energy, universal material substance. The
Olympians, when they finally appeared, mocked him, but relied on
his gifts of prophecy, for Earth supplies us with the future.

Demoted to a lesser god, a *daemon,* Pan was eventually entirely
debased into a demon, his role changed from "All" to rustic country god and shepherd, until finally he was made over into the devil,
Nature incarnate, the source, divorced from controlled, rationalized,
Paradise-Nature, where there are no creepy-crawlies, nothing to be-
devil or be-Pan us.

No matter that Pan has been transformed into Satan with his
goat's hooved, red-faced, horny, hairy image. Country folk nonetheless still pay tribute to him, with oblique customs and maxims to "let
the devil have his due," which simply implies giving the forces of
Nature—Pan—room to play and breathe in order to ward off ma-
lignant forces in the fields and gardens.

Pan was invoked as the deity who made the magical gardens of
Scotland's Findhorn grow lush in the most adverse conditions, and
at Perelandra, a horticultural research center in Virginia, where gardener Machaelle Small Wright has developed "co-creative science,"
a partnership between Nature and human needs, "based on the
principles of balance."

*   *   *

I deliberately leave portions of the garden unweeded, a wild shrine, benefices to Nature, with much the same intention as Navajo weavers who leave a glitch or mistake in the tapestry, called the "spirit hole," through which the divine can enter. A thing too thoroughly humanmade leaves no room for blessings. And it is certainly true that land, gardens or fields, can become overworked, so that it's a wise idea to let vegetable or annual plots rest and regenerate every few years.

In Ulster, an untended portion of a field or garden was called "the devil's half-acre"; in Wales, "the devil's offering." In Scotland, this preserve was the "gudeman's field," while the English called it "Jack's land," allied with Jack-in-the-Pulpit, Robin Goodfellow, and Jack-in-the-Green, the manifestation of the foliate head reliefs that ornament Medieval churches. The uncultivated fields could be likened to national parks and conserved wilderness, which have the same function in modern society. Before all the land is eaten up with our needs (not to speak of our material desires), some must be tithed to Nature and thus to Pan, or else we assure our own destruction.

In my yard, this place is largely the Enchanted Garden.

Seed growth was once thought to be dominated by Satan, who, in the absence of a specific or admitted Christian fertility figure, upholds the role of bestowing fecundity and health. Sown seeds were said to visit hell before they germinate. "Two sowings for the devil and one for the gardener" broadcast with a sincere incantation could allay the problem. Nevertheless, occasionally the seeds stay in hell and refuse to sprout.

> *This is for me,*
> *this is for my neighbor,*
> *this is for the devil . . .*

And gardeners everywhere leave bits of the harvest for the pixies, the fairies, the devas, the birds, the devil, or whichever manifestation Pan takes.

> *Men worship nature by the name of Pan*
> *A man half goat, a goat half man. . . .*
> *Some say that wisdom governs in the heart;*
> *some in the brain: none in the nether part.*

Apollo, the far worker, Olympian god of law, philosophy, the arts, and light, stole Pan's music and turned it to classical harmonies away from "vulgar piping"—the triumph of intellect over imagination, romance over sensuality, repression over emancipation, materialism over spirituality, and in the garden, formality over naturalism.

Despite Apollo's theft—when Nature and civilization separate—artists, writers, and gardeners continue to identify with Pan. Pablo Picasso's paintings of Pan (as well as satyrs and Minotaurs) reveal the indestructibility of Nature and art, of instinct and *jeu d'esprit*. "Art is never chaste," he said. "Art is dangerous. Where it is chaste, it is not art."

The same can be said for Nature.

> I bequeath myself to the dirt to grow from the grass I love,
> If you want me again look for me under your boot-soles.
> —Walt Whitman, *Song of Myself*

The Enchanted Garden

Rampant wild garlic has started its annual takeover in the Enchanted Garden. It's the scourge of my gardening life, yet such a sweet, fresh earlygreen, I leave clumps here and there.

For years, those blades seduced me. I let the garlic wander where it pleased. In those days, when I was overwhelmed supporting a family by myself, I was overjoyed at anything that looked to my eyes like a garden.

Little did I realize that if I gave the garlic an inch, it would try to conquer the entire yard. At last, I took the situation in hand and began digging it out. Every year, I remove more, tossing the bulbs into buckets of water, then washing them, pickling them, or roasting them.

One bulb missed, one wrong pull on a blade, and one garlic will propagate into hundreds. I pick a spot, sift the dirt where I've dug, search out strays, then replace the wild garlic with columbines, sweet woodruff, cranesbill geranium, plumbago, ferns, Chinese lilac, feverfew, daphne, and cotonester, until the Enchanted Garden has become thick with mostly shade-tolerant plants and evergreens to give it a sylvan illusion. I imagine Faunus capering here. In a recurrent dream, a Green Man, Pan, lives here and is available to me for visits, long chats, and piping concerts.

The Enchanted Garden is hidden by the Faux Forest. When I moved here, the space was the Candelarias' trash area, with stacks and stacks of used lumber around an old, picturesque brick incinerator. I cleared the trash, and let go the garlic and whatever else had been dormant, giving Pan his due.

The old grapevines trailed where they would, up and over the dead firs next door. The original wire fence was thoroughly rusted and crunched. The place was a mess. And, it was magical. It had its own identity. It was entered through a natural bower in the plum trees. The children named it the Enchanted Garden.

For a few years, it served as a favorite spot for the kids to hunt Easter eggs. And it was a pet burial ground.

Gradually, I began to understand that this disheveled place was becoming a serious habitat for birds. By letting it alone so long, its purpose had been decided for me. I wouldn't make it too much more open to the rest of the yard than it already was, and having just returned from a trip to Central America, I was inspired, dripping with visions of rain forests. I hankered for vines everywhere.

I raised redwood lattice where the rusty wire fence had been. Ten feet tall and anchored with 4x4s in cement, which to everyone's surprise, especially my own, still stands. The fence is thickly covered in concords, which we don't pick, but leave entirely to the birds. The robins dominate the area in late summer and fall, gorging themselves on grapes.

When Jerry Across the Alley renovated his house, it meant shrinking his luscious Japanese garden. One day, I spied a steep bamboo roof in his trash pile. Could I have it? Friends and I raised it on pillars to make a teahouse/bird blind. If we sit quietly enough, long enough in that spot, the action goes on freely around us.

The old grapevines, stems the size of tree trunks, have—with a little guidance—twined around the teahouse pillars and covered the roof. I laid in more groundcover of lamium, sweet woodruff, and ivy and added a splash of maroon nearby, with a tiny bareroot Japanese maple that leafs out every year, but does not grow taller. And no wonder, considering how much flora I've crammed in one space.

People rarely visit the Enchanted Garden. It's too isolated and overgrown, a "wild" place, Pan's place, though it's no longer untouched Nature, which in a city usually means only desiccation and the sad dregs of neglected previous gardens.

A mullein grows between the bricks of the old incinerator, which now houses woodbine. Mullein brings woodpeckers.

Modern civilization has split the world's wholeness into sections, subsections, headings, subheadings, microchips, sound bites, and salable parcels. Although the garden is, in a sense, artificial Nature, whole systems and natural principles operate here. The history of evolution, the past, present, and future, resides in our backyards. The garden responds spontaneously and honestly to Nature's forces. It lives without prejudice, without thought to "good" or "bad." It is not trite, trivial, or sentimental. The splits are dissolved, for each of us personally, in the garden. The "I am," "everything," and "all" are free to thrive here. Pan, the instinctual, the creative mind, sprouts and sprawls here.

Pan lives where he can. In the lowliest flowerpot and the grandest palace park. He lives *here.* Dancing, coupling, capering, piping, laughing and laughing and laughing. In the garden.

The Sun is low. The sky milky. The short grass is turning to emerald. The trunks of bare, deciduous trees are infinitely various. Large magpie and squirrel nests stir softly in exposed, forked branches. The ivy and evergreen trees, so stalwart in the dead of winter, seem suddenly exhausted, as if taking advantage of February to rest before the spring sprint.

The owl nests in February and was once the familiar of midwives and midwife deities. This is the month of midwives, mothers, and the secrets and poetics of the beginnings of beginnings.

In February, the ancient Greeks celebrated the Lesser, or first, of the Eleusinian Mysteries, rituals that were held in secrecy. Few clues are left to reveal the exact practices. They must have been intended to impart the greatest secret of all—the nature of Nature herself.

The annual festivals honored Demeter, Mother of Grain, and her daughter, Persephone—Kore the Maiden—ravished by Hades, Ruler of the Dead, who abducted her to be Queen of the Underworld. Mother and daughter had simultaneous attributes of earthiness and transcendence, held together by the soul.

A day of snow. I look out the bedroom window at the big flakes blanketing the garden . . . fast. My eyes adjust to a sharp-shinned hawk sitting on the coyote fence between Susie's and my yards. I blink. In that nanosecond, the hawk has whipped through the storm and snapped a house finch in its talons. It stops for another second on the fence, then flies into the west.

Two days later, most of the snow has melted. Under the icy mulch, I find spring bulbs straining toward the gaps and tiny peony shoots like scarlet lipsticks.

March

"What is compost?" I said. And the person explained in a way I could visualize it, recognize it as a miracle, a revelation. Masses, multitudes, millions upon millions, a culture of bacteria growing, living their lives, eating this problematical stuff, transforming it in a matter of weeks into a sweet-smelling treasure that plants would thrive on. I followed instructions, heaped the manure, watered it regularly, watched as it shrunk down then, after the prescribed number of weeks, picked up a turd, held it timorously to my nose and there—fresh and strong—odeur de greenhouse, astonishing.

—Jane Wodening, "Roscoe," *The Inside Story*

Wind Wallops the House

Branches scrape the gutters like fingernails on a blackboard. The windows rattle. The cats follow me, mewing as if I were responsible and could make it stop. If March were a Grimm's fairy tale and we lived in it, famished wolves would be howling at the cottage door.

No surprise that March is named for Mars, Roman god of war. Until the European calendar was reformed, March was the first month, goose-stepping ahead of the whole battalion, and for good reason. March is a powerful month.

The west wind roars through Susie's front porch, dislodging the lattice she's hung for privacy and light vines. It speeds, screaming on through my porch, as if through a tunnel. I long ago gave up the handsome redwood lattice for honeysuckle in favor of weightless chickenwire that can withstand these gales.

The wind sets my porch swing squeaking and flailing, then continues next door, where it's halted by a magnificent, fifty-year-old sprawling rugosa. No tenant or property manager prunes or props it. I'd let it spread, but whenever I work on the east side of the garden, that rose grabs me and slices my arms and legs like razors. You couldn't ask for a better guard dog. I cut it gingerly, where it reaches into my irises. I wear gardening gloves, which I loathe.

The wind sneaks through the few gaps in the snarled mass. Its journey thwarted, it rattles and thwaps a thorny branch on a drainpipe again and again. I stare, mesmerized, from my bedroom perch as bare trees sway, weak branches creak and crash to the ground. The pond ice has melted, but rather than lounge in sunny spots, the fish hide in the depths. There are mini-whitecaps on the water. I wish I had a toy sailboat, or better yet, two to race in this squall.

The laundry twists round and round the line. Clothespins, clinging to socks, fall into the campanula bed. A sheet rears off the line and flaps over the yard, landing like a hang glider on the plum trees.

"In like a lion; out like a lamb"—there's no guarantee of a sheepish March retreat in Colorado.

The garden gasps for nutrients. I stagger through the gusts feeding it bucket after bucket of fish emulsion, nitrogen to replace what was washed away with last summer's rain and winter's heavy snows. Susie steps out of her house and sniffs the air. Amused distaste curls her mouth. I shrug and smile apologetically.

In Ireland, it was customary to pile a dung heap in front of the farmhouse. A rowan sprig was stuck in the muck to preserve its fecundity and bring good fortune. My dung heap is behind the shed, protected from the wind and covered with plastic anchored with rocks.

Even our elegant home in Kabul had a dung heap, way at the end of the walled yard near the stable and the roosts where my brother and our house guard Ghulam kept pigeons. It was supplied with pigeon leavings and by a horse. After the auburn Arabian was gone, a rattling, wheezing truck, reeking of sheep, horse, and camel manure pulled up to the house every spring. The dung deliverers' tinny, junked Russian vehicle was painted orange, pink, and red, scrawled with blessings and prayers, the windshield trimmed with balled fringe.

The dung truck clanked into our yard and an astonishing number of young men and boys leaped out of the little cab armed with shovels.

> *O God of the sea,*
> *Put weed in the drawing wave,*
> *To enrich the ground,*
> *To shower on us food.*

With that incantation, coastal Scots walked into the sea, pouring ale into the water, after a night of feasting, drinking, and dancing, when the gods of wind were invoked to drive "sea-ware" onto the shore.

If the seaweed supply was insufficient, families in the Hebrides gathered to brew a huge cauldron of porridge, which they poured onto sacred headlands, as offering to Manannán mac Lir, the sea god. Its goodness would attract his insatiable appetite and bring him (as well as birds and seals) with a trail of kelp and wrack.

Wherever the potash-rich seaweed was gathered, a bit was left as a blessing at each door before it was spread in gardens and fields. Farmers blessed the soil by sprinkling it with incorruptible salt. Salt belongs to Manannán, who influenced the weather.

In Central America, the water hyacinth is used as garden fertilizer. There's an abundance of it, clogging waterways to the annoyance of electrical plants and other purveyors of progress. In pre-Columbian times, it helped feed highly populated cities by providing fuel for staple crops such as squash, corn, and beans.

"Waste not, want not," say the old wives. My mother and grandmothers chanted the aphorism ad nauseam. Yet for all her extravagance and privileges, my mother meant it. She was raised in poverty and a young woman full of unattainable material dreams during the Great Depression.

In her Virginia kitchen, she kept an antique Japanese urn half-filled with water, into which she dumped eggshells, teabags, and coffee grounds. She had no compost or dung heap—God forbid!—in the suburbs of Washington, D.C., so every few days, no matter the season, she emptied the urn into her blender and ground the rank contents to feed her garden, plant by plant. Tea and coffee add acids to alkaline soil. The eggshells provide calcium.

She filled empty milk cartons with water, shook them, and poured the contents onto the roses. She swore by the success of pouring a half cup of whiskey into the hole dug for roses. "Of course, it needn't be your *finest* whiskey," she said, "but bourbon works best."

Some gardeners collect the pulp from microbreweries. Spent hops and malt dust make nutritious mulch. Post-party dregs dumped into the flower and vegetable beds work, too.

I haven't yet been able to persuade the men in my family to pee openly in the garden. Human urine, before indoor plumbing, was a common fertilizer. It's full of nitrogen, phosphoric acid, and potash and is said to be wonderful for grapevines and newly planted fruit trees.

India's Ganges River was born when the Durga stood astride a valley and urinated. The urine of the god Shiva in the Himalayas becomes the rain that feeds into the Ganges, a coupling of piddle, another fertile mating. The ancient Celts, too, believed that rivers were the urine of the Mother Goddess.

Human excrement, with the pretty name of "nightsoil," is toxic. Our diets and the chemicals we ingest create *E. coli*, which makes it prohibitive for fertilizer. In some countries, processors are used to kill organisms and purify the feces into a benign substance called *poudrette*.

The wind tears on and on. Until it's quieted, I'm reluctant to empty the compost bin and sift its black contents onto my beds, reluctant to spread manure only to have it blow away. And even if I water it down, this wind will only harden the ground again within hours, preventing solid fertilizers from seeping into roots.

Wind was once believed to originate from holes in the ground or caves, like those where the Greek Delphic oracle or the Roman Sibyl sat while voices from the Earth traveled up between the seer's legs, through her body, and out her mouth as prophecy. "Listen closely to the wind," the books of childhood advise us, "and you can hear it speak."

Whistle three times with benevolence in your mind to bring a cooling wind, my grandmother said, or when a breeze is needed to accomplish a task.

"Be careful," she warned. Witches also whistle for the wind to speed them on their brooms toward wicked deeds. The devil has the power of the air.

"A windy March will bring a beautiful May," she promised without explaining why. She may not have known the reason, but was simply transmitting folk wisdom passed down through generations.

Winds scatter seeds and can send them on journeys across entire seas (while birds transport them from place to place for hundreds of miles in the mud dried in their claws). In old Breton and Estonia, gardeners and farmers threw knives, pitchforks, or sickles to prevent the thief who rides the wind from carrying off the hay and seed corn.

Whistling for a mitigating wind has been less than successful . . . for me, anyway. Yet March is the busiest month, so these chinooks should give us plenty of energy and motivation for the garden tasks to come.

Winds deliver dreams. When I finally fall asleep—having stomped outside in a temper with my pruning shears to stop the angry thwapping of the rose against the drainpipe—I dream the garden air is crowded with vibrant American goldfinches, swarming around salmon azaleas.

At my parents' last house in Virginia and in our Japanese homes, there were hundreds of azaleas. It's been difficult living without them. A hardy variety, developed at the University of Minnesota, at last made it possible to grow them in Colorado, though their bloom time seems short. I've kept the whites and yellows thriving in soil that is far too alkaline, by watering them weekly with specially brewed pots of coffee or black tea.

Now's the moment. The obsession's on me. This year, I'll plant salmon azaleas on the edge of the Faux Forest glade.

When at last the raging March chinook stops—always abruptly—the garden is bone dry. I give everything a deep drink, then dress the beds with compost and manure. I fold the nourishment in with a whisk, so as not to disturb roots. In shady spots, the ground is frozen, despite the wind, but the manure dressing will help thaw it.

The red wigglies I bought by the dozens at a bait shop—on the recommendation of a friend who swears they work harder and faster than earthworms at breaking down solid compost material—are in fine fetor. Their population has at least quadrupled. I scoop as many as I can from the compost bin into a bucket and "transplant" them to other areas where they're needed to sift and enrich the soil. I chatter at the worms, "selling" them their new homes like a real-estate broker.

"Daffodil snows" finally tumble from the sky. In Colorado, snow usually counts more than rain, although global warming seems to generate more humidity each year. Increasingly heavy spring rains alternate with weeks of scorching dryness, causing confusion for the gardener and trauma to the plants.

Morning snows are melted by early afternoon, when the sun comes out. The ground is just damp enough to encourage the tulips and hyacinths, which are four or five inches high. The narcissus is about to bloom, but a bed of daffodils my father planted for me, eighteen years ago, has been in full glory since February, withstanding every hostile force.

Daffodils—trumpet narcissus—were said to have covered the Greek Elysian Fields of the Dead, and are the flower born from the vanity of Narcissus, a young Greek demigod, who fell in love with his own reflection and pined away unable to grasp it. The hyacinth sprang from the blood of another beautiful Greek boy, Hyacinthus, brained with a discus by the jealous West Wind.

> As for me, my vulva,
> For me, the piled-high hillock,
> Me, the maid—who will plow it for me?
> My vulva, the watered ground—for me,
> Me, the Queen, who will station his ox there?
>
> Oh Lordly Lady, the king will plow it for you,
> The king, Dumuzi, will plow it for you.
>
> Plow my vulva, man of my heart!

At the king's lap stood the rising cedar,
Plants rose high by his side,
Grains rose high by his side,
Gardens flourished luxuriantly by his side.
—*Song for Inanna's Vulva,* Sumerian

Soil

I love dirt and all it does for us, from nourishing our food to providing clay for the plates we eat on and the bricks that shelter us.

Responsibility for the soil's fertility belongs to the gardener. Long ago, it was understood that Nature is not an inert object merely to be exploited, but a living partner to be revered, cared for, and respected as one would a partner or a child. In many ancient cultures, no king could rule until he had symbolically coupled with Mother Earth. (Such a ritual ought still to accompany the inaugurations of all leaders.)

Soil was known to be a living, breathing being on the Earth, the womb or the skin of the Mother. To disturb it without ceremony and offering was a dangerous undertaking. That danger still exists. Propitiation offers an opportunity for thinking before we act. Sustainability = sustenance.

Old gardens where organic fertilizers were used continue to produce, season after season, centuries on. Modern agribiz farms and gardens pounded with artificial fertilizers become sterile within a few years and pollute and poison the entire environment around them. Once I walked onto the lawn—actually thick mowed weeds—where my Aunt Kate's mother, Celinda, kept the vegetable garden, started a century ago. I reached down and dug a little. The soil is splendid.

"Watch where you dig, honey," Kate laughed. "Anyone who tries to develop my land after I'm gone will get a big surprise out there: twenty-two suitcases holding kitty corpses!"

Before Indo-Europeans understood paternity, the masculine role in reproduction, only women could break the soil and do the planting. As bearers of children, women were considered to be the

Source, Mothers of Abundance, self-fertilizing, inexhaustible funds of vitality, the life force itself.

In Neolithic times, Mother Earth was mated to a Sky-Father, who sent the fertilizing rain, the seed that energizes the sacred marriage. The male god revivified Nature and took the job of weather making. In India, the "he" source of procreation was united with Prithiri, the Earth Mother. In Greece, she was Gaia, who gave birth to her consort, Uranus the Heavens. As time went on and civilization grew, Zeus the Cloud Gatherer came to reign over the elements from Mount Olympus, coupling again and again with Gaia's fragmented and therefore disempowered personifications—Aphrodite, Semele, Hera, Demeter, Hekate. In the tales, the coupling mostly took the form of rape—a sad similarity to and prototype of the way Nature is abused today.

In Egypt, the roles were reversed. Geb the Earth God united with Nut the Sky Goddess, an act repeated each time the ground was hoed.

In the Fertile Crescent, the goddess ruled. She was Cybele, mother and lover to Attis in Phrygia. She was Ishtar, mated with the shepherd-god Tammuz in Babylonia, and in Sumer, she was Inanna, whose husband was Dumuzi, "the faithful sun of the waters that come from the Earth." She was mother and bride, entirety and eternity, supreme Nature, her love for the virile male god simultaneously sexual and maternal, which together give rise to the creative powers of Spring. Only she could rescue him from the Underworld. Only she could resuscitate him to renew Nature.

In the Sumerian myth of Inanna, there is a fascinating passage in which the goddess, preparing for her wedding, is told she must marry a shepherd. It's as if we've come precisely to a point in the history of Western civilization where settled agriculture comes head-to-head with nomadic herding (an ongoing battle through history, like that in the American West between farmers and cattle ranchers). That conflict is repeated in the Biblical story of Cain's jealous murder of his brother Abel, when God rewards the agriculturalist over the shepherd.

At first, Inanna refuses the shepherd and insists she will wed a gardener/farmer (terms then nearly synonymous). He grows plants and grain and is not "coarse," like the shepherd, who represents raw Nature.

Dumuzi is adamant about how much more he can offer the bride and finally confronts the gardener, a meek man who wants peace and friendship, refuses to fight, and offers Dumuzi pastureland and water. Inanna is eventually persuaded to marry the shepherd, the virile man, the "wild bull" whose meadow dwelling is "fragrant." The rebuffed gardener brings gifts to the wedding.

To marry the gardener would have canceled Nature out of the equation. The union with raw, "coarse" Nature ensures continued growth.

Green. Fecundity. Transition. Newness. The gardener has a green thumb. One who is young or naïve is "green."

Spring arrives on a green mist. In the Christianized Celtic world, the fairies inevitably appear to humans wearing green. The fay-knight who challenged Gawain of the Round Table, in the anonymous Pearl Poet's fourteenth-century masterpiece, was green and so was his horse.

The Austrian philosopher Ludwig Wittgenstein admonished us not to "stay up in the barren heights of cleverness, but come down into the green valleys of silliness." Green is "silly": carefree and uncontrived. In Middle English to be "silly" was to be blessed, innocent, and hapless.

In ancient Greece, March was referred to as "Green Demeter," after the Grain Goddess in her Spring aspect. Grains were "Demeter's fruits" (and in Rome, "gifts of Ceres"). In images of the goddess, she carries the yellow grain and scarlet poppy, which grows profusely amid the crop. Paint disappears across the millennia, leaving archaeologists to guess, and some speculate her gown and hair were tinted green.

I imagine Demeter's stolen daughter, Persephone, with green flesh like Yama, the Hindu god of death, who carries a mace in one of his four hands and a noose in another. He is green to signify decay, and like Persephone—Wife of Death, Queen of the Underworld, who revisits Earth each year—Yama returns as fertility that becomes nourishment.

The March sky is now a hard, cloudless, Alpine blue. The wet snow sinks into the soil. The grass is suddenly vibrant, phosphorescent, *silly*. The cats graze the young grass tops. I pick at it like hors d'oeuvres, pulling blades out of their sheaths and chewing on the succulent ends. The children made grass whistles by holding the blades between their thumbs and blowing, an ear-piercing trick my father taught them.

The fruit trees are budding. Tiny, tightly wrapped sprouts poke from branches. The Manchurian bush apricots are already in bloom. The weeds, too, are inspired, as healthy as I could wish any of my plants. We curse the weeds. Ancient Greeks uttered curses when sowing certain plants, such as cumin and basil, to avert misfortune. This preemptive strike was meant to anticipate and forestall disaster. Other cultures were known to curse the seeds of medicinal herbs as they were planted, in order to strengthen their bitter taste and thus their potency.

(An ancient Greek ploughing ritual also included curses uttered against any who denied their fellow humans the basic necessities—food, fire, water, shelter, love, health.)

The weeding that began with asters and dandelions in February continues, more and more frantically, as more and more little intruders pop their insolent heads out of the ground.

Weeding, I'm in my element, truffling in the dirt, transported by this lowly task. I could weed uninterrupted for hours and often do. On my knees or balanced on my heels and haunches, in the manner of our Japanese gardeners and Mali, our Afghan gardener, whose hennaed red beard blended with the zinnias. The dyed whiskers were a sign he'd made the *haj*, the pilgrimage to Mecca required of all Muslims.

Observing outer objects
we find our own minds.

Weeding is like clicking off prayer beads. The repetition carries me out of body, out of worry, away from troubles and temperament. I start each day's work by weeding. Before long, I'm devoured in the green.

Humble tasks, we're told, lead us closer to the divine, an idea on which monastic life, for one, is built. In myths, folk and fairy tales, the lesson is reiterated again and again as milkmaids, Cinderellas, or lovely queens distorted by hexes, and ash lads, farmhands, or fools transformed into princes discover the redemptive power of anonymity, of no-Self.

Weeding provides gentle stimulus to the spirit and imagination, in addition to its devotional, restful benefits. And weeding, again, is sorting, when we can heal ourselves from hard times, practice forbearance, and let go.

Weeding is the first step in my reductive method of "designing" a garden. I tend to plant far too much, too close, most always on a whim. I forget that little things grow big. Like a kid, I can't be bothered with too much planning, though for some people planning is part of the joy of gardening. For me, it takes time away from play. In every aspect of my life, including the garden, I've wanted to let things expand to their own limits, then prune and shape them. Across these many years, I've become a knowledgeable gardener, and I'm also a deliberately rudimentary one.

On the other hand, perhaps my problem is, as my husband has written in a poem, "Nature's too slow; people get bored."

In a year or so, I'm faced with transplanting (lately to Susie Next Door's yard), in order to realize what it was I may have had in mind in the first place. By then, the plot has revealed its capabilities, given its size, location, and the quality of the soil. In the end, the garden always designs itself.

This ability to *achieve* the garden exactly as I picture it, its insistence on its own will, its relationship to things outside my control (such as weather), confirms—again—that gardening is indeed a fine art (whether "Sunday" or professional), not merely pastime. Labor toward an idea is ultimately accomplished in the garden's own terms. The poet W. H. Auden said that a poem is never finished, "only abandoned." And so it seems with the garden. But it is the rigidity of a design idea, an expectation of *how* it should look and feel, that must eventually be abandoned. Gardening, like any art, is a process not a product.

*   *   *

Somewhere between fertilizing and weeding, there are repairs. Fences and stakes. Lattices and arbors. Tools. All get the once-over for rust, paint, winter, and wind damage.

Recognition of the male principle brought us the plough. No longer was planting a role assigned to women. The plough reflected the phallus, which broke the ground and made it ready to receive seed. With the invention of the metal plough came digging that was unnecessarily deep. And heat from metal harrows (the word *harrow* also means to "inflict great distress or torment"), as well as rotary tillers so popular in gardens today, kills off microbes and insects who live in the ground and keep it fertile.

I'll stick with a shovel, a hoe, a trowel, a broomstick broken at just the right angle to draw seed trenches and poke holes, a kitchen whisk, pruning shears, a tree saw, and a pair of retired sewing scissors.

In another dream, my hands fall off. I'm frightened and run to my Tío Yomi for help. He attaches a trowel to my right wrist and a pair of garden shears onto my left. Now I can work in the garden, but each time I dig the ground, my wrists bleed. Little by little, I become more skilled with the strange prostheses, but the blood still gushes. At last I work my way to the pond. I dip my bleeding wrists, trowel, shears into the water. Goldfish gather around my wounds and nibble them. Horrified, I pull my arms out of the pond and my hands are restored.

> In this fateful hour,
> Between myself and the powers of darkness,
> I place all Heaven.
> And the sun, the snow, fire and lightning
> And the winds, the sea, rocks and earth.
> I place them between myself and the powers of darkness.
>   —*The Rune of St. Patrick,* Irish, date unknown

Saint Patrick's Day

I hoe, carve seed trails with my broomstick. March 17 is the first "official" planting day of the season. I often cheat and take a gamble with lettuce and spinach seeds in earlier weeks if the ground isn't frozen. During temperate February days I push my luck as far as it will go by transplanting. Flexing the muscles, turning the soil, poking holes in the dirt . . . nothing feels healthier, nothing sloughs winter off more joyfully.

Planting is the best part of gardening. There is the happy satisfaction of watching things already planted return and take their places again, each year becoming more integrated with the environment. Adding something new, whether seed or seedling, carries with it a transcendent ecstasy, equivalent, I think, only to giving birth.

Putting in peas on Saint Pat's is probably the best-known of all American garden rituals. It is an Irish-American tradition—peas were a luxury an oppressed peasantry could in no way afford. I plant seeds of beets, snow peas, turnips, arugula, radishes, and cilantro. Kale next to pink cosmos, collards, this year with a stand of white daisies. Mustard greens, mizuma, onions, carrots, and lettuce.

Radishes were highly prized by ancient Greeks and Romans, who dipped them in salt or ate them with butter. My husband likes them that way, too, or any way he can get them. The snooty gentlewoman gardener emerged when my mother sneered that radishes are so easy, they'll "grow in your fingernails." Yet vegetables—radishes, lettuce, onions—that are little trouble and provide a quick source of nutrition, however base, are customarily the ones most lionized. The same is true of ordinary flowers—bachelor's buttons, poppies, goldenrod—which offer reliable beauty year after year.

My grandmother said that planting too much lettuce brought bad fortune and the woman who did so would be childless. How much is "too much" lettuce? By contrast, in ancient Egypt, lettuce was used medically to help childless women conceive.

When the Greek youth Adonis was killed by a boar, the goddesses Aphrodite and Persephone fought over his body until Zeus declared the boy would spend half the year above with Aphrodite and the other half in the Underworld with Persephone—another in the long, important parade of death and resurrection tales symbolizing the seasonal cycle. Aphrodite laid the boy's body on a bed of lettuce: its quick growth, fast bolt, and withering signified the youth's short life. At the Festival of Adonia in ancient Greece, lettuce was featured in the funeral rites.

*   *   *

Saint Paddy's is also the day to plant the first crop of potatoes. If the gardener missed the exact day, the problem could be rectified by chanting "praise be to Saint Patrick" each time the potato was dropped in the hole.

On the rocky Irish Aran Islands, where there is almost no soil, there are potato gardens, generations old, in neat mounds surrounded by stone walls to stop sea gales. (Robert Flaherty's classic 1934 film, *Man of Aran,* describes the trouble folk went to for mere spoonfuls of dirt.) Some of these gardens are situated within the ruins of ancient churches and monastery huts, and some in Mesolithic settlements, where the fierce pre-Celtic tribe of the Fir Bholg built massive stone fortresses on the cliffs. Seaweed was, and may continue to be, the fertilizer of choice for some island gardeners.

I planted potatoes . . . once. Colorado is said to be prime for growing them. My crop was so puny, if I'd needed it for sustenance, I'd have had to immigrate *back* to Ireland.

In the late 1990s, the Russian post-Soviet economy collapsed, the people stood on the brink of famine. "There's an art to being poor," a Siberian woman told a BBC interviewer with surprising good humor and infinite wisdom. "It is an art to live with no money at all."

Potatoes are the Russian barter goods of choice. They'll keep in a cool larder (not nearly so long as grain) and delay starvation awhile, until they sprout and develop fungi. Ironically—considering the millions who fled Ireland for the United States—the first major Irish potato famine was caused by a fungus brought to the island on an American steamship.

In the annals of gardening jokes, "1001 ways to cook zucchini" is a standard. It's no joke when it comes to potatoes, which, since the Spaniards found them in Peru in the sixteenth century, have become one of the four major staples of the human diet, with maize, wheat, and rice.

Without iron, beasts of burden, or the wheel, the Incas nevertheless developed complex systems of mathematics, architecture, astronomy, agriculture, and 3,000 varieties of potato, which is native to the Altiplano. Most of these varieties are lost.

Pachamama was the Inca Earth Mother, still called upon by indigenous peoples of the Altiplano. She is the Old Woman of the Forest, who lives inside the Earth. She is Chagra Mama, the Garden Mother, the one women call *comadre,* companion. She aids their pregnancies and births, helps them herd and make pottery, and teaches them to be good gardeners. She gave the people potatoes and all the other delectable foods. For good measure, she bestowed intestinal gas on them, too.

Maintaining a really lush flower garden at either of our homes in La Paz was rough. Small front yards were pampered for show. Backyards were another story. Thus, my mother hit upon the idea of planting potatoes to make a guaranteed backyard flower garden (fertilized with llama dung). When it was first introduced into France, she reasoned, the potato was planted exclusively as an ornamental. Its starlike blossom is delicate and lovely.

I remember our cook, Suzanna, shook her finger at my mother and yelled at her during the long weeks that followed the potato-garden harvest, when we—"wasting not and wanting not"—ate potatoes night and day. My father had a new joke every suppertime, playing off the Spanish words for potato, *papa,* and daddy, *papá.*

> *St. Patrick turns up*
> *the warm side of the stone.*

Saint Pat's is the day for pruning the roses, whose leaf buds are beginning to show. And for cutting silverlace vine, which in my garden stretches across the mattress-spring trellis to the west and climbs the telephone pole, much to the consternation of the linemen, who prune that portion for me.

Brussels sprouts can also be planted today. Kate knew a man who planted cabbages on Saint Patrick's Day, but only before dawn, while wearing his p.j.'s, which somehow guaranteed a fine crop. How modest he was compared to those who swore by planting naked as the best way to assure healthy vegetables. The unclothed body can sense the right planting temperatures. Plunk your bare butt on the March ground, and the reasoning behind, as it were, this folk belief will become coldly apparent.

Green as I would have you.
Green wind. Green boughs.
The boat on the sea
And the horse on the mountain.
With shadow around her waist
She is at her railing, dreaming
Green flesh, green hair.
—Federico García Lorca, "Romance of Sonambulo,"
Gypsy Ballads

The Vernal Equinox

Green Supper Day. A custom brought to us by my stepdaughter, whose mother celebrates Spring Equinox with a dinner all of green foods, white wine from the green grape and a recitation of Lorca's great poem.

The table is covered with a sage-green cloth, the candles are green. My husband's little grandson toddles in with a fistful of dandelions for the table. Like so many bold wildflowers and intrepid weeds, dandelions shrivel, instantly shy, suicidal, in the confines of a vase.

The Vernal Equinox on March 21 is celebrated as the new year in Islamic countries. Until the Julian calendar changed to the Gregorian, it was also the European new year.

This is the day to prune the grapevines in honor of Dionysus, Lord of the Vine, God of Forgetfulness. God of Trees. The Greek Green Man.

His adventures as a mythic figure in the ancient Greek tales feature infanticide, matricide, patricide, child devouring, and general mayhem. As a warrior, Dionysus traveled over Europe, Asia, and North Africa, spreading the vine cult, agriculture, and the arts, which go hand-in-hand. The insanity pervading his travels is, of course, the effect of too much wine. The tales seem to remind us that wine taken as a condiment is healthy, and as a sacrament, holy, a gift from the gods. Taken thoughtlessly in massive quantities, it destroys families and children and the childlike wonder and clarity within ourselves. The Greeks, in fact, produced marvelous wines, but drank it watered, saving a last, few, undiluted mouthfuls for the end of the meal.

Dionysus' priestesses, the Maenads, sought sexual union with him and feasted and drank with rampant ecstasy. Their victims' blood fertilized the grapevine. At the festival of Dionysus, Greek women retreated to the mountains, where they ranted and raged. Perhaps that day of overconsumption gave them permission, for a change, to vent their anger and pain. The vitality of wine is like that of blood.

Dionysus is among the world's many sacred savior kings, ritually killed and resurrected each year on the Vernal Equinox, a cycle obvious in the garden.

In ancient Rome and Italy, the Bacchanalia—the Roman festival of Dionysus—mingled practices from Greece and Phrygia. Dionysus was already familiar to Italians as Liber Pater, when the Bacchanalia arrived in Rome. Liber Pater—the Liberator, who frees us from winter—was an ancient, solemn vegetation god, whose festival, Liberalia, was celebrated on March 27.

Mars, after whom the month is named, was the state-sanctioned god of agriculture . . . and war. The Roman Senate understood that if troops are deployed during the planting season and the seedlings destroyed, victory is assured.

The Bacchanalia gave voice to the unrestrained processes of Nature, of Chaos, with its annihilation and regeneration. Singing, dancing, frenzy, orgies, and drinking celebrations spread rapidly throughout Italy and are still found in Europe, in such festivals as Germany's pre-Lenten *Fasching* (where a child born nine months later is called *Faschingskind,* its paternity unquestioned).

Bacchanalia was esoteric and excessive and vented the social and political frustrations of the controlled populace of an overdeveloped civilization. Enjoyed by everyone from the nobility to slaves and criminals, it clashed with the state cult. By 185 B.C.E., the Roman Senate took measures to outlaw it with capital punishment for anyone caught celebrating Bacchanalia or worshipping the god. The cult of Dionysus nevertheless survived into the Christian era.

Priapus, the Greek garden god—He of the Giant Genitals—was the son of Dionysus and Aphrodite.

*   *   *

The ancient Persians sent one another gifts of eggs at the Vernal Equinox. *Nawruz* may have its roots in Mesopotamia, when rites of Dumuzi/Tammuz—incarnations of spring's creative powers—were enacted. The rains renew vegetation; the procreative forces of Nature vanquish the dark and fallow.

> *Ajuzak leaves her cave at sundown. Step by crooked step, she carries her crone's body to water, dips her long, black hair in the water, whirls it in stringy arcs. Once, twice, three times, she dips her hair. She shakes and the water cascades to the ground.*
>
> *She pulls the black goatskin coat tight across her shrunken shoulders and over her dripping head. She wraps her dusty spiderweb veil across her withered face, which is as worn as the world.*
>
> *Her knotted fingers tear at the clouds, splitting them apart. Thunder clatters. Lightning stings the horizon. Ajuzak's gnarled toes squash the muddy earth as she roams across the skies and fields and hills. Her eyes dart left, right, forward, and back.*
>
> *On the eve of Nawruz, mothers in Afghanistan hide their children from the evil eye of Ajuzak.*
>
> *When Ajuzak washes her hair at Nawruz, the rain comes and spring planting will be fruitful.*

Ajuzak the Witch brought rain. She could drown life with floods so that children, themselves new life, were especially vulnerable.

On *Nawruz* we got new clothes, ate sugar cakes and visited or were visited by friends, each wishing the other a happy new year over hot, milky cups of *chai*. And once we attended a reception held by King Mohammed Zahir Shah at Darulaman Palace, an architectural carnival of Persian, Hellenic, French, and Arabic influences, where the tulips, thousands of them, were equally outlandish . . . and awe-inspiring.

Where and how my mother got the notion of celebrating Lady Day with a women's dinner is beyond me. This somewhat obscure West Country English festival on March 25 is associated with the return of the healing herbs. My mother showed no interest in herbs. It was the party she was after.

My father rolled his eyes and grinned. "She's mad as a March hare," he muttered, while my mother skipped around the house singing

> *Sumer is icumen in—*
> *Lhude sing! cuccu.*
> *(Spring is coming in—*
> *sing loud, cuckoo!)*

The "boys" were excluded from the fête, packed off "to entertain *themselves,* for a change," my mother sniffed. In an era when activities exclusive to women were pretty much limited to shopping, visits to the hairdresser, and the occasional tea party, my mother's annual "girl Bacchanalia," as she called it, was a daring feat. (Less isolating, more community-oriented quilting bees and sewing parties virtually disappeared after World War II.)

If the weather was good, a canopy was stretched in the backyard over a banquet table. My great-aunt Mil, unlike my grandmother, had shed poverty and taken on lofty airs by marrying well. Three times.

Mil had no children, and left my mother her gold dinner plates, cutlery, and gold demitasse set.

These were unwrapped and carefully washed and the table set with the best linens. Flowers everywhere: on the tables, the mantel, at each woman's place, floating in the goblets. My mother fussed and flew from chore to chore.

One by one, the ladies arrived. To my little girl eyes, it was as if all the most gorgeous and powerful queens in the world had converged on our house. Embassy wives and other friends, decked out in velvet, satin, shantung, organdy and crunchy taffeta, jewels, baubles, furs, and frills.

At tea, which was stuffy, or bridge, which was quiet, or cocktail and dinner parties, which included the men, these women were demure. By the second course of Lady Day dinner, they were cackling like thieves.

By dessert and champagne, they were jitterbugging and leaning against one another exhausted from laughter. Would they go home with their shoes worn to shreds, like the Twelve Dancing Princesses who sneaked off each night to a secret place of freedom?

At midnight, the ladies began to drift away on clouds of chiffon, crêpe de chine, cigarette smoke, and crème de menthe. My father had tiptoed back into the house and gone to sleep. I stuck around, lurking in corners, as long as I could keep my glazed eyes open, trying not to be seen and sent to bed.

Maybe it was then—there are so many possibilities—that the garden began appearing in my imagination as a place to make the glamour and adventure of fairy tales come true.

A lull. The last three days of March are called "blind." What can safely be planted, has been. I wait, anticipating, dreaming, digging, pruning, fertilizing. The tulips and hyacinths are watched pots that won't boil. Breezes come and go and so do the snows.

The soil is fragrant. The trees are still leafless, twisted in patterns like runes.

April

Whan that Aprille with his shoures soote
The droghte of Marche hath perced to the roote,
And bathed every veyne in swich licour,
Of which vertu engendred is the flour . . .
　　　　　　　　　—Chaucer, *The Canterbury Tales*

The Fool's Dare

I unload four flats of petunias and a few four-packs of orange pansies and place them around the garden, on borders, in planters. Always on April Fool's Day.

Some years, I'm fooled. If there's a lingering frost, I'll have to start all over. But most Aprils, although it's chilly at night and in the early morning, the cold doesn't linger. That space between the intensive first plantings in March and the next truly safe and frost-free sanctioned moment in May is frustrating. The petunias give me a taste of the satisfaction I crave in these push-me-pull-you spring months.

Where's my gardener's forbearance? The local garden columnist doesn't even broach the petunia subject until May and then she advises caution.

I want what I want when I want it. I've never been particularly patient, partly the blessing of energy and partly the curse of being a diplomat's daughter, a princess ever discomfited by a remote pea.

What quietude I do possess comes from and in the garden. I can't afford large shrubs, vine and trees, so I purchase scrawny striplings and whips or visit nursery salvage sales and pick through the miserable, unwanted leftovers baking in parking lots. Then I wait . . . wait . . . wait for them to revive and wait some more for them to grow. It's a lesson in fortitude. I keep a "plant hospice," a bed where I foster the abused orphans until they're healthy enough to transplant to permanent homes. This, too, forces me to slow down.

It took me a while to develop the confidence to plant flowers—annuals, such as marigolds, cleome, and zinnias, and some perennials—outdoors from seed. I spent an inordinate amount of money on potted annuals—and I still buy some, like petunias and tomatoes, which require a long germination period and the proper indoor conditions to start. The seasoned gardener will find this revelation ludicrously elementary, but for me, it was simply a failure of experience. And patience.

I haul a bag of composted manure around the yard. Wheelbarrows no longer fit my paths. I move from bed to bed, arranging stands of princely purple, carmine, and alabaster petunias. The pansies won't last the heat to come, whereas the petunias love high summer and don't mind cool spring and autumn nights. I'm not especially fond of pansies, but my husband likes them and I try to interest him in the garden any way I can. It's the wilderness he worships. He needs no garden go-betweens, no shrines, no mediums, no detours to the divine, but marches fearlessly into the heart of Nature. What he loves most about our garden are the birds and wildlife it attracts right here, smack in the middle of the city.

In ancient Babylonia, King Sennacherib created gardens, parks, and simulated marshlands in the capital of Nineveh. He knew his efforts were successful when herons roosted in his ersatz environment.

My garden is fulfilling in much the same way. It's a year-round home to hundreds of birds and has become a regular layover for migrants. As for herons, Jerry Across the Alley tells me that a few years back, one visited his pond—not much bigger, but more open than mine, and fronted by the street, which acts as a runway. The heron picked off some chunky koi and goldfish, before he was frightened away.

Jerry was not pleased. Nevertheless, when he put a bronze weathervane in the shape of a heron on his roof, it was a badge of triumph.

Years ago, I was planting petunias in the front yard, ignoring my children's endless April Fool's Day tricks, when they roared up to me with half the neighborhood kids in tow.

"Mom! Mom! There's a porcupine in the garden!"

"Uh huh," I mumbled. All day, we'd had salt in the pepper shakers, rubber cookies, plastic spiders, and false alarms followed by twitters and giggles and "April Fools! Fooled ya, Mom!" This is the only day a kid can "cry wolf" and parents, not wanting to spoil the fun, have to come running.

April Fool's Day—or in Britain, All Fools' Day—is said to commemorate the crow, who set out to find land from Noah's Ark and failed. Yet the bird most associated with the day is the cuckoo, who returns in April and is so elusive the poet Wordsworth wondered, "shall I call thee bird/or but a wandering voice?" An April Fool was originally a person sent on an errand to fetch something nonexistent like hen's teeth. One year, my children's favorite fool's errand was to send their friends home to "ask your mom who's the admiral of the Swiss Navy."

Like the other holidays when folk make "fools" of themselves, dress up, anoint mock kings, and the like, April Fool's Day marks a vacation from life's serious conventions. And the fool symbolizes a fresh beginning.

For me, this is Petunia Day, which can turn out to be a joke.

"Mom! Come on! It's a porcupine! Come *on!*"

"Just a second, let me finish this," I said, turning the trowel in wet ground and patting a petunia into the hole. I envisioned a stuffed toy hanging on a tree, gales of laughter, and "April Fools! Fooled ya, Mom!"

After what must have seemed a century to the kids, I followed them into the backyard, my mind on the next planting, far from these shenanigans. As soon as the petunias and pansies were in, I'd broadcast dill in select places, lots of places, part of my ongoing effort to attract butterflies. Then, maybe put those evening primrose seeds in the ...

"Shhh! Over here! Shhh!" I had to admit the children were convincing. One of them ceremoniously parted the long stems of a spirea and I peered where he pointed.

A porcupine. A real porcupine. Lying flat as if it were playing 'possum. How the kids knew it was a porcupine surprised me. They were quiet, respectful—awed—and sympathetic. It wasn't much of a hiding place. I'd recently pruned that spirea to within an inch of its life and it was only just budding.

"We put the dog in the house."

"I'd better call the Humane Society," I said and went inside.

Just as I hung up, a falsetto shriek bounced off the trees. My four-year-old ran screaming, red-faced, helter-skelter toward the house heedless of the flowerbeds, holding out her hand, two quills stuck in her tiny palm. She'd tried to "pet the porcupine to make him feel better," she sobbed. A fool's errand, indeed, poor baby.

I brought her into the kitchen, shoved a lollipop in her mouth and luckily managed to pull the quills out whole. Before I could dress her wounds, she skittered back outside, hopped nimbly over the lettuce patch, skipped into the gang of kids, who were lined up to greet the parks and wildlife rescue team. She leaped on her big brother's back to get a view over the heads of the bigger kids. The rangers lobbed a leash around the porcupine's neck and gently guided it into a box.

Now my son's eyes widened and tears welled. "Will they put Porky to sleep?" he gasped.

Murmurs, howls, and protests issued from the other kids.

The rangers, facing a potential preschooler riot, assured us that "Porky" would be returned to the wild.

Raccoons, squirrels, coyotes, skunks, and various species of birds have adapted to city life, but the appearance of an animal as wild as the porcupine is a blessing in an urban garden, a yard just six blocks from the downtown center. The kids built a circle of stones to commemorate Porky's hiding place beneath the spirea. They decorated it with plucked grape hyacinths and dandelions.

Twenty years later, the circle is still there, sunk into the dirt and minus my daughter's thumb-sized teddy bear offering. The violets have spread in such profusion that in April the Faux Forest floor is flat-out purple and the cairn invisible.

And there's another carpet of violets on the west side, thriving in the lightless corridor between Susie's house and mine. Violets are no longer a particularly fashionable groundcover. The ones at my house were probably planted by Miss Hicks, the chiropractor, in the early part of the century. They withstand every adversity and would take over if not for the sweet woodruff, wild strawberry, ivy, and vinca major I've added to vary the textures. All are voracious, especially the strawberry. All more or less tolerate dry shade and for some reason—so far—haven't consumed one another. When the violet flowers are exhausted, the woodruff sends up its lacy blooms.

We gather the first violets in spring and make wishes on them. Some folk eat the seeds and some believe that taking violet flowers in tea or tincture will cure cancer. A poultice or a wreath of violets placed on the head is said to stop its aching. In the Middle Ages, violets were crucial to the medicinal herb garden.

I toss violet flowers, periwinkle, lambs quarters, plantain, and baby dandelion leaves in the blender with pineapple juice, a spring tonic recipe passed on to me by an old German woman who used herbs and laying on of hands to heal.

In April I lurch out of winter, clumsy and thick-witted. On Palm Sunday, I'm driving along, ogling my neighbors' gardens, paying scant attention to this street I know so well. I don't notice the Day-Glo cones or detour signs. I'm on "Church Row," admiring the block-beds of tulips, hyacinths, and daffodils that link Congregationalists, Methodists, Lutherans, and Episcopalians and are warmed to early blooming by the church buildings. It's a candy box, somebody's idea of Heaven: gaudy and merry as clowns. Candy-box gardens are not for me, but in spring, they're nearly unavoidable. I'm wondering how my tulips will look this year, when I turn my head back to the street and a brown, fuzzy shape materializes.

Brakes slam. Tires squeal. I stop the car inches short of hitting a donkey, the star of this interdenominational Palm Sunday pageant.

The congregations stare in horror at this maniac, me, who's run over the palms decorating the pavement, the donkey's path. This infidel idiot who's nearly transformed the bearer of the Son of Light into roadkill.

The donkey never turns a hair.

A few less charitable churchgoers yell and shake their fists. The Episcopal priest, whom I recognize, smiles at me, raises his hands, and conducts the flock away like a traffic cop, while I back sheepishly down the block, turn the corner, and hightail it home.

That afternoon, I write the priest a note of apology and hope he reads it aloud or posts it. The next day, a friend, who has a wry sense of humor and happened to be attending the service, brings me a clay donkey from a Mexican pottery shop. I place it next to a statue of the Virgin in the fern garden, as close as I can come to palms, and vow to the god of donkeys (or whoever's in charge of beasts of burden) that I'll keep my eyes on the road from here on out.

My grandmother held that on Palm Sunday, the church must be swept and the dust scattered into the church garden, for it is considered especially blessed fertilizer. The parish ladies gathered with brooms and mops and gave the church a thorough going over. Granny pocketed a dust bunny to bring home. It sat that night at the feet of the Blessed Mother, until morning, when she took it to the garden and planted it with her cabbages.

Not being a churchgoer, I've translated the custom to suit myself: on Palm Sunday, when I'm not mowing down donkeys, I sweep my kitchen floor, pick out bits of plastic, carry the dustpan across the yard, and stir the bunnies into the compost.

April is the sighing month. In March, the stirring green skittered along the ground like green dew. In April it rises. The air is green mist, a fine, soft shimmy of green in the budding trees, which touch the sky so it's green, too. How could green get greener? Lime green, silver green, olive, sage, blue-green, emerald, pea green, jade. Green = verde = veritas = truth.

Now milkmaids pails are deckt with flowers,
And men begin to drink in bowers.
The mackerels come up in shoals
To fill the mouths of hungry souls;
Sweet sillabubs, and life-lov'd tansy . . .
—Easter verse from *Poor Robin's Almanack,* 1740

Snow

So much for green.

Nothing to do in the garden. Nothing but fret about the white stuff pouring out of the sky.

I consent to a two-day drive in the country, "on the lam from the Palm Sunday lynch mob," my husband teases. We take an overnight hot spring in the mountains and return to find sunshine and the garden blasting with fresh growth from the moisture and everything inches higher. How did it happen so fast? It's said that April's is the "germination moon," which stimulates the seeds and wakes the sleeping roots.

The anemones remind me of vividly glazed doll's bowls. I'm surprised they survive this quicksilver climate, but here's ranunculus, too! Just a few of the dozen I planted, yet those are miraculous.

Every single daffodil is wide-eyed now and glowing. Hyacinths, bleeding heart, forget-me-nots all piercing the ground. More signs of columbines. The Oriental poppies have formed their testicular buds and each day they get rounder. I check to see the tomato cages are secure around them. They are unruly, rowdy, and greedy. I explain to my daughter that they have to be muzzled so others can live. She promptly names me "the prison matron of poppies."

The Iceland poppies—short and far more polite—are in full glory. The redbud tree blazes. Its graceful branches dip in and out of my father's memorial mugho.

The phone rings, but I'm blissfully unaware of it as I thin the leaf vegetables. We'll eat the thinnings as salad tonight and once a week until the plants are full grown. Then we'll harvest leaves every evening, until one hot day when the lettuce, mizuma, arugula, spinach, and cilantro shoot up in seedy stalks like rockets.

I drop the sprouts into a colander. My husband's feet appear. "Jenny," he says. "There's a call."

He has that look on his face, *that* look, of sympathy, concern, friendship and love. I hate that look. Something is terribly wrong.

The family friend phoning from Ohio says Kate has had a heart attack.

Should I go? Should I get on a plane this instant? Wait, she says. She's insistent.

I slam out of the house, grab my shovel, turn around and around with it, like a dog deciding where to land. I head for the Enchanted Garden. Start digging under the pear tree with a fury I rarely experience. Digging in Earth to get an answer—will Kate live? Will my dearest auntie make it through? Will my last close adult, my last retreat from growing up or growing old, leave me? Is she lonesome? Frightened? In need of a loving bedside companion? I dig and dig discharging my fear and grief.

Rage. If Kate dies in April, it will indeed become the cruelest month. But so will any other in which she dies. I've always thought of April as the kindest month, the charitable month that frees us from the winter cage, unlocks the cell doors. Rage . . . and the garden absorbs it all.

Within a few hours, I've dug a second pond. Sitting on the berm, breathing hard, massaging my toes in the clay, rubbing my heels against an exposed pear tree root, I sense Kate will make it. She is ninety-one this month and I must face her death someday. But not today. Not yet.

Tomorrow I'll lay leftover roofing liner from the big pond into this hole over the few bits of carpet and rag rug I can scrounge from the cellar and shed, with a few old throw pillows, to protect the liner from stones and roots.

In contrast to the big pond, which is banked with red sandstone and moss rock, I'll trim this one's edges with granite foraged from Boulder Canyon, where a shoulder was cut for the road. They might be fortress stones.

Next, I buy three ivory foxgloves to plant where they can be seen from other parts of the garden through the bower. My real intention is this: foxglove is *Digitalis,* the plant from which a cardiac stimulant is synthesized. It is my healing consecration to Kate's heart.

When we talk, two days later, I tell her about the foxglove and how scared I was.

Kate laughs. "Well, honey, I'm grateful, but how about zinnias or impatiens? Much more my type. To tell you the truth, I'm not really fond of foxgloves. My mother called them 'witches thimbles' and she liked them in the garden, but considered them unlucky to pick. They grow wild on the isles, you know. Wildflowers were never to be brought in the house. Elder and hawthorn flowers in the house, she said, would bring bankruptcy or tax audits, a stock market crash, some drastic financial trouble."

"Fine. I won't cut the foxgloves," I sniff.

"They do have one advantage," she chuckles and quotes:

> *When you see the foxglove blossoming,*
> *put your fishing tackle in your boat*
> *and go off for mackerel.*

"Who said that?" I ask. Kate is a font of poetry. She knows Thomas Gray and Edna St. Vincent Millay, Spenser and Shakespeare and Swinburne and Donne, Phyllis McGinley and more limericks than were ever written.

"I have no idea who said it, honey, but it does make your foxgloves more appealing, doesn't it?"

"If you like to fish."

"When I *do* die, honey, I'm leaving you my prize stuffed bass. The one over the den door."

A few days later, a package arrives containing a large ceramic vase painted after a van Gogh scene of a French village. The skewed buildings are multicolored, the path vivid orange-yellow. There is a note:

> *Jenny crossed a yellow daffodil*
> *With lily-of-the-valley.*
> *Because it's so unusual*
> *She calls it Daffy Dali!*
>
> For your foxgloves. Love, Kate

Foxgloves are the archetypal fairy flower. *Peg's Faery Book,* published in Australia where I was born, was my favorite in early childhood. On every page—whether as cradles for fairy infants or fairy caps and petticoats—there is a foxglove. The "fox" is a corruption of "folks" or "fairies," as it is in foxfire, ignis fatuus.

Squeeze a bit of the juice of the foxglove on a sick child's tongue and in its ear, then place the plant on a shovel at the door, swing the shovel three times while shouting, "If you are a fairy, away with you!" If the child lives, it will soon recover. If it dies, don't be dismayed. It was a fairy, after all, a changeling the Folk switched for your own infant.

In some parts of rural England, people believed that foxglove leaves placed in children's shoes and worn for a year would prevent scarlet fever. My brother and I popped the flowers on the palms of our hands, a venerated ritual among kids wherever foxglove grows.

> Consult the Genius of the Place in all,
> That tells the Waters or to rise, or fall . . .
> —Alexander Pope, *The Genius of the Place*

The Nilus

Four Aprils before my rage gave birth to Kate's pond—after years of yearning, imagining, reading, drawing, inventing, pacing, sighing enviously at Jerry Across the Alley's garden—I finally made up my mind to dig a pond, the Nilus.

The "water element"—as landscape designers refer to it—has long been an essential component of gardens. It provides cool relief in summer's relentless heat, particularly if there are fountains. In Japanese gardens, the delicate trickle of water, with birdsong, bee buzz, the rustling of leaves, offers a gentle orchestra.

Among its benefits, a pond acts as additional attraction for animals. If the garden is to be a substitute habitat, then water is vital.

Water, like the moon, is *yin* in the ancient Chinese tradition, contrasted with Earth, *yang*. Water is simultaneously strong and yielding, feminine, inviting, and stately. In the Hindu Vedas, water and the moon are *soma,* sleep, dream. The moon is mirrored in my pond with the phone poles, the barn-red, rough-lumber shed walls, the nightgown hanging above the shed door—a shield whose lace heraldry is an emblem of the dominant female principle in this place. Its reflection floats on the water, like the Lady of the Lake.

I watch the changing scene in my pond like a child examining shapes in mud puddles. Double exposures of goldfish swimming in clouds. Vines or water lilies and iris springing from echoes of morning glories, silverlace, iris, clematis.

And the pond refracts myths, resonates with primordial events, the beginning of time, the birth of fertility. Aphrodite rises from water. The waterlilies (erroneously labeled lotuses by early Egyptologists) are the Flower of Isis. Lakshmi, Hindu goddess of love, luck, and wealth, of agriculture and fellowship with the land, rose from an actual lotus flower.

First, there was the question of where to put a pond. At last, I decided on the west side, next to the Fiesta Dinner Theatre, a pavilion of sorts in the corner of the saltbox shed. Here, I'd torn down flagging walls and replaced them with warped lodgepole pine left long, long ago by a friend who'd had no place to store or raise her tipi. Grapevines make a roof over table and chairs, reminiscent of Italian restaurants we'd encountered on the road during family vacations, gazebos sitting on hills overlooking the sensual Tuscan countryside.

The Fiesta Dinner Theatre was named for a joke about the stereotypical expectations of middle-American audiences, a joke repeated all night during a gathering in the garden with a group of visiting Mexican performance artists. Afterward, I painted the table and chairs bright purple and blue, and parts of the retaining wall shocking pink and yellow and turquoise. The Dinner Theatre and its surroundings give me an excuse—as if I needed one—to use the garish colors of the tropics.

On summer mornings, I work at the table under the grapevines, watching the pond, the birds who come for their early baths, the squirrels, the fish. I would like to turn this entire tumble-down shed into a summerhouse, where we can sleep and eat, looking up at the stars through the electrical lines.

I wanted the pond out of sight. Like other subdivisions in my garden—the Enchanted Garden, the Colony, the Medicinal Garden, the Fairy Ring—we'd have to "travel" to it. Unlike European garden ponds—the fantastic Baroque watering holes in Italian villas or the squared, soldierly pools of French classical parks—this would not be a centerpiece, but a retreat.

The pools in ancient Persia and Egypt were oases, earthly equivalents of Paradise, the garden's focal point. Egyptian garden ponds, channels used for irrigation as well as pleasure and refreshment, were called *nilus.*

There's no accessible underground water to sustain lush vegetation on the banks of my Nilus. I tossed the diggings to the side and built them into hills. Ironically, these banks are among the driest spots in the garden. Having no engineering skills, I didn't think to make a mudflat to accommodate salamanders and frogs. I wouldn't have known how.

I dislike heavy machinery, so that eliminated bulldozers. I had no money to hire young, muscular *braceros,* so that left the digging up to me. I trooped out to the area one April with a pick and shovel, and miraculously, by summer's end, I had a fifteen-foot-long pond with an island. Wherever I could, I dug down four feet, giving the goldfish room to live there year-round without freezing. They hover in a kind of yogi suspension across the winter. We call this pose "carp asana," and imagine them floating under the ice with their little fins in *namaste,* as if they were praying.

When I stepped back and surveyed my magnificent hole, I realized I'd dug the pond right to the very edge of the shed and within two feet of the west-side fence. Poet-stonemason John Wright came to the rescue and built a lovely sandstone terrace out from the shed wall. It curves into the pond, giving it shape. Across from it, accessible only through the water, vines climb rusting mattress-spring trellises.

The silverlace is glorious later in the season, but I wanted to block the view of the Dumpster next door. With no one's permission, presumptuous as can be, I planted two old-fashioned lilacs on Susie's side of my trellises. She now cares for them.

Morning glory on the berm against the coyote fence, blue carpet juniper, more irises, mountain bluet, Russian sage, lavender, and asters. I built a bench of sandstone and flat rocks right into the hill and upholstered it with woolly thyme, again reminiscent to me of Tuscany. Various creeping sedum are stuck into clay between the rocks and dripping toward the water. The rest are grasses and bamboo.

Bamboo is the first plant I recognized and could name. My mother was crazy for it and carted roots of it everywhere we lived. It spreads like wildfire in the most unlikely places. On more than one occasion, my mother plucked a plant from some exotic park or other. (She also took hotel towels.) With her diplomatic immunity from customs agents, she smuggled the rootlets to the next garden she'd inhabit. Environmentalists have since revealed this practice of introducing alien plants and animals to be incredibly destructive. I'm not convinced that knowledge would have stopped my mother.

With no outdoor electrical outlet and the pond so far from the house, I couldn't afford a pump, so I ran a hose from the faucet, hidden behind the flower beds and threaded it into the hollow of an old cottonwood trunk from which I extended a bamboo pipe. The "delicate trickle" when I turn it on is more like the roar of a broken fire hydrant, but at least it refreshes the goldfish and replaces evaporated water.

There are water iris and waterlilies, but the raccoons eat the water hyacinths, so I've given up. There's duckweed, which country folk and my family called Jinny Greenteeth. It grows like a carpet across the pond's surface and has to be thinned constantly. It's nonetheless irresistible.

Little swimming, bobbing insects simply "appear" in the pond, convincing me that the ancient Greeks were right to believe in parthenogenesis.

Hundreds of tiny fish arrived in two buckets one day from the newborn fry in a friend's pond. With the help of raccoons and neighborhood cats, their population has been whittled to a supportable number, until now there are a steady ten. I don't feed them, but we did name them: all Sparky or Butch. The Sparkys are albino or spotted. The Butches are gold and bigger. Last summer, my daughter spotted a Butch with no eyes. We watched it lurch around the water by the rocks for days, until one afternoon, it was gone. We decided not to speculate on goldfish cannibalism.

This April morning, I walk out to my pond and realize I've reproduced a lagoon near my uncle's house in Chile. My garden is built of "pretend," and it is also built of remembrances.

All gardens are dreams, time revisited, memories rearranged.

> A garden enclosed my sister, my spouse,
> A spring shut up, a fountain sealed . . .
> —*Song of Solomon*

The Coyote Fence

In April, the city collects piles of prunings and the broken mess left by heavy snow to shred for mulch. When pickup times are announced, there's a frantic, last-minute chorus of chain- and hand-saws, the groaning of felled trees, which in olden days people believed were cries of pain.

Ladder under one arm, tree saw in hand, I shape the fruit trees and scour the yard for wind and snow breakage and branches that will block sun or the paths of Art the Mailman and my husband, both over six feet tall, who accuse me of pruning to my puny height of five feet four. I apologize to the trees, but when I scold resisting branches—"This is for your own good!"—they respond by whacking or poking me.

The Faux Forest is of special concern now. The plum crowns are overgrown, sprouts everywhere. What's a Faux Forest if one can't meditate on the colors of bark and the swerve and camber of trunks and peek through them at hints of the Enchanted Garden beyond?

The city resembles a logging camp, towers of tree debris fronting every house. I built my coyote fence partly from my own prunings and partly by scavenging the neighborhoods in April. Then I wired the straight, strong branches against the existing chainlink. The coyote fence, with its many gaps, is not meant to keep things out, but to invite them in. Susie and I chat through a wide cavity, where we also leave gifts, necessities, and notes.

I built the fence for annual and perennial vines in the west-side sunshine to attract birds, bees, butterflies, and dragonflies. The vibrance and activity from both Susie's and my gardens occasionally stop passersby in their tracks. One way and another, there's always an exchange.

Japanese *torii* gates were designed to provide resting places for birds and to frame daybreak to warn the gods of the sun's approach. Their purpose is also to mark the border where the sacred is enclosed. Ordinary private gardens throughout Japan (and now elsewhere) use *torii* to indicate that a numinous space is about to be entered. Besides the lesser function of delineating property and discouraging trespassing, garden gates—like the entrances to tombs—serve as doorways into (An)other world.

I scavenge an old porch column, persuade my stepdaughter to dip her hands in paint and put prints all around it. She's a great sport and lets me use her feet as molds. The concrete feet (toes sticking out, like Osiris trapped and wrapped in the papyrus tree) stabilize the column on teetery ground. I raise the post, then suspend a dowel for a lintel and over that weave cattail leaves for a roof. It will have to serve as my *torii* for the time being. The squirrels are delighted with their new bridge.

Many primal peoples made cutting trees a crime. An ancient German law forbade the peeling of bark. The offender's navel was cut out, pinned to the tree, and the criminal forced to circle it, wrapping his intestines around the trunk. In some places, to break a bough accidentally was a sin. Knocking on wood for luck harks back to ancient tree worship.

I've done only the lightest pruning—mostly dead material, amputations for the tree's health. My removal pile is the smallest on the block. I'm now saving my prunings to replace poles in the coyote fence when the wood rots away and to use as filler for berms. There are no natural hills in my garden. Berms and boulders help modify the terrain.

For years, I refused to prune. I was—and still am—wedded to the notion that trees are sacred. And I craved growth, any growth. I suppose I was in the process of developing my reductive gardening method. I ignored the saplings or they eluded me. In no time, elm and sumac trunks crushed the house gutter, menaced the windows, scraped the roof. Typically, I had given no thought to these obvious practical matters.

Sooner rather than later, there'd be no room for garden and no sun whatsoever. There'd be no house! At last I was forced to remove the elms butting up against it.

Very wrathful was the vine
Whose henchmen are the elms;
I exalt him mightily
To rules of realms.

In Italy, *ulmus* was used to support young grapevines and so became the tree of the Wine God, Dionysus. Thus, in this verse from the "Battle of the Trees," the elm is servant to the grape, the youthful, headstrong chieftain. The word *henchman* is also defined by Webster's as "a member of a criminal gang."

The American elm pops like a gangster out of seemingly nowhere. I'm constantly sawing tall trunks I hardly noticed the year before, when they were hidden saplings. I leave high stumps as props for ivy, woodbine, or clematis. But until the vine takes hold, the intrepid new elm growth must be constantly clipped. In moments of surrender, I simply shape the elm and sumac suckers into shrubbery and prune them often. They are surprisingly attractive rising out of ground ivy and sweet woodruff.

Farmers in England believed that "when you see the elm in leaf, take your seed bag and sow your barley"—an April aphorism. Elms are said to be excellent medicinal plants. I've never tried it, but I could easily supply a folk pharmacy. When strands of hair or toenails are affixed to the tree, chills and fever are cured. If the bark is boiled for two hours in new milk, the drink will cure jaundice. The bark boiled in water and put on burns will mend the wound.

There are mystical bonds between individual human beings, communities, and trees. Pioneers moving farther west on the North American continent felled as many trees as possible, until they were suddenly confronted with the terrifying, seemingly bare and infinite prairie. Right away, they *planted* trees. And so have I, wherever I've lived. I inaugurated this house by planting first a rowan—or mountain ash—and a redbud.

Kate's Pond is approximately five feet in diameter and only a foot or so deep, too shallow for goldfish. Cats and 'coons would sweep them up overnight.

One of the latest east-side renters has tossed a large, ailing calla lily in the trash. There's nothing wrong with it that the pond won't cure. Within a few days, new shoots have sprouted and in a month, with increasing heat, it will thrive and bloom. A serendipitous addition.

The berm behind the pond will take sweet woodruff, a friend indeed when it comes to shade. Feverfew may be worth a try, too, but it's really dark here under the dead pines and grapevines.

Hosta and columbine. A path cobbled with bleached cattle bones found on a hike in Idaho's Bitter Root Mountains pocked with Irish moss. Two cinderblocks and a plank make the form for a bench, which, as the season progresses, I'll pack with dirt and plant with thyme, as the Elizabethans made garden seats with chamomile. I tried that once. It collapsed under the weight of a portly guest.

I pull on shorts and trot off to clean the Nilus.

It's freezing! I pace the pond perimeter working up my courage. Kerouac, the cat next door, has been fishing. Whenever I catch him gazing dreamily into the pond, I throw tennis balls at him. Now, I wish I'd made friends with him, so I could get close enough to give him a dunking that would really teach him a lesson.

I toss the half-consumed goldfish corpses onto the garden. Still avoiding the plunge into the chilly Nilus, I rake leaves off its surface, flinging the wet stuff onto the banks.

At last I'm ready. I step into the pond and start sneezing. The live fish, the Sparkys and Butches, dart away. More Butches than Sparkys survived the winter.

The Nilus is a Bermuda Triangle for trash. And Styrofoam peanuts! Someday every inch of the globe will be covered in layers and layers of Styrofoam peanuts!

I pull pots of irises and waterlilies out of the water and set them on the terrace. I use a bucket to scoop silt from the bottom of the pond. Most of it "belongs" to the goldfish, part of the environment they're producing here, and mustn't be removed too enthusiastically. Ankle-deep, the silt seems to nurture the water irises, which have outgrown and strayed from their pots. It's rich with goldfish poop, leaf mold, and algae. I toss it on the pond banks, where it will enhance the clay—my version of seaweed fertilizer.

The hotter it gets, the clearer this murky water will become.

Meanwhile, the fish lap up the algae, and when mosquitoes and water striders show up, they'll devour those, too.

Waist high in cold, cold water, my nose running, I weed parts of the "outer bank" I can't otherwise reach. When I haul myself out, dripping and shivering, I quickly repot the waterlilies and irises, using my hatchet to separate the iris roots.

> Although it is the Pharaoh of old who is the tyrant of
> the Haggadah, it is not he alone of whom we speak
> tonight . . . We speak
>> Of the tyranny of poverty
>>> and the tyranny of privation,
>> Of the tyranny of wealth
>>> and the tyranny of war,
>> Of the tyranny of power
>>> and the tyranny of despair,
>> Of the tyranny of disease
>>> and the tyranny of time,
>> Of the tyranny of ignorance
>>> and the tyranny of color.
>>>> —"Pesach 1997," compiled by Naomi Harris

Easter

Feast of the Ovaries. Every celebration we attend this month includes eggs. In my grandmother's day, no eggs were eaten during Lent, but were saved up for the Easter feast to come.

My mother was a twin, born in June 1917. My grandmother knew she'd have twins, when at Easter, she opened an egg with two yolks.

Osiris rises "out of the egg in the hidden land," brought back to life by his sister-wife Isis.

The word *Easter* comes from *Eastre* in Anglo-Saxon, which in turn, comes from Germanic *Austron,* a dawn goddess whose holiday was celebrated at the Vernal Equinox. "Star," "astro-," "estrogen," "ovary," and "egg" are all related.

At Passover—at the house of a friend, who holds a "mixed seder" of gentiles and Jews—I sneeze and cough and read my lines in a voice like a dry sponge rubbing a screen door.

A celebration of the Jews' escape from slavery in Egypt, Passover is all about triumph over injustice. And the *seder* is an intimate communion of tribe, family, and friends, the home. It's earthy, whereas Easter church celebrations seem to me lofty and empyrean, too far removed from food and ancestors, daily life and dirt, the sacred realities of the season.

Sacrifice is the key to rebirth in every culture, the "disembodied shadow," as Nathaniel Hawthorne wrote, "nearest to the soul." From the Paleolithic to antiquity, from offerings of blood and tearing of flesh comes modern Christianity with its demands for sacrifice of the corporeal pleasures across the weeks of Lent.

Dionysus was also called Liknites—He of the Winnowing Fan. In one of his incarnations—for he was "thrice born"—he was a Holy Child laid in a *liknon,* or winnowing basket. It is not uncommon that grain and fertility gods are cradled in mangers or seed-bearing vessels, nor that their sacrificial flesh is eaten in the form of bread.

In the Baal-Anat cycle of ancient Palestine, in the Greek Adonis and Dionysus myths, with Tammuz in Mesopotamia and Osiris in Egypt, the gods die, are dismembered, their limbs and seed spread. They lie dormant and are brought back to life by the goddess: Cybele, Isis, Ishtar. In each, as illustrated in this retelling from ancient fragments, there are close similarities to the Christian myth and rituals of the death and resurrection of Christ, with wine for blood, bread for flesh.

She Who is Light, Nana, eats almonds. They travel through her body, body buoyant as the moon. Attis slides out of Nana's womb onto the brown plain of Earth. His newborn body touches the ground and the ground turns green. Thus, soft grass cushions his entrance. Cybele—She of the Earth, Mountains, and Holy Madness—receives him in her arms.

Attis grows fast. Wherever he steps, Earth springs new green and lush. He is God-without-a-Father and Cybele takes him for her lover.

They travel in Cybele's lion-drawn chariot from Phrygia to Rome. There, Cybele conquers the invader Hannibal with her black stone. For thirteen years, the stone radiates from its Place of Victory, radiates defeat for the Carthaginian.

Attis loves Cybele and he loves another. He seeks a trysting place with his nymph, but nowhere can they hide from Cybele. She sees the lovers. She shudders. She moans. She shakes until the ground around the couple cracks. She quakes until Attis' mind shatters.

He rushes to a pine tree. Eternal and everlasting tree. He tears with his nails at his member. He rips at his testicles and penis. He rends them from his body. He leans with rattling sighs against the tree. He dies and violets grow where his blood flowed.

Cybele's priests carry Attis' body in procession into the city. They lay him in a sepulcher, washed and clothed in a shroud of new, white wool. They pray a day. They fast a day. And on the Day of Blood that follows, they mourn with loud and bitter lamentation, clashing cymbals, beating drums, dancing to awaken the dead. They drink wine—his blood. They eat bread—his body.

Cybele mourns in secret. She cannot close her hearing to the pleas of her people to make the dry Earth moist and verdant.

A day of fasting. A day of vigil. The sepulcher is opened. It is empty.

The priests march round and round the stone bed with lanterns and incense. "Rejoice!" they cry to the people. "The god is saved. And we too will find salvation from our toils."

Sorrow gives way to joy. Cybele embraces Attis again. Green and genitalia restored.

The cycle could continue only with our participation, our arts dedicated to the divine, our atonement, our prayers. And human sacrifice: the Day of Blood.

Even as human sacrifice became less common among cultures, nevertheless customs of bloodletting and pouring blood on the garden continued. Not long ago, when livestock was slaughtered, its blood was sprinkled on the soil. In Ireland, in 1678, four men were tried for "sacrificing a bull in a heathenish manner," as a healing ritual. Blood, scholar E. O. James wrote, is "soul-substance, responsible for the phenomenon of life."

It's also an excellent nutrient.

"A straight shot of vitamin B12," a friend notes, as I pour handfuls of bloodmeal here and there. The stuff stinks when it's wet, like butcher shops and killing fields.

In addition to the nitrogen injection, bloodmeal turns out to be the only thing that will deter the squirrels from digging up my seeds. They're as repelled by it as I am and will avoid squash hillocks or trenches topped with bloodmeal.

Plum. Crab apples. Apples. Peaches. Pears. In full bloom. This may be the most glorious moment of the season.

The apple trees are heaped high with their sweet disorder of pearl-and-rose-hued blossoms. The one destroyed by Susie Next Door's landlords is returning from a curved limb left behind. It resembles a blooming serpent.

A peach tree has sprouted against the east-side house. It's as tall as I am. Where did this shower of pink against that brick-red wall come from? Did I once spit out a pit? Or was it a raccoon or squirrel? The children? How long ago? An April miracle, growing out of a pile of rocks over black plastic. Another sapling I didn't notice till now. The heat from both houses must have helped hatch and nurse it.

> *Who does not sigh,*
> *when the withered cherry flowers*
> *flutter upon their heads?*

Balmy rain takes me home to Japan, to sudden haiku inspired by cherry blossom time. To slow days when my mother, my father and I joined the annual crowds of awed gawkers strolling through parks. The sun shone on the cherry trees. They looked like the paradise of the Snow Goddess who lives in crystal caves on Mount Fuji.

Now I sit at the den window, mesmerized by the crab apple blooms—white and red and pink—all in a row along the west corridor. My whole vision is an unbroken mass of flowers.

Gloom turns to snow. Will the flowers freeze? Will this be a replay of last year's storm, which smashed the yellow and orange "Emperor" tulips and flattened them? My heart sinks. I want so much for this spring to live up to its grand start.

In a few hours, the snow melts. The blossoms are unaffected. Worms languish on the wet sidewalks and stone paths, scuttling awake at our approaching footsteps. A hungry raccoon emerges at dusk and slinks slowly along sucking earthworms one after another. We stand at the window and watch her. The raccoons usually wait to come out until dark. I'll bet she's pregnant.

Five years ago, I found a tall bouquet in a flower shop, the biggest, juiciest, sunniest yellow tulips I'd ever seen. They were nearly spent, buckled, and opening, half price and irresistible.

If they lasted just another day, it would be worth it. I put them in a vase on the coffee table, lit a candle, and so as not to lose time admiring them, I sat all night reading beside them. One by one, petals flopped onto the table. At 3 A.M., I had a pile of yellow tulip petals and an epiphany.

I rushed to the magazine recycling box and dug through until I found the right gardening catalogue. I blew every single penny I'd saved that month on a hundred yellow "Emperor" tulips.

Until that night, I'd not cared much for tulips. They seemed prissy, too organized, almost bureaucratic. Yet here I was, in the grip of "tulipomania," the disease that overtook Holland in 1634, when the bulb business went bananas. Everyone, butchers, bakers, candlestick makers dealt in tulips and a single bulb of rare *Semper augustus* sold for 5,500 florins or $2,500 dollars.

My—much cheaper—bulbs arrived in two weeks. I planted them in the glade. The plums and sumac leaf late, so there'd be no danger of shade to blot them out. They would be the crown jewels of my April garden. But would even one hundred tulips outdoors against all the busy growth of violets and twine of tree trunks be sufficient to saturate and satisfy my eyes as that bouquet had in the closeness of my living room?

The month is nearly over and the yellow tulips glow in the glade like lamps. Alert and sparkling golden goblets. More than enough for a May banquet.

SUMMER

May

Welcome May-time.
Fair season. Perfect aspect.
The sweet o' the year . . .

Welcome vigor and sap . . .
The green field echoes.
Ah, mad ardor of the iris and the lark.

—Irish, author unknown, ninth century

May Eve

Fruit trees in bloom must never be pruned. "If you want the fruit," my granny intoned, "don't pick the flower." (Why do grandmothers intone like bumper stickers? Or is this our memory of them?)

On this day, I break the rules, clipping branches of the crab apples for the *beltane* celebration tonight. I do this every year, party or not, exactly on May Eve, and decorate house and garden in a gesture to celebrate the fresh season, the year's new shape. With four crab apple trees, the birds are well supplied. How much of this fruit—for which I can find no culinary use but jam—do we humans in this household need?

> *Of all the men she could have had
> she chose and married a perfect cad.
> She'd searched the orchard through and through
> and picked the sour crab.*

Beltane is the second of the four great Celtic seasonal festivals, spring's birthday party, the first day of summer in antiquity. *Beltane* means "bright" or "goodly fire," the one that anticipates the sun's increasing heat. Fires kindled this night tickle the sun's journey up the horizon toward climax at the Summer Solstice. Wild creatures emerge tonight, on *beltane,* when the Green Man, the Forest Man, the antlered Stag God, couples with the Lady of the Green, the Queen of Crops, Maiden of Blossoms. Together, they fertilize the land.

Fragile April is ripening into a more vigorous, less ethereal beauty. Leaves unfold, blossoms glide to the ground like light snow. No moment in the gardener's calendar is so magnificent as May.

The asparagus is ready to cut. Three-year-old roots in a sandy bed, left unharvested for two seasons after planting. A tender treat for May Eve supper. I don't grow much, just enough for one unforgettable meal. It's more fun to forage for wild stalks near streams and ponds, to discover where the asparagus hides, then hoard the delicious secret.

Lily of the valley, "fairy ladders" like pearly popcorn, grace a shady corner. They're tight and too close. Last year, I transplanted a group to the Enchanted Garden, where they'll bloom beside a stand of vibrant basket-of-gold next to the teahouse. They've got to be thinned again. I move some to the new hosta and fern berm on the east. And some for Susie, too.

In Cornwall it was the custom for young people to dance wearing lilies of the valley, romping and skipping through cobbled streets and in and out of houses and gardens.

I've used lily of the valley to treat cuts, laying the leaves over the wound, holding them in place with a bandage. They seem to quell the bleeding and numb the pain.

Golden-spur columbine is now the centerpiece of the sunny Poetry Garden. An Arizona native, it needs hot shade or semi-shade, and won't continue this abundant flowering if we have heavy May rain.

She loves me, she loves me not . . .

A white Shasta daisy has already bloomed, an early riser and spikey complement to the golden-spur columbine whose head resembles that of its namesake, *Columba,* the dove.

A white iris has also opened. There's always a scout in every iris patch, one brave prospector, sliding from its sheath to test the weather.

The bleeding hearts, white as well as pink, have bloomed everywhere there's sun. The ones in the Faux Forest will take another week or more.

Chinese lilacs in the Enchanted Garden are too young to bloom with much conviction. My mother advised plucking flowers of new shrubs to enable the plant to put energy into stem and leaf growth. I reach to do it. I'm too fainthearted. And curious to contrast this lilac flower with the other varieties.

I've never seen a bigger lilac than the one that fronts Kate's kitchen. Standing alone in sunlight, it's nearly a hundred years old, conical, and so tall I climb a ladder to reach the top. There are others, too, smaller and mostly white, which Kate's mother, Celinda, favored. Kate isn't "fond" of the whites. They lack the scent she loves.

White lilac is considered unlucky to wear except on May Day for it means the wearer will never marry. Kate never married, never wanted to. She was engaged several times before she "got cold feet."

What kind of lilacs—Persian?—were balanced in a basket on the turban of the boy who stood outside our Kabul house? We had sufficient lilacs in our own garden, yet my father was so charmed by this flower-crowned vision, who recalled ancient pictures of the Greek god Dionysus, that each morning as he left for work, he bought a bunch to give my mother or take to the embassy. A photo of that handsome, grinning boy hangs in my study. He was in his teens, just my age. Some days, I'm overwhelmed with homesickness and sorrow, wondering if his lilacs still grow, if he tends them yet, or if the scented glory was lost amid bombings, fire, and smoke.

In my mind, the lilacs of Afghanistan will bloom forever in the rubble. The magnificent bushes that graced ancient palace gardens in Kabul, Kandahar, Herat, Jalalabad, Peshawar. Gardens designed after the great Persian and Indian courtyards and pleasure parks, yet wilder, idiosyncratic. Each conqueror brought another culture to the "roof of the world"—Darius the Persian, Genghis Khan, Alexander the Great. The many tribes left their marks on the faces of the people, on the landscape, and in the architecture. And when the Afghan warrior-poets invaded other realms, they yearned for home:

Whatever worlds I conquer,
I can't forget your beautiful gardens.
I remember the lilacs
and forget the greatness of the Delhi throne.

Among Europeans, lilacs were commonly believed to protect a house. A hedge of alternating Persian lilacs and Mongolian apricot shields my front garden from the sidewalk. A Canada hemlock's bowed branches embrace the old-fashioned lilac against the porch. The hemlock rises past my daughter's second-story window. She's hung blue and green bottles on its branches, in the African-American tradition of the spirit tree. Evil entities of the night are trapped in the bottles. Morning sunlight burns them away.

The Mongolian apricot bloomed two months ago, and sports feisty, dark-green leaves with scarlet spines. It's the lilacs' turn and they're budding.

"No frosts, please, please," I whisper. "Be kind, weather god. Don't zap these beauties. Be a nice garden god, a strong lilac deva. Hang in!"

I've recreated the "scaredress" early, to show off for the party. This year's worn nightgown is a Georgian-style number, shredded lace, torn and blackened hem. I hang it on crossed 2×4s and stuff the arms with straw. For *beltane,* I tie the antlered skull of a deer onto the scaregown's shoulders. The skull is a gift from my mountain woman sister-in-law, who found it in the woods.

Crab apple branches shade the Austrian rose, Russian sage, rudbeckia, and coneflower by my front walk. I'm clipping the branches when I hear a sharp, high voice.

"May I have some?"

I jump at the sound and whip around to face it. A young woman stands on the sidewalk, blond hair washing down her back, arms outstretched. She's dressed in soft colors and Stevie Nicks layers, pearly beads hanging from her earlobes and around her throat and waist. Her skin is so fair, she's almost invisible. Her eyes are blue as cornflowers.

"May I have some?" she repeats and smiles confidently, as if fully aware that these flowers are being cut for her.

"It's *beltane*," she adds, reminding me to be generous in such a generous season.

I'm speechless. Startled at how this wraith resembles the Other-worldly women I'm characterizing in the book of stories I'm currently working on. Obediently, I fill her arms with crab apple branches, a pile so high she could dust them with her eyelashes.

She thanks me and proceeds down the sidewalk, trailed by red, white, and pink petals. I catch my breath and sit on the stone wall. Did that really happen? Did some Flower Maiden really appear out of nowhere demanding blooms? I set to pruning again. The fairy lass—probably a young Wiccan on her way to a *beltane* festival of her own—took all my cuttings.

Susie Next Door steps into the front yard, gloves and shorts and ratty sweatshirt, a shovel in one hand and trowel in the other. My Susie. Solid and beautiful as an oak. Graceful, earthy, feet square on the ground. Pragmatic.

We explore her sunny front yard for new growth (mine, with its lilac/apricot hedge, roses, herbs, the seventy-year-old silver maple on the hellstrip and separate microclimate, is a week or more behind). We find the very beginnings of reseeding annuals, calendula, fever-few, various poppies, and much that's not yet identifiable.

Several years ago, in desperation at the ragweed turf, Susie attacked the front yard with a commercial packet of "wildflower" seeds. Cosmos, the majority of these seeds, have taken over. In May, they make a feathery lawn. By midsummer, they'll be a misty pink veil separating her from the street.

She readies the ground for sweet Williams and begonias to line the brick walk leading to her front door. She laments the overgrown, unruly juniper bushes and together we prune them back as far as we can. I'll commandeer the clippings to mulch vegetables, again to add acid to this bland soil.

We take a quick survey of the backyard, which Susie is reclaiming with my contributions. She's added more seeds to those I broadcast in November. She's created a vegetable garden, planted morning glories, and found prominent homes for perennials from my overgrown yard.

Not much has happened yet with the seeds. Some may take

years. Nevertheless, there are signs among the weeds. Eventually, it'll be a splendid garden, with mowed paths between the wonderful disarray of wildflowers and self-seeding annuals anchored by the perennials.

Right now, dandelions dominate. Where Susie disrupts the soil, digging them out, the poppy seeds broadcast in November will sprout. Like so many of us, poppies lie dormant until ploughing, digging or hoeing—until, that is, a "crisis" takes place.

I haul crab apple branches into the house and balance them in vases for tonight's celebration. By tomorrow morning, the blossoms will droop and drop. They make it clear they don't belong and don't want to be indoors.

I tie twigs into circles and crosses, hang them above the entrances, the fireplace, and the woodstove.

The rest I drag to the Nilus to "dress it," an ancient custom throughout the world. At *beltane,* if I do nothing else, I "dress the wells," a ritual homage to the life-giving spirits of water.

> *Knots of May we've brought to you,*
> *Before your door it stands.*
> *It's but a sprout,*
> *Well budded out*
> *By the work of Nature's hand.*

In South America, vibrant colored threads and streamers hang above wells and springs, beside rivers, lakes, ponds, pools, and water tanks. And there are shrines on shores, where statues of the Virgin Mary or random patron saints are adorned with the *compesinos'* most precious possessions. Would these be better used in some practical way to defray poverty? Or has faith become the best hope?

The tradition predates Christianity. Lake Titicaca has been found to contain precious objects sacrificed by the Inca to the holy waters. In Mesoamerica, the *cenotes*—lagoons—contain the remains of sacrificial humans, as well as gold, pottery, and effigies of the gods. The River Po, which begins in Northern Italy and flows to the Adriatic Sea, contains all manner of offerings and human and dog sacrifices along its route. Some of these sacrifices were made far into the Christian era.

In Tissingham, England, the custom of well dressing continues to be an annual event on Ascension Day, forty days past Easter. Processions, bands, dancers, and television personalities convene to dress the well with pictures of Biblical themes, wet clay tablets "painted" by everyone in the community, with wildflowers, seeds, leaves, and mosses. The paintings are spectacular folk art.

Springs, streams, creeks, and freshets are under the care of the goddess-saint Brigit. The Well of Brigit in Fouchart, Ireland, among others, is a place of eternal magic and ceremony, where folk hang rags and leave gifts.

Of the thousands of holy wells in Britain and Ireland, only a few survive, the ancestors of today's wishing well. Most have been plowed, planted, or neglected. Nevertheless, well worship is by no means extinct. There continue to be well-dressing ceremonies, where bowers of flowers, rushes, and other greenery are proffered annually. The offerings are simple and spontaneous, single tokens from passersby. The joke's on anyone who steals a well offering: the thief merely adopts the trials and tribulations of the one who left it.

Today, we "take the waters" hoping to discard our illnesses, mental and physical, at spas. Some of these were once holy wells, where curative miracles or an appearance by a saint-goddess may have occurred. Among the most famous in Europe is the grotto at Lourdes, France. Saint Winefred's Well at Holywell in Wales is much visited since she was beheaded sometime in the Middle Ages by evil Prince Caradoc for refusing his advances. Where her head fell, waters gushed from the Earth.

The White Lady is still spied ascending from holy wells. The story of Winefred—whose name is related to Guenevere and apparently means White Goddess, White Shadow, or White Wave—may be a Christian mutation of an older tale. The nineteenth-century poet Gerard Manley Hopkins, a Jesuit priest, honored Saint Winefred and her well in fragments of an unfinished play.

In the Christianized Arthurian stories, the Lady of the Lake is none other than a latter-day White Lady of Waters, perhaps Brigit herself. The Lady of the Lake guards Arthur's mighty sword, Excalibur, just as Brigit was matron of blacksmiths and iron.

It was under the water that the Greek smith god Hephaestus had his first forge, built for him by his foster mother, the goddess of the sea. In ancient Greece, the Naiads ruled the fresh waters as the Dryads ruled the trees. When Nature goddesses were shunned—or transmuted into saints—nymphs presided over the waters, with gnomes, trolls, and other supernatural creatures who guard shores, confluences, estuaries, and bridges.

My streamers take the form of vines surrounding the Nilus. Silverlace, clematis, grape, barely beginning to bud. The heavy pruning that grapes love in March is always slightly terrifying. I forget they'll grow back with redoubled strength and observe these stubs in desperation. Morning glory seeds go in on May Day. They're soaking in a cup of water to soften the pods and quicken the sprouting process.

My rags are faded Buddhist prayer flags—white, blue, red, yellow, and green—stapled in a vertical row on the coyote fence. The wind sends the prayers wherever they need to go without my interference. Prayer is too much a matter of pleading and bargaining. I take satisfaction in not knowing what this Tibetan calligraphy means, or what the prayers say. The flapping flags are private communiqués between the deities.

Spike by spike, the blue fescue, in need of haircuts, perk up from their winter doldrums. Taupe and rust-colored bearded iris will also soon highlight the pond, tucked among tapered blue Japanese iris. Meanwhile, the miniature yellow iris are come and almost gone. They're jaunty and I like them, yet they've always struck me as willful, somewhat disagreeable characters, like gruff dwarves guarding underground treasures.

I tie the crab apple branches with multicolored ribbons saved from birthday packages and balloons, and arch them across the water, then interlace the shorter pieces to steady this bridge—a symbolic link between seasons. In many mythologies, there is a bridge between life and death, and a mystic body of water must be crossed to make the transition. The Prophet Mohammed said it was necessary to cross a bridge thin as a hair to enter Paradise. In Egypt, the final voyage was made across the sacred Nile. In Greece, the River

Styx took the dead into Hades. In gospel hymns there are countless references to "crossing the river."

My father loved Arthurian legend. He doted on its lyric imagery, and he was especially moved by the struggles between might and right that take place in the stories. He was a born idealist, and a veteran of World War II, when good and evil seemed clearly delineated—as they seem in the old tales. He read me so many Arthurian tales—so many versions of every adventure—that May, in my mind, is the Arthurian month. The tales reach far into antiquity, borrowing from older myths. All stories are made to be retold and are always slightly refashioned with every teller. Like plants, stories evolve and so do their meanings. However archaic the tale, it will have infinite interpretations for any era.

Guenevere of the gray eyes, the Flower Daughter, awakens on beltane and calls for her green gown. She calls for her horse to be dressed in green. She calls for her company and they set out a-Maying.

She picks flowers in the meadow and forests. Her company runs off in pairs. Their giggles and delighted cries arouse Melwas, the Summer King, from his winter sleep.

Melwas shakes off his brown cloak and dons the green. He stands, stretches, and his glazed green eyes fill with a golden vision of the queen. Guenevere, singing to herself, fills basket after basket with May blossoms.

Melwas is struck with love, as if by a puncheon. He mounts his steed and gallops toward her. He swings Guenevere onto the saddle. She screams for her company. Her screams are muffled by the green cloak Melwas wraps around her. One couple spies them and rushes back to court.

Gawain, Champion of Women, is first to the site of the Summer King's castle. He tries to cross the Bridge of Swords. He tumbles into the river.

Lancelot comes next and minces nimbly over the Bridge of Swords. He enters the castle. He searches every nook and cranny and finds only spiders, cobwebs, and dim-lit corridors leading to labyrinths.

Arthur arrives on his loam-black stallion. He, who has the bless-

ings of the Lady of the Lake and wields her iron sword, Excalibur. He spurns the Bridge of Swords, spurs his horse and bounds the river. They gallop into the castle, narrowly missing the speared gate as it creaks closed. Arthur dismounts. A path opens, leading him far into the cavern of the Summer King. Arthur fences stalagmites and stalactites. He follows the peals of Guenevere's cries. He reaches the green bower, where Melwas has deposited her. The Summer King rears and puffs his chest. Where he stood, a white bull appears and charges.

Arthur the Stag jumps out of the white bull's steaming course. The bull snorts past, head lowered. Arthur slices Excalibur through the bull's thick neck.

Arthur carries Guenevere back to the upperworld. Green floods the Earth in the same measure as the bull's blood billows and streams across the cavern floor.

Melwas rises from the blood of the white bull. The Summer King is resurrected.

In the Enchanted Garden, the sweet woodruff is going full tilt. The lamium preens under spirea and near the teahouse. The woodruff will liquidate everything in its path. I transplant it continually throughout most of the summer. The ground under the redbud and mugho was impossible to populate, except with woodruff transplants.

Last week, I picked a basketful to marinate in Rhine wine. Deadly sweet May wine is customary in my family, and I've prepared several bottles for tonight's guests as a ceremonial drink (one sip too many and you regret it).

My great-grandmother was said to have made "angelic" May blossom wine from hawthorn flowers, distilled across a year from May to May.

My grandmother made bathtub gin.

The puffy, purple giant Chinese alliums have detonated. A member of the onion family, it seems to be jockeying with the wild garlic for territorial governorship of the Enchanted Garden. The garlic makes a hazy, lime-green carpet, archetypal newness even the woodruff can't suppress.

A month since I planted them, Kate's foxgloves have sent up their flower stalks. Ferns and lilies show no signs yet, but Rocky Mountain columbines illuminate the granite rocks facing Kate's Pond. The moss and thyme I pushed into soil between the stones are settling in nicely.

I dress Kate's Pond with coral and white impatiens, pulled from their pots and plunked directly into the water, roots anchored in the spaces between the rocks and one or two stuck into the calla lily pot. I bounce in the water, as if some force were trying to levitate me . . . not a pond troll, but the cushy throw pillows I'd used as hasty underlining.

My daughter adds a pink plastic lobster and a blue frog, "offerings" to the raccoons. They love toys, she says. She should know, having volunteered all during high school at the wildlife rescue center. Occasionally, late at night, we hear the toys squeak.

Yesterday, during a rain storm, I had a notion to shape bake-in-the-oven clay images of Sheela-na-gig, an Irish female icon who displays her genitals on church walls and lintels and is sometimes called the "Celtic Kali," creator and destroyer, though no one really knows her origins or meaning. Her hands open her vagina so wide it obliterates her torso. The sidewise grin on her big head suggests she has the answer to the vast enigma of fertility, a mystery only she understands.

I paint the figures with red sand from the mountains, mixed to a paste with gesso, and place them in strategic crevices in and around Kate's Pond. The plasticine is surprisingly durable and won't break in the 'coon kickball games. The raccoons are quite as likely to eat the impatiens as they did my water hyacinths.

My Brigit-pals and other friends leap, whooping, over the *beltane* fire in the old iron cauldron placed strategically in the center of the newly dug bed. Someone appoints himself Keeper of the Flame and stokes it. Across the years, I've known two women who jumped the fires with a wish to become pregnant and did. I suspect at least one conceived in the Enchanted Garden. I hope so. I want my garden to be magic and meaningful in others' lives, too. Marvelous things happen this night when lovers traditionally vanish into woods and fields. "Mad-merry" May marriages made in the greenwood. (And one made under my apple tree.)

This was the marrying month. After the Christian era, it became ill-luck to marry in May—that licentious time when the libidos of every sentient being are zestiest.

"In the bestiary of the heart," Lawrence Durrell wrote, dwells "the little hairy sexer, Pan."

In ancient and not-so-ancient times, livestock were herded round the *beltane* fires to ensure their fertility. At *beltane,* as at *samhain,* the hearthfires were allowed to go out and were relit the next day from communal bonfires. And dancing, always dancing: around trees and sometimes *on* them, as on the Meavy Oak in England, whose top branches were kept clipped flat for a platform built at festival time for dancers, then feasters who ate and drank at treetop tables.

A guest starts a percussion band in the Fiesta Dinner Theatre with my drums, bullroarers, kalimbas, and rattles. Reggae blasts from the stereo in the living room and people boogie in the front hall. As the night gets colder, partiers surround the fire singing hits from the fifties and sixties—"Teen Angel," "My Boyfriend's Back," "Leader of the Pack," "Wake Up, Little Susie." A pitch pipe would be useful. We'll either kill the garden or it'll be the best ever.

Contrived mimicry of ancient rites at these celebrations of the garden calendar seems unnecessary, as long as we mark Nature's occasions in some fashion. Honoring the past and our traditions is essential. By fashioning the celebration to fit our own era and culture, we offer the sincerest, least distracted salutations to the divine. Earth-based spiritual practices are needed desperately in our culture. The ancient traditions act as a road map, a loose itinerary, cultural mnemonics. Return to Nature worship may be the only way to save Nature. Yet spiritual colonialism or retro-ritual aren't required to make it real. Instead, we should, as the poet Ezra Pound advised, "make it new."

When the partiers leave, I dump the cauldron contents into the new vegetable garden and, in the moonlight, turn the embers and ashes over with peat and manure.

Make a holiday!
Don't tire of play!
No ones takes his goods away,
none return from beneath the clay.
　　　　—*Song of the Harpist,* Egyptian, Middle Kingdom

May Day

My kern dollies come out of the shoebox, where they've slept since November on the shelf with my gardening journal.

On May Day, as at the Spring Equinox, effigies of Death were drowned or torn to pieces. Others, like my dollies, were more gently buried with new seed.

Parsley makes a fine, frothy edging plant with sweet alyssum around the leaf vegetable bed. And parsley is a healthful partner for roses as well. I shift a few parsley plants that made it from last year to the new *beltane* bed and together with marigolds, they'll protect the tomatoes. With hyssop, borage, basil, coriander, and especially lemon balm, parsley is among the honeybees' favorites.

> *How doth the little busy bee*
> *Improve each shining hour,*
> *And gather honey all the day*
> *From every opening flow'r!*

My mother quoted the first verse of Isaac Watts' children's poem repeatedly as a reminder to us that hard work has its rewards. The bee, like the ant, has been an emblem of exertion, productivity, planning, and organization for generations. They are real examples of how the wild is necessary to keep the garden alive. Honeybees are liminal creatures, for they're partially domesticated. "My" bees seem to know me. They never sting, unless I step on them (mud quickly applied to the wound is the best remedy). Without them, although wind and other flying insects help, pollination would be drastically reduced.

Bees are considered the wisest, most intelligent of insects, if such distinctions can be made. What, finally, are wisdom and intelligence?

The goddess Demeter was also known as "the pure mother bee," and her priestesses called bees, *melissae*. Actual bees were thought to be the departed souls of the *melissae*.

Bees were revered, even worshiped, throughout the ancient world. The Wine God Dionysus was reared by nymphs who fed him honey. Honey, as well as being the only known sweetener and having potent properties in mead and wine, was once also the only known preservative. It was a monkey who presented *madhu,* honey, to the Buddha. A child born among the Sikhs of India is baptized with a honey kiss to the lips and honey rubbed on the tongue.

Honeybees are besieged by severe weather and parasites and have been beleaguered for decades by pesticides. Their population in our gardens has seriously diminished and the loss is tangible. Scientists, meanwhile, are grooming the blue orchard bee to take over, though nothing can ever make up for any creature reduced or made extinct.

Three years ago, there was a parasite epidemic and a sudden, eerie quiet in my garden. A friend, whose yard may have been an apple orchard, had so many bees, their buzz was deafening—and as uplifting as Beethoven's Ninth. The mite blight left a depressing silence in her yard, too. There was far less fruit of course, and a kind of dullness hovered over every plant all season long.

The fabulous blossoming of fruit trees this year hints that the bees could be back on the upswing. Not in droves as before, but there are signs of action.

There was an old, old man who lived near our farm in Pennsylvania and kept hives. He showed me the carcass of a dead queen. She was as big as my thumb. He was proud of this majestic creature and kept her in the box that had held his wife's wedding ring. His bees were "alfalfa-fed." He brought me a jar of honey every fortnight. When he died, his children turned the wooden hives around so the bees would not see his corpse carried out of the house.

On May Day, my mother had a Maypole erected in the garden. In the Southern Hemisphere it was, after all, only early autumn. The Maypole is simply a remainder and reminder of tree worship.

A May King and Queen were chosen by our mothers from

among the children who excelled in school. I never got the honor though once or twice I got to be a princess. (Good enough for me, if there was a costume, preferably with a tiara.)

In many British and Irish May Day traditions, the May King and Queen begin as cinderfools, tending the May Eve fires. The next day, like Cinderella, they "graduate" to royalty.

I remember flowers everywhere on May Day. The happy shrieks of children. The tangle of May Pole ribbons, when some child lost count in the dance or, not knowing left from right, trotted off in the wrong direction clutching her ribbon and tangling the others. The laughter of the adults. The picnic food you could eat with your hands, no table settings, no need to remember which fork to use for what. Paper napkins! No cloth serviettes to unfold carefully across your lap. There was the mock-solemn crowning of the King and Queen of May—a secret held by the mothers until the very moment. The King and Queen—she wearing an old lace curtain for a veil—and all their retinue paraded around the yard in cardboard crowns. And our old rocking horse—the traditional hobby horse of May Day—carried about on someone's shoulders.

Whistling, singing, cracking of whips, blowing of horns, bells, noise ushered in the May Day, as it does most other holy days worldwide. And just as at other festivals on the European garden calendar, seasonal battles were enacted.

In German villages two persons, one dressed in ivy as Summer, the other in straw or moss as Winter, staged a public combat. In Sweden, companies of mounted troops, one in furs, the other in fresh leaves and flowers, battled out the seasons. In Turkey, the "good spirit" of Spring, took on the "bad spirit" of Winter. *Les Rouges* engaged *les Noirs* among the Basques of Southern France. Some places held dance contests. In any of these "matches," Summer naturally won.

Traditional sporting games were surely the forerunners of the games we played at our May Day festival.

This is the hour of the May King, Jack in the Green, Robin Hood, the Green Knight. He is the carved, foliate head that decorates Medieval churches (occasionally, the figure is female); his forefathers are Attis and Dionysus, Pan and Osiris, Dumuzi and Jesus. Creative power.

Two days of intense heat have hurried away my daffodils. The sun beating on the crowns of the earliest tulips forced the slender, closed chalices to open wide, gasp, and tumble. The golden "Emperor" tulips at last bewitched me. I've begun planting tulips throughout the garden. They are tricky little soldiers that seem to enjoy fooling us. Into a bed of, say, entirely pink blooms a red, bacon-striped tulip will suddenly appear, thumbing its nose at the gardener.

Feathery scarlet, "nameless" tulips I filched from the city land-scapers' garbage are opening in the Enchanted Garden. Nearby, the "Queen of the Nights" are taking their thrones, dark radiances be-side a group of Oriental poppies, which rarely flower in time for the orange, ruby, and aubergine complement I planned to resemble col-ors I imagine in a story from *The Arabian Nights.*

The first smells of mowing permeate the neighborhood. My lawn paths need clipping, but I'll have to wait. Wherever I've dug dandelions, I've placed grape hyacinth bulbs in the holes—purple Q-tips scattered in fresh emerald.

Today, I plant purple stock, Queen Anne's lace, and lunaria around my sea lavender, again inspired by winter flower arrange-ments. These are marvelous prototypes for mixing and matching flowers in the garden, although consideration has to be given—out-side the hothouse—to whether things will bloom simultaneously or in reasonable sequence.

On May 15—our frost-free date—I'm ready to plant the *beltane*-bed with tomatoes and a kern dolly. Just before my husband disap-pears into the woods looking for migrating birds, I send him to the nursery. I've given him a note that specifies, among other things, "three tomato plants, Big Boy, yellow plum, and cherry tomatoes." He returns with three *flats,* sixty-two tomato plants! I'm busy else-where and don't notice the mistake until he's gone. He has the car and I'm in no mood anyway to hassle with returning this embar-rassment of "love apple" riches.

I spend the day telephoning friends offering them four-packs—

"oh, *do* take more than one . . . you can't have enough tomatoes! Yum, yum," I add, smacking my lips as an extra incentive. Everyone gladly accepts. Even a friend with only what she calls a "postage stamp garden," terraced in brick, takes a few tomatoes to plant in pots.

(When I finally see him again, my husband blames my notoriously bad handwriting.)

Iron near tomato plants is said to help the fruit ripen during inclement weather, and so, just in case—this being Colorado—I stand a horseshoe next to each one, upright, so the luck won't run out. The horseshoes are evocative of the crescent moon, once a sign of the goddess and later a symbol of the Virgin Mary.

The fine weather holds. It's not unusual to have snowfalls this late in May.

Orioles. Wrens. Warblers. Siskins. Tanagers. All turn up in the garden across the seasons. Today, I'm looking out my bedroom perch when I spot a tiny, then two tiny, then three tiny yellow flashes on the thistle feeder over the Nilus. Goldfinches. *Astragalinus tristis tristis,* sad sad star chicken.

I glance at the azaleas. They're blooming. Hundreds of bright orange and salmon blossoms on each bush, gleaming like a coral reef.

Day after day, there are more goldfinches, flying Easter eggs, soaring lemons with black scored foreheads, wings, and tails, dropping from low-hung branches, flitting through the sky, circling the house, now and then resting on the azalea bushes.

My March wind dream come true.

P ink lace with frills is stylish in Spring
E levating all around to grandeur
O pening soft petals in continuity
N ever remember snowy days in February
Y ellowing petals under the summer sun's heat.

—Nell Geiser

Nell

Reserved and earnest. Fourteen years old and one of the few people I trust to work with me in my garden or care for it while I'm gone.

The time's come to hire some help and I'll have no one but Nell. She seems to intuit the complications of my garden. She approaches it with respect and patience. If she's a little awed by the imbroglio, she doesn't show it. She keeps a journal of each visit, complete with crisp, fine poems and lovely sketches. She is a budding eco-activist and talented violinist, so it's a particular pleasure to show her the fiddleheads, the first signs of ferns.

She's organized, where I'm not. She remembers, for instance, to turn off the soaker hoses, invisible and silent and easily forgotten by me. Without Nell's maps and her memory, her quiet, strong powers of observation, even I, who planted this seething shambles, would be lost.

A job sends me out of town in mid-May. I'm devastated about leaving my garden for a minute at this most crucial time of year.

Throughout my sojourn, I can think of nothing except the garden. Nell's in charge. Her poetic journal—and the photos she's generously taken—document what I'm missing:

May 17—*The soil and woods darken and take on an air of richness. [After watering], the flagstones steam and white and purple irises brighten. Their petals drop slightly under the weight of the water. The tall, purple columbine turns down its face . . . shapely petals, deep, bright color . . . a jewel. Yellow and brown irises have bloomed near the house.*

May 21—*Dark purple irises have bloomed in the backyard. [Oriental] poppies look as if they're about to pop into being. A mass of peonies has effloresced. One flower is fully opened and full of pink frills. Four or five others are in various stages of unfurling their petals in a glorious welcoming of the sun.*

May 25—Today I was at the Boulder Creek Festival—a Mecca of hot bodies eating greasy and sweet foods on a scorching day. What a relief to arrive into the coolness of the garden. Some lovely orange poppies have bloomed near the back of the house. Also, more irises and more peonies are ravishing shades of many colors. The honeysuckle is doing beautifully and all this you'll get to see soon! Today, I'm doing the sprinklers and tomorrow the watering with hoses . . . as it has been slightly rainy weather. WEATHER REPORT: for the first full week of your absence, all was sunny and heated to the bone. But on Thursday last, a mighty rain did shake all life in violent jubilation. More, but less, came Friday, and Sunday too, and today, Monday, they say a p.m. thunderstorm will hit.

I return to the arresting scent of lilacs all over town. A rhapsodic explosion. The fragrance of lilacs, John Berger wrote, is "not so far from the smell of cows in the stable . . . smells of peace and procrastination."

My garden is plush with peonies and poppies and irises—a carnival of "poor man's orchids," hundreds of them.

And daisies, pink valerian, lupine, leopard's bane, geum, forget-me-not, and coral bells. The kale is as high as an elephant's eye . . .

The garden celebrates Floralia at its peak, tumultuous, voluptuous Nature festival of the Roman goddess Antheia, She of the Flowering Plants, beaming, prosperous, impulsive maiden cousin of ransomed, guarded, stern Persephone.

Talk about being "struck with love, as if by a puncheon"! I can't stop hugging Nell.

June

... offerings of flowers
are pleasing to the gods.
They loathe those who come before them
with uncrowned heads.

— Sappho, Greek, sixth century B.C.E.

Dominion of Dreams

Birds sing but less rapturously than in May. The garden still invites unusual species, but the great migration is coming to a close. The goldfinches have all gone and the azalea blossoms are fading.

The thrill of May is its mad merriness, more settled than April, more sudden and urgent than June. In June, time seems to slow a bit, to steady, and all spring's potential is fulfilled.

I've been asked to participate in an "eccentric, secret garden tour," organized by an artist/master gardener friend. I'm flattered and a little bit frightened. No one has ever come here with a critical eye.

I spend all week before the event tidying up and planting perky annuals in every nook and cranny. In a mere few days I've become "yard proud," dressing areas of the garden just for the tour. Will the creeping phlox be flowering between rocks like the pressed hues in a watercolor box? Will delicate places be tromped and trampled?

What a shame that by June all evidence of the "Emperor" tulips have disappeared under a spreading carpet of violets no longer blooming either. There's so much exploding growth here, this fretting is a waste of time.

Poppies, irises, and peonies are the June garden superstars. "Big" and "bright" are the current watchwords, and leafy backgrounds are too young to compete. Later, things will cool down to more subtle shades against darker greens—until fall, when the garden explodes again with relentless thick-petaled yellows, such as sunflowers and gaillardia and the earth-fire colors of harvest blazing in the chrysanthemums.

"A June garden's easy," another of the participants says ruefully. "Mid-July would be a bigger challenge."

Early June is a time of profound inspiration, when planting is more or less risk free: not too wet, not too dry, and the season still lengthy enough for plants to settle in and give their best. Theoretically, those garden tourists who have yards of their own will want to rush home directly after the tour to throw themselves into the work, buzzing with new ideas.

Inspiration is always to the point. Before the tour, I visit the Denver Botanic Gardens and one of my favorite displays: the peony garden.

There are 3,000 peony cultivars, about 1,300 available commercially. The Gardens, while not vast, exhibit some of the rarest of these, with blossoms that glow as if with inner fluorescence, incandescence as if their centers were lit by fireflies. There are peonies like waterlilies of the land, peonies like pillows that fell from the Milky Way, and peonies that seem not at all three-dimensional, but like outré paintings.

I have merely the basics. Even those seem exotic to me: red "Felix Crousse," white "Madame de Verneville," and purplish-crimson "Karl Rosenfeld," as well as a red Chinese peony I inherited from a friend. Most will be open by the day of the garden tour.

My first peony—a light pink "Sarah Bernhardt"—will be at the peak of its aria. It came from Susie Next Door's house, twenty years ago, during the era of the tree-planting landlord. He gave me a peony root, bits of iris rhizome, and a few handfuls of vinca minor

for one of the first of many "new beginnings" my garden has en-
dured. The vinca went into the front yard, where it's now a handsome, voracious, evergreen sward along the front walk.

I plopped that first peony root into hard ground beside the back
steps. And I do mean *plopped,* with no idea of proper peony planting protocol. It thrives in the warmth generated by walk, steps, and
foundation and never fails to give us blowsy, buxom blooms.

A friend in New Mexico, a gardener who can make the driest
desert bloom, hates peonies. I'm astonished. Apparently, they remind
her of grim family graveyard visits back in Nebraska on Memorial
Day. And she remembers them planted plunk in the middle of
lawns, alone in beds that related to nothing, uglified by their austerity, yet oddly precious. This custom isn't restricted to Nebraska. Peonies are frequently planted that way to give them the brightest
sunshine, as well as to show them off to best advantage.

To me, they're best mixed with other flowers—the red Chinese
with the pink Oriental poppy, and irises in another shade of pink as
well as coral, for instance, make a spicy show in a small bed lined
with the succulent dragon's blood and grape hyacinths. My peonies
are all scattered throughout the flower beds, some prominent, others puffing out like balloons escaping the riots. I'm giddily proud of
them this year. Later plantings took years to bloom. This is normal
for the long-lived peony, but I've also retarded three of my plants by
transplanting them several times.

In China, peonies are the flower of longevity, and no wonder.
Like oaks, they can far outlive the gardener or the garden. By contrast, in England, there's a rural belief that an odd number of peony
blooms *portend* a death.

One of the most felicitous peony gardens I know is a formal
composition of white peonies with pink, black, and white irises and
blue delphinium, bridal veil, candy tuft (and later blooms of white
and purple clematis with lavender rose-of-sharon), subtly shaded
like clouds against a gray house.

My first peony by the back steps—in a yard that was unbearably
stark—looked much like the lonely lawn plantings that so prickle
my friend's memory. One season, which I recall as my "Sleeping

Beauty Year," during a period of introversion, when I wanted to hide myself, my house, and my mind in flowers, I built an arbor over the steps for a climbing "Blue Girl" rose and started a Himalayan musk rose creeping along a sumac branch overhanging the walk. It's rather like a wedding each time we enter the back door. The fragrance— theoretically—improves our moods. Later, I planted a yucca, which flowers only every five years or so, but whose leaves offer a spiked contrast to the soft "Sarah Bernhardt."

Behind it all is a hopelessly trashed area under the kitchen window birdfeeder, decimated by scavenging squirrels. I've tried everything, including cactus. Nothing deters my little furry monsters from this seed bonanza, not even dreaded bloodmeal.

As the tour date approaches, I become self-conscious about the mess. I build a short wall with cinderblocks, and disguise it with an old piece of wrought iron fence. I string vinca along the fence to hide the squirrel sabotage.

Sadly, another rhododendron has died. I dig the miserable little root from the ground, sigh over its skinny, starved branches, which briefly showed signs of green, then recanted. I had great hopes for this P.J.M. variety, especially bred for high-altitude, arid climates like Colorado's. The hardy new azaleas settled well, but I'll not try the P.J.M. again. The few I've seen blooming here are planted right up against the radiating heat of foundations. For me this is three and three's a charm. I'll have to satisfy my rhododendron cravings with trips to the botanic gardens or to my daughter and stepdaughter in the Northwest.

Certain plants won't grow for certain people, no matter the effort. Each planting of Russian olive has failed—the last time beside the Nilus as a "dry" substitute for the weeping willow I really wanted. If word ever gets out that I'm a proven Russian olive assailant, I'll be the darling of the Forest Service. The invasive Eurasian oleaster, though splendid, is—with tamarisk, which I also can't grow—quickly edging out indigenous plant life in the American West.

Wisteria can't stand me. Astilbe loathes me. Coleus and four-o'clocks have nothing but contempt for me. Russell lupines sneer at me before turning up their toes. And there are more, all of which will grow in Boulder . . . for others. Neighbors. Same vicinity. Opposite results.

For years, morning glories—which my mother considered pests—despised me. Its cousin bindweed does not. Then one season, for reasons I can't fathom and won't question, just when I'd sworn it would be my last attempt ever, the morning glory seeds of all types—even the fragile moon flower—sprouted and took off running. Overjoyed, I've become, for the present, a morning glory maniac, obsessively dropping seeds everywhere there's an excuse, even in a self-watering planter under my second-story study window, where they trail toward the roof.

Of course, our relationship to plants isn't just dependent on personalities. There are matters of where, how, and when we plant, as well as a particular season's weather conditions. Or, it takes experimentation, moving things around till the right spot is found, amending the soil and so on.

But sometimes, there's simply bad chemistry between plant and gardener, mismatched vibes, as there can be between people. The best advice in this case, with people or plants, is to let go and take the long view, admiring from afar.

I am filling the empty spot left by the dead P.J.M. with a big pot of lisianthus, when the first garden tourist arrives. I don't notice she's an hour early and so think, with great relief when no one else arrives for another forty-five minutes, that this tour will be sparse and manageable.

By noon, two hundred people have moseyed through my yard and more are coming. Some seek out "the gardener" and want to chat, ask questions, share ideas; others ignore me and walk along the paths, silently or talking quietly with their companions. A brief hullabaloo when someone nearly loses her three-year-old in the pond. Kate's lavish foxgloves have garnered the most attention. I find myself telling the folklore of foxgloves again and again, enjoying the look of recognition that passes over people's faces when I describe them as "fairy caps" or "cradles."

No one challenges my gardening methods. No one's pushy or unpleasant. It occurs to me that visitors to the botanic gardens are equally nice and well-behaved. People touring gardens are peaceful and happy—even if they arrive in a state of stress, their anxiety seems to disappear instantly. The atmosphere encourages kindness and sweet manners.

By the end of the day, more than four hundred people have passed through my garden. Nothing has been disrupted, though one very narrow spot on a path looks the worse for wear along its edges. The low hum of crowds has subsided. I sit on the pond bench alone, delighted at how gardens can transform moods, heal, and make us happy, when a young woman appears at the gate. She's familiar, someone I've seen earlier. She's shy and stutters a little. She tells me her grandfather recently died. She has only a studio flat and the parks are too noisy. Could she sit quietly here awhile, maybe in the Enchanted Garden, to meditate and mend her heart?

I leave her alone beside Kate's Pond to soak in whatever the garden has to give. I'm unspeakably gratified by her presence. I hope she comes back whenever she needs to.

> As for the heated man . . .
> He is like a tree growing indoors;
> A moment lasts its growth of shoots,
> Its end comes about in the woodshed . . .
>
> The truly silent man, who keeps apart,
> He is like a tree grown in a meadow.
> It greens . . . its fruit is sweet, its shade delightful.
> —*Instruction of Amenemipet,* Egyptian

Plant Persona

According to our local newspaper garden columnist, this is the time to snip the candles of conifers to prevent them from growing too big. Beyond the yucca, beyond the "Sarah Bernhardt," an Austrian pine sets yet another texture. There's another pine on the banks of the Nilus. I've kept them low and bushy with the candle-snipping technique, then trained their long, curvaceous arms to spread low by pulling branches to the ground and anchoring them with string and big staples. Why, I don't know, since doing so gives me the "*bonsai* creeps." *Bonsai,* the Japanese practice of dwarfing trees and shrubs is the gardening equivalent of footbinding.

Although I've rarely seen a Japanese garden I didn't like—and have learned something about Japanese gardening technique and aesthetics—my adoration isn't quite unconditional. While the Japanese do, indeed, sincerely worship Nature—and call their garden designs "borrowed landscapes"—there's an awful propensity toward controlling Nature. On such a heavily populated island, this is partly pragmatic to keep things manageable, as well as beautiful. It's nevertheless disillusioning to realize that in Japan, coral reefs, for example, are being turned into airports or to discover, as the poet Gary Snyder did, that there are no songbirds in Japan—they've eaten every one.

Of course, there are highly manipulative gardening practices worldwide. Some folk recommend plucking the buds of the peony, for example, to triple the size of the remaining blooms. They grow outlandishly immense.

I have no gigantism desires. Behemoth watermelons, three-story sunflowers, pony-sized pumpkins . . . big lacks nuance and, these days, is too often gained through chemical and genetic tampering, a practice far more horrifying than *bonsai.*

However its day-to-day manifestations—the difference, as with all spiritual practices, between the ideal and the real—the ancient, native Japanese Shinto religion venerates Nature. It is one of the few faiths today that actually looks to Nature rather than beyond. Most Japanese folktales feature a plant spirit whose behavior was true to what was thought to be the nature of the plant. The belief that plants have souls is by no means exclusively Japanese—though in Shinto, it's official. Gardeners everywhere perceive the spirits and make intimate acquaintances with them, calling them, among other things, "devas," "fairies," "*dames vertes,*" "pixies," "pillywiggins," "fées"— hundreds of names to describe the divine essence of plants.

Of Nature's offerings, horticultural humans liken ourselves most readily to plants and plant life. Plants are not only benign and pose no threat, except in extreme circumstances, they can also be studied closely and to a great extent, controlled. Animals, on the other hand—whose spirits are identified generally with nonagricultural or horticultural/hunter-gatherer communities—are perceived by agrarians as able to kill and eat us, and as competitors for territory and food supply.

Plants act as metaphors for individual personalities, emotions and behavior. In Victorian England, illustrator Kate Greenaway listed hundreds of behaviors and emotions matched with plants in her *Language of Flowers.*

The orchid, bamboo, pine, plum, and chrysanthemum are considered by some Asian cultures to be lucky and represent the best of human virtues. The plum is like the "superior," ascetic human being, undaunted, unobtrusive. The bamboo is gentle, hardy, indefatigable, flexible, straight, humble, modest, and consistent.

Orange blossoms recall the past. Cherry blossoms connote happiness and hope. We can be strong as an oak or infrangible as an orchid. This story about a peony was told to me repeatedly:

> *Princess Aya is betrothed to the second son of Lord Ako. One night before the wedding, she walks through the garden, accompanied by her maids. She wonders about her bridegroom. How he looks, if he is kind.*
>
> *The moon shines on her favorite peony bed beside the pond. She lingers and bends to smell the fragrance. Her foot slips and as she is about to tumble into the pond, a young man appears and snatches her upright. He is clad in a robe embroidered with peonies. He vanishes before the princess can thank him.*
>
> *A few days later, Aya takes to her bed. She is too ill to stand, her fever rages. The best physicians cannot cure her.*
>
> *Her waiting maid begs an audience with Princess Aya's father. "I am sworn to secrecy" she tells him, "but I am afraid for Aya's life." She confesses that Princess Aya fell in love that night by the pond with a young man wearing robes embroidered with peonies. "You must find him, Lord, or Princess Aya will die."*
>
> *Aya's sickbed is moved to a pavilion by the pond next to the peonies. At night, musicians play their flutes and kotos behind a screen, while the princess stares with hot, glazed eyes into the flowers. Each night, a young man appears to Princess Aya. He wears the same silk robe embroidered with peonies. Aya weeps with yearning and her fever increases.*

One night Aya's father orders a servant to dress in black and hide in the peony bed.

The music starts, the princess turns her head toward the peony bed. She is weak, waiting for her vision. The mysterious young man appears and as he reaches to touch Aya, the servant grabs him. The servant binds the young man's arms. He cries for the palace guards. The princess sits up in bed, alarmed, fully awake.

The servant clings hard to the young man. A heady fragrance emanates from the captive. The servant grows dizzy and slumps to the ground. The Lord's guards come running. When the servant regains consciousness, all he holds in his arms is a large peony.

"My daughter," says Princess Aya's father, "I see that it was the spirit of the peony which visited you and saved you from falling. Now you must take this flower and treat it with all kindness."

The princess returns to her bed in the palace and places the peony beside her in a vase. Each day, she grows healthier and the flower flourishes.

When she is well, Lord Ako arrives at the castle with his second son. Princess Aya marries her betrothed.

At that very hour, the peony dies.

The Oriental poppies and bearded irises are so reliable in this mercurial climate, there's every reason to grow as many as possible and seize the June moment.

By now, I have hundreds of irises and each one is energized. Whatever it was—Nell's exquisite care while I was gone in May, the right combination of rainfall, sunshine, and temperature, last year's vigorous thinning of overgrown rhizomes—the garden is breathtaking, awesome, in the original sense of the word. These extravagant hosts of color occupy all portions of the garden, except the shaded western corridor between Susie Next Door's house and mine.

Irises are said to free the soul from the body and are thus popular in cemeteries. Greeks and Romans decorated tombs with the iris—named for the Goddess of Rainbows, Iris. Iris, and not Aphrodite, was said by some to be the mother of Eros.

On the western edge of my oldest vegetable garden, there's a set of white irises—with just a hint of sky blue in their petals—that have not needed thinning in the ten years since I planted them over my parents' ashes.

Those first bearded irises—old-fashioned purples, not at all fancified with stripes or fluting—which came from Susie's house, long before Susie, have been separated repeatedly and many returned to their ancestral home (where their foremothers died of neglect). Susie now has stands of her garden's great-great-great-etc. grandchildren thriving within her wildflowers and as borders along her new paths.

I've also replanted these passion-purple progeny in the hellstrip and as a border in the Colony—the section of Susie's front yard I coopted years ago when I could no longer bear the ragweed.

I confess it wasn't just the ragweed. Like a marauding imperialist, I also wanted more space in the front, where there was unalloyed sun and where I could create a kind of aesthetic climax in my front yard. So I began, not at all discreetly, to invade. Just a little way, mind you, with sedum, blue fescue, morgananium, artemesias, and other silvery plants. My first attempt to make a purely xeric zone.

To show the landlords—who may not have noticed anyway—my good intentions, I ran a stone path through it all, pulled the ragweed in the remainder of their front yard and cleared and leveled the path leading into their backyard.

"Don't forget, that's not our property," my husband warned. "If the landlords want to tear out your plants to put in a badminton court, you're just going to have to accept it."

He's right, of course, and it would break my heart.

For the first year or two, I had merely a nodding acquaintance with Susie. Renters come and go so frequently, I couldn't be bothered making friends. Susie stopped periodically to chat while I planted the Colony. Our first conversations were commiserations about the dreadful state of that unloved yard.

It's simply not in Susie's nature, so to speak, to bypass the chance to connect with the Earth or to beautify her surroundings. Before that spring ended, she'd taken up the gauntlet and planted wildflowers in the remainder of the front yard. Nor did she stop there.

The backyard was her next challenge and together we conceived how to do it with little or no expense.

The landlords know a good thing when they see it. They welcomed the backyard reclamation program she proposed. They even agreed not to drop by unexpectedly with chainsaws for their annual random massacre. Still, Susie warned, we had to be cautious. You never knew when they'd show up with some harebrained plan, trying to be helpful or suddenly possessive or paranoid. "It's our team versus theirs," she said.

As it turns out, they trust and admire Susie and have given her carte blanche.

More land! And new spots to plant thinnings I might otherwise have to throw away. It takes a coroner's certificate before I'll admit a plant is dead and ready to be discarded. To toss out live plants is absolute anathema.

Susie and I immediately started digging beds and transplanting. She planted wildflower seeds and cosmos and I spread seeds from my November basket. The landlords laid five paving stones on our paths, anonymously.

In Flanders fields the poppies blow,
Between the crosses, row on row . . .
The larks still bravely singing fly
Scarce heard amid the guns below.

Since the nineteenth century, poppies of all kinds have been associated in Europe and North America with war and those who died in battle. The seeds sit dormant for years, then sprout when the soil is disrupted. The association of poppies with heroic death probably started with the Battle of Waterloo in 1815, when red poppies appeared after the bloody field in Flanders was plowed.

Lettuce, opium, lactos, galaxy are among words that mean *milk*. Squeeze the center of a lettuce, and it will exude the same white juice as the poppy stem.

Susie and I have tossed hundreds of corn, alpine, Shirley, California, Iceland, and Oriental poppy seeds in her garden. Inspired, or just unable to quit, I started a poppy "field," in a strip between the shed and the alley.

My Oriental poppies are mostly traditional, bright orange, explosive, intense. In recent years I've tried the pink, red, and purplish Orientals, fragile, extravagantly hued tissues planted where they'll not be lost in the cacophony: the tall pinks with the low, red Chinese peony; the "Raspberry Queens" in the Poetry Garden next to the golden-spur columbine. It both pleases and frustrates me that poppies refuse to last in a vase. Pleases me, because it indicates a determined wildness that no amount of cultivation can imprison. Frustrates me, because I want them in the house, would paste them on my skin or wear them on my nose. I cauterize the stems before I put them in water, but they won't last more than a day or two.

My grandmother and I made poppy dolls, little ballerinas and princesses, contrived by turning the flower inside out, using the split stalks for arms and legs, tying grass around the dolly's "waist," and drawing a face on the seed box with a pin. We had a little house for them under a boxwood, where we made furniture from leaves, pebbles, and acorns.

She called poppies "Headaches." This was typical in Ireland and England (where picking poppies was also said to cause blindness, earache, and nosebleeds), probably because of the poppy's reputation as a soporific. In Ireland, it was considered particularly bad for unmarried women to touch them. The belief must have something to do with the vulnerability of young women to the aggressive desires of men, and is perhaps related to old customs of abducting brides, willing or not.

After all, Persephone, picking flowers one morning, was drawn to poppies planted by Hades to attract her. As she plucked them, he rose from underground and stole her away. I imagine her bobbing and dizzy, woozy, unable to scream or fight. That myth, or the memory of it, has surely been passed around and handed down in locally peculiar versions.

In one variation on the tale, the poppy was created by Somnus, god of sleep, to help Demeter rest and forget after the fervent, disappointing search for her daughter. When Demeter awoke, soothed and refreshed, the crops sprouted again from the ground. So it was that many European farmers believed poppies in the field were essential for the well-being of the grain.

A modern version of the poppy-abduction tale occurs in L. Frank Baum's *The Wonderful Wizard of Oz,* written in 1900 and made into a film in 1938. The Wicked Witch of the West causes poppies to materialize on the path of the girl and her allies, who fall asleep. The nasty winged monkeys seize the opportunity to carry Dorothy to the Witch's castle.

My mother thought poppies were "too weedy" and wouldn't grow them. Nevertheless she adored looking at them and owned a thirty-foot-long Japanese folding screen, painted with orange-gold poppies, her most prized possession. Catatonic with grief, she gazed at it constantly after my father died. What had it meant to them as lovers and partners for more than thirty years? No one but they could know, least of all their child.

> A rose is a rose . . .
>
> —Gertrude Stein

. . . is a rose . . .

. . . speaking the language of roses. Pink for simplicity and happy love; red for passion and desire; white for innocence and purity; yellow for jealousy and perfect achievement.

I have none of the tolerance rose devotees need for pampering and fussing. I have less patience with the chemicals rosarians seem to require to produce perfect, pest-free blossoms.

It's said that garlic should be planted with roses to keeps pests away. Kate tells me there's a local belief that planting roses with a lump of fat or salt pork will . . . do what?

Make them plumper, of course.

"Don't laugh," Kate says. "My mother planted them with goose grease. And she had wonderful roses, over by the barn and the well house."

They're still there. I've pruned them. Their old stalks are so tough I needed a saw.

There are roses in France, planted in the Middle Ages, going strong.

My roses are stock and proven varieties, hardy "Max Graf,"

"Spring Gold," "Austrian Copper," rugosas. By any name, they smell as sweet. Season by season, I transplanted the originals, growing here when I moved in. My rose "career" started in earnest when I needed to find something that would survive the poppy blitzkrieg. Having put so much energy into such largesse, the poppies die back after flowering, leaving a stickery mess (and return late in summer as green mounds). While they bloom, the sprawling plants overcome everything else anywhere near them.

In a few small beds, I've planted late-blooming gladioluses around them, which I hope will fill the empty space and take advantage of the poppy cages for stakes.

What to plant that would survive the Oriental poppies in the larger beds and replace them when they turn papery brown? Clearly, "light" shubbery was called for: two bird-attracting, hardy, highbush cranberries, whose height has been decelerated by the intrepid poppies, and a washed-violet, single-petaled rose-of-sharon.

These are languid growers. Something else was needed, which would respond to urgency. My solution was roses, planted between the poppies and up the coyote fence.

Roses evolved in Central Asia sixty million years ago. Their fossils have been found in Oregon and Colorado. They've been cultivated for five thousand years, first in China, where the red rose was called "Flower of the Goddess." At Troy, the "Queen of Flowers" decorated the shield of Achilles, as well as Hector's helmet when they fought their final duel.

Another political botanical emblem, the English Tudor rose unites the white rose of York and the victorious red rose of Lancaster after the brutal Wars of the Roses in the fifteenth century. Lewis Carroll's 1865 send-up of that thirty-year massacre in *Alice in Wonderland* includes the gardeners painting the roses red. As one of them explains to Alice: *"Why, the fact is, you see, Miss, this here ought to have been a red rose-tree, and we put a white one in by mistake; and, if the Queen was to find it out, we should all have our heads cut off, you know . . ."*

Alice hides the gardeners in a flowerpot.

Today, the rose is an insignia for far-flung nations from India to

Peru, where Santa Rosa de Lima became the first native-born saint of the Americas in 1671. Many roses sold on Saint Valentine's Day are imported from Colombia.

When they dined, ancient Romans draped their guests with rose garlands, washed in rosewater, ate rose puddings, and drank rose wine. When privacy was desired, Romans hung a rose to indicate confidentiality or bribed one another into silence with a bouquet of roses, thus leading to the *sub rosa,* "under the rose." Romans showered rose petals on important people and religious statues, notably those of the Phrygian Cybele, whose statue was honored with a "snow of roses."

Typically—and not unlike our own faddish immoderations—the Romans overdosed on a good thing. The rose, worn by priestesses of Venus, came to symbolize degeneracy and debauchery to the early Christians, who disdained it until the Middle Ages when it underwent another transformation as a symbol of the purity of the Virgin Mary. (The rose as an emblem of goodness and virtue is seen as well in the fairy tale "Beauty and the Beast," when Beauty's hapless father picks a rose for her from a stranger's garden, but must then exchange his daughter for the flower in order to save his own life. The characters of rose and maiden are alike.)

The rosewheel is a kind of Christian mandala, as the rosary is the rosewheel of Mary. The role of roses in the West parallels that of the lotus in the East as an emblem of nascent life. Roses were said to have been made red with the blood of Christ, just as numerous other heroes gave theirs to generate flowers: Adonis of the anemone, Endymion of the bluebell, Hyacinthus, Attis of the violets.

In the Dark Ages, as Christianity gained speed, flowers in a church were considered by zealous laymen to be a pagan custom. Monks, however, decorated altars with bouquets and on Holy Days, priests wore chaplets and wreaths, particularly of roses.

King Midas—He of the Golden Touch—was said to have grown a sixty-petaled rugosa. Mine are not so glamorous. The stalwart *Rosa rugosa,* like the one that guards the east-side house next door, was first imported to England two hundred years ago from Japan, where it had been cultivated for one thousand years. It is named for its crinkled leaves—"rugose," from the Latin *ruga*, meaning wrinkled. It acclimates immediately to all situations and has been hybridized by ever-intrepid rosarians, who crossed *R. rugosa* with climbing tea roses, floribundas, noisettes, centifolias, and others, creating roses of all shapes, sizes, and scents. Rugosas are drought and disease resistant, trouble-free. Just my kind of plant.

Late afternoon sun lances the poppy bed. The shell-pink roses redden amid the gold, the scarlet roses turn a darker ruby. The climbers have yet to bloom against the coyote fence. One is thrusting a thorny arm toward the bench, ready to snag the first head that rests here. A branch of the honeysuckle I've been weaving into the back of the bench is also out of line, threatening to goose anyone who makes it past the rose.

In this untidy bower, roses straggle where they will, while the poppies battle for the entire territory to themselves. And underneath, fuzzy, luxuriant white lambs ears ignore the whole mess. Larkspur and tansy, only a few inches high, prepare to step in.

> Glory forever,
> Bright moon.
> You are
> The glorious lamp of the poor.
> —Scottish Highland moon greeting

The Moon Garden

We sat on the grass and spooned, crooning a tune to the moon one June, the summer after the Nilus was finished. The black sky glowed. Clouds indigo. Light puddled on a hillock nearby.

"An opinion is like a moon in a song," my husband said and leaned back with binoculars to trace whatever stars he could through the light pollution.

"Why a Man in the Moon," I muttered, "considering the moon's female origins as Diana, Luna, Ishtar, Selene, Phoebe-the-Shining and all?"

*   *   *

In Polynesia, China, and Japan, the moon's occupant is a woman. To the Mayans, she was a woman weaving. In Mesoamerica, Mongolia, and India, there's a Hare in the Moon (her cycle matches the gestation time for a rabbit). Or a toad. The spots on the moon were sometimes described as trees, sacred groves of Paradise. The Quechua and Aymara peoples believed that Moon Maiden coupled with her brother Sun and their offspring were the royal Inca of Cuzco.

My husband handed me the binoculars. "I can see the rabbit. And the toad. And the groves," he said. "See if you can find a weaving woman."

I couldn't.

I was, however, inspired to plant a Moon Garden on the beaming mound of pond diggings.

There's never been a culture on Earth that hasn't paid homage to the moon or understood her (and rarely "his") phases as essential to the welfare of crops, trees, and flowers. Activities throughout history worldwide are influenced by those phases (from cutting hair to cutting vegetables). Old Farmer's Almanacs, which give careful moon-planting instructions, make intriguing winter reading.

Even the most pragmatic and scientific of us knows that the full moon causes strange events. Medical professionals on emergency duty steel themselves for additional disasters, especially violent altercations, on the full moon.

It's said that more births occur on the full moon. My great uncle Willie had a favorite Holstein milk cow on his Ohio farm who never failed but once to give birth on the full moon. Her calves were named Luna, Looney, Moon-calf and Minerva, a.k.a. Minnie. The one born on the waning moon was named Roger. My cousin called him Steakbone, in anticipation of his destiny.

Just as the moon was responsible for birth, she devoured the dead. And she was the Land of the Dead, the vessel that contained departed souls. In the pre-patriarchal age, the goddess of the moon, Joseph Campbell wrote, "was herself the mythic garden, wherein Death and Life—the Two Queens—were one."

There has never been a time or place when the moon was not

perceived as a deity. She has infinite names as the primordial Great Mother, whose rhythms determine the pulse of plants and the ebb and flow of women's bodies. Even in the Christian era, the Virgin Mary is associated with the moon.

I have a friend who claims her garden is entirely devoted to the moon. It is planted in a spiral, with a round mirror on the ground in the center. She plants and harvests, she tells me, by the moon's phases—seeds and seedlings go in on the waning moon, or forty-eight hours before it waxes. Her garden thrives.

As the wind delivers dreams, the moon has dominion over them, determining their content. Perhaps stories, like this one from Japan, originate *on* the moon. Certainly most have been told *under* the moon.

> One night, Moon Goddess visits Earth. She leaves her white feathered robe on the bank of a river while she bathes. A fisherman snatches the cloak and refuses to return it. The more she pleads, the more determined he is to keep it, for these glowing white feathers are a treasure, a marvel.
>
> The fisherman offers a bargain. If she will dance before him, he will restore the robe.
>
> "I'll dance the dance that makes the Palace of the Moon turn round and round," she says, "but without my feathered cloak I can't dance a step."
>
> The fisherman accuses her of planning to fly away before the dance.
>
> "Promises made by mortals are easily broken," she says. "But there's no falsehood among the Heavenly Beings, no lies in the stars, or the sun and moon."
>
> The fisherman is shamed. He hands the goddess her cloak of white feathers and she begins to dance. She dances and sings. She sings of the Moon. She sings of its wonders. She sings of the mighty Palace of the Moon, where thirty monarchs rule, fifteen in robes of white for the waxing moon and fifteen more in black for the waning. She dances to the moon.
>
> After a time, her feet rise from the sand and the goddess is lifted into the air, the white feathers of her cloak gleaming against the pine

trees and the blue sky. Up and up and up she goes. Singing. Past the summits. Singing. Higher and higher until the fisherman can no longer hear her voice. Higher and higher, until she reaches the glorious Palace of the Moon.

The moon was still visible in blue sky when I crawled into the cellar and retrieved a large, old wire Chinese birdcage, with towers and turrets, elaborate as a palace, big as a doll house, which had held a sick cockatiel given to me by a friend to mend. The bird died, the cage was relegated to storage.

I placed the birdcage at the top of the hillock and planted ivy and woodbine inside it. On Susie's side of the coyote fence, where there's blazing sunlight, I planted a handful of moon flower seeds, which crept between the cracks and hovered in branches above the birdcage, giving the illusion, if you squint, of magnolias. I created a miniature moon gate, in the Chinese tradition, using a hollow log, packed over with dirt and planted with creeping veronica. I built a wee path, steps of mica, red stones, and sand dollars climbing up the hill to the birdcage. Then I covered it all with white verbena, which slinks down the pond banks. In early spring, Grecian windflower gives the hillock the look of the proverbial "field of daisies."

Over time, the red rocks and sand dollars have mostly disappeared into the dirt and under the groundcover. The mica has crumbled into occasional glitter.

Bloomsbury writer and English gardener extraordinaire, Vita Sackville-West, famous for her single-color productions, wrote of an all-white garden through which, she fantasized, a snowy owl might fly across the full moon.

To one side of the cage, I planted a marguerite daisy. In moonlight it resembles an airy clutch of butterflies. Below the hillock, snow-in-summer segues into the larger garden. Silverlace trails the fence en route to the pink climbing rugosas.

Pure white flowers in the Moon Garden seem too stark. Whites with slight, translucent, icy hues add mystery and enchantment. There are chette campanula with shell-pink edges and blueish-white monkshood. Soloman seal, whose white blossoms seem to have been tipped in green paint, complements the cloudy peony draped against a large ivory rock.

It's a gossamer place. When the moon is full, it glows like a bowl spilling with pearls.

> *If you find nine peas in the first gathered pod,*
> *you will have luck and blessings from God.*

We're living on peas and beans, kale and collards and radishes. Chives, wild garlic, turnips, baby carrots, baby cukes, and infant zukes.

I weed the front yard, thankful to my yoga classes for my agility. Things are tight in here. I grope for stray asters, dandelions, and ragweed, when my fingers grasp something mushy. I jerk away, afraid it might be a dead mouse or bird. It's an apricot. The Mongolians that flowered way back in March are bearing fruit for the first time.

In the pond, the goldfish are romancing. The females, engorged with eggs, are pursued relentlessly. One Butch-ette is especially popular. A Butch tails her round and round and round. A Sparky tries to get in on the act. Butch turns and thrashes him, then hurries back to his sweetheart.

Rain off and on. At Summer Solstice, the arid High Plains weather will begin in earnest.

> Every spirit builds itself a house; and
> beyond its house a world; and beyond its world
> a heaven. Know then, that the world exists for you:
> build, therefore, your own world.
> —Ralph Waldo Emerson

Light Is God's Daughter

June's joys will always be overshadowed by my mother's death on the Summer Solstice.

I flew to Virginia, to the house she'd refused to leave, where she insisted on living alone with her memories, her garden, and my father's grave. It was the grave under the dogwood tree in the woods she wouldn't leave, though I asked her to move to Boulder.

"We can move Daddy, too," I promised. "We'll bring him with us." No go. This was her *place,* where all her life and all the other places we'd made home had finally coalesced.

Before I could enter the front door, I sat on the steps leading to the creek, which my father built with blue Spanish tiles, and sobbed until my chest was empty and my eyes ached. At last, I found the courage to go in past the front flower garden with its bridal veil, lilacs, peonies, irises, flowering almond, vinca, roses, and magnolia tree. It was meticulous and magnificent. Transporting herself with a walker, my mother had somehow managed to care for her garden. The woods behind the house were wild, her beloved bamboo scattered everywhere.

I hesitated, then opened the door at last. There in the hall was a celadon vase filled with giant white carnations. White carnations are a Chinese flower of death, used at funerals and on shrines. She often displayed carnations in memory of my father.

After the memorial service, my son and I crossed the creek on the Japanese bridge, into the woods, carrying shovels and a trowel to exhume my father's ashes from under the dogwood. They'd shifted and slipped under the moist ground, so that we had to dig a larger hole than we'd anticipated before we found the lacquer box, intact, wrapped in plastic. We put my parents' ashes together in an old cedar saki box with a wedding picture and I brought them back to Colorado. The house was to be sold.

I remember thinking, as I locked the door forever, that the garden would live on. The soil my parents had nurtured, the Christmas trees they'd planted, all this land had been touched by them. The landscape might be altered, but their spirits will be here. I wondered if whoever bought the house my parents built would learn its history and know their names and preserve this cultural and horticultural legacy. Like the box containing my father's ashes, that legacy would gradually sink and shift, yet reappear for anyone who looked.

As I walked slowly away, I bent to pull a weed or two, then careened into the woods, where I picked an azalea and cut a stalk of bamboo. I pressed them in my mother's girlhood copy of *Through the Looking Glass.*

My Brigit-friends gathered at my house to make a ceremony of mixing my parents' ashes. I'd been assured the urn would be big enough for two. They didn't fit. I couldn't start all over again, I just couldn't. I verged on tears, when the women took the situation in hand and marched us—my parents' leftover ashes and me—into the garden. I sprinkled them in each corner and poured a little mound in the place where next day I planted irises. My parents had, after all, helped plant my garden in the early days, when I was trying to raise kids alone. The rest of the ashes, my friends suggested, could accompany me wherever I traveled. My mother and father had been gypsies, global citizens. In the past decade, I've lovingly left them in Ireland, Latin America, California, and Vienna, my grandfather's favorite city.

A month later, Kate and I stood with Aunt Bridie, alone at my father's family gravesite in Ohio. I dropped to my knees and lowered the urn into the squared hole under the tombstone marked with the names of my grandmother, my grandfather, my great-grandparents and great-greats and grand-aunts and uncles, ancestors all around, and now my mom and dad. And Kate recited Charles Swinburne's "The Garden of Proserpine":

> *Here, where the world is quiet;*
>   *Here, where all trouble seems*
> *Dead winds' and spent waves' riot*
>   *In doubtful dreams of dreams . . .*
>
> *She waits for each and other,*
>   *She waits for all men born;*
> *Forgets the earth her mother,*
>   *The life of fruits and corn;*
> *And spring and seed and swallow*
> *Take wing for her and follow*
> *Where summer song rings hollow*
>   *And flowers are put to scorn . . .*

July

[Take] parsley, sage, garlic, chilbolls, onions, leek,
borage, mint, porrette, fennel and cress, rue, rosemary,
purslane.

Lave and wash them, clean, pick them, pluck them
small with thine hand and mingle them well with raw
oil, lay on vinegar and salt and serve it forth.

—Recipe for a "salat," *The Forme of Cookery,* compiled by
the master cooks of King Richard II of England, 1390

Realm of the Senses

I make my way through the medicinal herb garden with scissors
and paper lunch sacks for separating leaves and flowers.

This is the first harvest of healing herbs. I hang some from the
kitchen walls and ceiling to dry, and in winter I'll pulverize them in
an old hand-cranked coffee grinder for teas.

Others work better as tinctures. I stuff the flowers and stems into
mason jars, pour an appropriate liquor over them and in a few
weeks, I'll strain and bottle them for home use. Wildberry schnapps
with horehound for cough medicine, diluted heavily with fruit
syrup to make it more palatable; valerian in heart-warming brandy
for sleep and jangled nerves; skullcap in vodka; calendula flowers
soaked in olive oil for sunburn.

I'm nowhere near a real herbalist. A *real* and quite renowned
herbalist, Brigitte Mars, lives down the street and keeps an overgrown, unkempt garden in the hellstrip outside her home. She's a

gatherer, a wildcrafter. The weeds have particular meaning to her and particular uses.

I'm a "first-aid" herbalist, at best, with just enough knowledge (and a substantial library of reference books) to remedy my family through ordinary aches and pains, head colds, and muscle strains.

Of the hundreds of herb books—from reprinted ancient herbals to contemporary tomes, how-tos and folklore—among my favorites is Rosetta Clarkson's thorough *Magic Gardens,* shamefully out of print.

It was through Clarkson that I discovered a custom of bedding during the time of Henry VIII, using bones as supporting boundaries. Having collected more animal bones in the woods than I knew what to do with, I dusted them off and encircled the mint garden with them, fitting them together like a puzzle. If they were to stand up and come to life, they'd be a weird specimen, "Creature from the Mint Lagoon," with vertebrae for feet, jawbone arms, and shins patched into a skull.

As personal objects, such as shoes and pieces of iron, have been found in the walls and chimneys of old houses, so have horse skulls been found beneath the floorboards of Irish houses. (The skulls gave a room acoustic resonance for step dancing.)

In Henry's day, shanks were popular—presumably not post-mortem souvenirs from his many wives—while jaws were considered vulgar. As pennyroyal creeps over the bone border and into Irish moss between the stones on the path, and the bones bleach, they present a rather spectacular, not to say spectral, scene.

The bones entomb water-loving woolly mint, chocolate-, apple-, spear-, peppermint, but absolutely not catmint. I'll have no rolling felines in my garden beds. Kate demands to know what the point is of gardening if you can't keep the cats happy? The mint garden is located near the faucet, which I allow to leak a bit in order to help it stay damp. Ancient herbalists attributed multifarious healing benefits to mint. The Greeks believed it would even cure elephantiasis.

I make an elaborate, solo ritual of herb planting and harvesting, tincturing and drying. I love the alchemy, the transference and practical magic that comes of touching, smelling, gathering and putting them to use. To know something, however little, about herbology, to nurture medicinal and culinary herb gardens is yet another way to participate in and interact with Nature. Here is her goodness, direct and clear, everything we might want and need for health and good living contained in these profoundly efficacious plants.

My hands tingle with their powers, their oils permeate my palms. When I complete this harvest—and there'll be another in the fall, when I take pieces of the roots of such plants as echinacea—I reel out of the garden, high as a kite on the intensity of the mingled scents. Southernwood and angelica dominate. No wonder it was customary to burn angelica in the house and strew it on the floors each morning to perfume away the odors of cooking, hearth, animals, and bodies (at a time when bathing was rare). The angelica seeds I tossed in Susie's yard produced a plant of giant proportions that's throwing out a perfume I can smell down the street. The old herbalists constantly preached the curative effects of merely inhaling the fragrance of an herb garden—early aromatherapy.

In medicinal herb lore what's sometimes at work is sympathetic magic, so that some plants indicate their affinity for healing ailments according to their physical characteristics (for example, the phallic Jack-in-the-pulpit is believed to be an aphrodisiac). Or the taste of a plant—sour, pungent, sweet, or bitter—in Chinese herbalism and Indian Ayurvedic medicine provokes like kinds of cures. A bitter herb, for instance, is likely to be an internal cleanser.

My kitchen herb garden consists of thyme, tarragon, rosemary, hyssop, oregano, cilantro, marjoram, summer and winter savory, salad burnet . . . the usual suspects, each with its own wizardry for transforming food into nectar, as well as illness into well-being, for many cooking herbs have healing virtues, too.

I plant whole rows of basil to replace the bolted leaf vegetables. Basil is unspeakably tasty, of course. And according to Nita Hill, its essential oil serves to "empower and enliven." Among other benefits, it is "excellent for mental fatigue." I keep oil of basil on my desk next to herbalist Tess Schauffler's rosemary tincture, which snaps the lagging brain to attention.

Basil is sacred to Hindus as the plant of Krishna and Vishnu. But in ancient Greece, it was a plant of poverty and misfortune. In Italy, basil was a love token.

Although I've played around with new varieties that appear annually in nurseries, and grow two or three explosive Thai basil plants—a zinger in salad with peppery nasturtium leaves—I'm devoted to Mediterranean sweet basil, which I learned to savor from my husband's Italian family.

I'd rarely ever cooked before meeting the Bagli clan and took for granted whatever was in my food as long as it tasted good. One of the first things I learned to make was pesto from my mother- and sisters-in-law, decades before it was available in grocery stores. The family cooked pesto with Velveeta, which may explain why Nonna drank homemade champagne every night for her digestion. Why Velveeta? I recently asked my sister-in-law.

"It had to do with how fast it melted," she said. "And—believe it or don't—the taste. People used to beg for the secret of why that pesto tasted so good, but Aunt Angie just looked at them diabolically and refused to answer."

I remember rending basil, garlic, and hard lumps of Parmesan in my mother-in-law's kitchen with a meat grinder by hand. We took turns, Mother, her three daughters, and me. I keep a meat grinder permanently attached to my kitchen sideboard. Like memories, it's become a knickknack, a dust catcher, a distant, precious fondness. The food processor does the job in less than half the time, effortlessly. Making pesto is an efficient activity now, without the smells, the dissolving laughter, the teasing, the mess, the babies underfoot, the triumph of the meal, Velveeta, cheap Cribari wine, and handmade noodles in that fine Pennsylvania house.

When my daughter-in-law in New Mexico has a child, she tells me, she'll be eligible to enter the society of women in her family, who gather to mix, knead, shape, and fry hundreds of tortillas at Christmastime. I envy her the warmth and solidarity of that company, which seems to be gone from my life. The old ladies around whom younger women and families congregated are passing.

I try to imagine myself as an old lady in my garden, surrounded by my family, participating in and enjoying this, my spiritual legacy to them. The reality may be very different and a good deal lonelier. Then the garden will serve me even better than it does now to cushion *involuntary* solitude.

*   *   *

Lavender, bronze fennel, parsley, yarrow, and evening primrose grow among the flowers. Diverse artemesias—generically labeled "sage" in Colorado—gleam in sunny, hot places. Oregon grape (with a reputation as a blood purifier) acts as cover for ground-feeding birds, who dine on the berries.

Sweet woodruff, myrtle, thyme are at work everywhere; pennyroyal and chamomile trickle around rocks . . . and bones. Just as I weed, then wash and dry dandelion roots for tea, I treat the mallow as an ornamental, rather than the intrepid trespasser it's inclined to be. Its leaves are rough and stout, elaborately fluted, and it offers a pretty, pinkish-white flower. I transplant it to the hellstrip, where such an indestructible groundcover is needed and where it blends with lavender cotton. I thought I was unique in this, but a friend who grew up in the Midwest recognized mallow as a groundcover used at his family farm. He knew, as my kids did, about eating the flat round seed pods like nuts.

Rue, comfrey, lemon balm, and garden sage line a lawn path, a low, healthful, scented hedge of contrasting greens leading to a shady corner with feverfew (itself a healing herb), coral bells, and Asiatic lilies. Eating one sprig of garden sage a day is said to enhance longevity.

The balm plumps into perfect domes and is a ubiquitous seed-spreader. A whiff of it sends the blues packing. There is no olfactory pleasure like the lavender and lemon balm together at their aromatic apex.

Comfrey, endlessly adaptable, also thrives in the shade of the Faux Forest, hiding gaps where the old chicken-wire fence pokes through. I've transplanted some of the comfrey's many*many*many offspring to a spot by the coyote fence, where it adds its pendulous flower to the tintinnabulation of Carpathian harebell, peach-leaf, Serbian and Danesblood bell flowers, Canterbury bells, foxglove, and balloon flower (with a smattering of asters, marguerites, cranesbill geranium, and forget-me-nots). Bursts of blues drift into the fern garden, where bare spots close to the fence host plumbago (not a medicinal that I know of, though its name sounds like a disease).

There are many plants commonly considered only ornamental, but which are vital in sophisticated herbal medicine. Among them are peony and yellow flag iris. Trees such as oak or chestnut or ginkgo are important, too. How to handle and employ them is a natural science far beyond me. Peony root is considered in traditional Chinese medicine to be particularly effective for the kidneys. I've found it in the mysterious and foul-tasting, yet effective herbal combinations my acupuncturist gives me.

> *Not even the woods and the wilder faces of Nature are without medicine; there is no place the Holy Mother of all things did not distribute healing remedies.*

So the Greek Pliny (23–79 C.E.) observed in his *Natural History*, though we seem to have forgotten this truth.

The ancient Egyptian medical papyri record ninety-four herbs, predating the pharaohs, for cosmetics, medicines, food, and decoration. Among them, garlic and onion were prized, as were cucumber, cumin, caraway, elderberry, castor beans, and spices. One formula in the papyri calls for frankincense to remove facial wrinkles.

Henna was employed, then as now, for coloring hair and nails, as well as decorating the skin with marvelously intricate floral imagery in temporary tattoos. When my niece married in Tunisia, the women gathered to paint her hands and feet in the most gorgeous, intricate patterns.

Pomegranate was also a treasure among the Egyptian physicians, whom Homer called "more skilled at medicine than any of human kind." Centuries later, the Prophet Mohammed said the pomegranate would purge the system of envy and hatred. In autumn, when pomegranates are available in the grocery stores, I eat them daily, as we did in the Middle East and Central Asia. We make a pink tea, halving and boiling the halves, husk and all, in water with honey, then straining the liquid and adding a dash of rosewater.

Herbs were also a potent ally in the religious rites of the Egyptians, Greeks, Romans, Celts, and countless others throughout the world. The Greeks described their gods as "sweet-smelling, emanating the scents of herbs and flowers." Prometheus stole fire in a hollow fennel stalk to give to human beings. Today, in rural Greece, charcoal is transported in the stalks of giant fennel.

In almost every lore, herbs enchant, charm, work miracles, and are spiritual vessels, each with alchemical and astrological meanings, each with its own association to the gods. As plants have spirits and souls, and act as metaphors for human feeling and behavior, they also have power to transform attitudes or situations when consumed or employed in specific ways.

To the ancient Greeks, the ingestion of thyme brought bravery and gave life energy (what the Chinese call *chi*). Borage gave courage, its name derived from the Celtic word for courage, *borrach*. According to some Native American traditions, yucca—made into a hoop or a hat—can render the wearer invisible. Burdock (also planted in Japan for food), sorrel, and chamomile are among the throngs of plants that will attract money. An astonishing number of plants can be used to attract love—proof positive of how fundamental love is to our lives, and how essential fertility rites of all kinds are to our well-being and symbiosis with the Earth.

The *Ancient Herbs* catalogue from the J. Paul Getty Museum gives the recipe for a delicately herbed leek, onion, and split-pea dish, called *Pisa farsilis,* enjoyed by the Roman emperor Nero, who believing that leeks improved his voice, ate them before giving oratories. (After he kicked his wife Poppaea to death, he depleted Rome's supply of cinnamon with which to bury her.)

In Medieval Europe, leeks were worn as protective amulets. When bitten, leeks broke hexes. It's no secret that wearing garlic discourages vampires . . . and everyone else.

My medicinal garden erupts behind the lilac and Mongolian apricot hedge in the front yard. Ajuga trails from the sidewalk and beneath the shrubs toward this sheltered, aromatic place, which I'd originally wanted to model after a Medieval monastery garden. Monastic gardens of the Middle Ages are probably the most frequently cited herb gardens in the many Eurocentric gardening tomes. Few herb-growing practices and garden designs elsewhere around the world seem to be much documented.

The monks' knowledge of medicinal herbs was pilfered from the province of women, who'd been learned in healing arts, but who, as the Church spread, were reduced to increasing dependency on an expanding guild of medical "doctors." As that club became powerful and wealthy, women without means were neglected, yet also left ignorant of how to care for themselves. A first-aid acquaintance with herbs and natural healing is for me, therefore, liberating and empowering.

Scholarship in recent decades records the history of these Medieval physicians (the old word for doctor was "leech") as a deadly, invasive, and aggressive bunch. Besides killing more patients than they cured, these early M.D.s insisted on the persecution and execution of women competitors, who continued to practice medicine. This accounts for many of the notorious witch burnings during the Inquisition.

Nevertheless, monastic herb gardens were exquisite. Medieval illustrations inevitably show gardeners at work, emblematic of the universal belief that toiling in the garden is an act of devotion. In the more secular Renaissance, these figures disappear from garden paintings, as gardens became increasingly art for art's sake and the practical, spiritual, and aesthetic separated.

Regardless of healing politics, many monks were aware that there is simply no adequate substitute for the closeness with Nature, the feeling of spiritual and physical wholeness that comes from growing herbs.

How could I possibly have imitated the monastic garden's cloistered quadrangle, paths, raised stone and brick beds, and central cistern without giving over most of my yard to it? Contemporary gardens, if they have any space at all, must accommodate a great deal, and in my case, also make room for fantasies and fancies. Yet compared to what most people have these days for land, my eighth of an acre seems like an estate. A number of friends without gardens keep window boxes of cooking and healing herbs in two-inch pots and couldn't do without the fragrance, the pinches here and there in cooking, and the favor they bestow on a home.

Rather than building walls and parterres, I divided my medicinal garden, and "magically enhanced" it, with masks I've set in the dirt. Stalks shoot through eye holes; flowers blossom in mouths. Like herbs, masks carry powers of transformation in sacred dramas. The ingestion of herbs often allowed the masquerader to be transported to other realms.

Neither do many of the plants in my medicinal herb bed bear much in common with those of the Medieval physic garden. Unknown to European monks, for example, were *gotu kola,* an herb used in India, or *dong quai,* a Chinese staple, particularly helpful in women's ailments. Bloodroot, or Indian paint, is a Native American herb, used as an expectorant.

I wish I could grow mandrake—so named for its human shape—a favorite herb to which an astonishing number of magic and medicinal qualities are attributed, from anesthetic to aphrodisiac. It was said to cure "every infirmity, except death." (Isn't it fascinating that we continue to consider death an "infirmity," which we could get over if we only tried harder?)

The veracity of these cures isn't necessarily what's important when growing herbs. Rather, as one Medieval herbalist noted, "most of [these remedies] I am confident are true, and if there be any that are not so, yet they are pleasant."

The monastics are present in my medicinal garden with St. John's wort, mother wort, skullcap, valerian, lovage, costmary, hops, wormwood, the dog rose (thought to cure rabies), apothecary roses, white peony, and a background of field lilies, standing in for the traditional Madonna lilies. Medieval gardens were dedicated to the Virgin Mary, planted as her Paradise on Earth.

Roses were sacred to the Blessed Mother and would cure "the feeble, phlegmatic, choleric, or melancholy, quicken the spirit and take away blemishes."

Long before European settlers reached American shores, indigenous peoples used roses for healing. Petals were mixed with bear grease to cure mouth sores, the powdered petals were applied to fever blisters, flowers soaked in rainwater soothed sore eyes, and the inner bark of the root was applied to boils.

Kaya-Nu-Hima was the Japanese goddess of herbs. Polydemna was an herbalist who supplied Helen of Troy with an antidepressant. The herbs themselves instructed Airmed, the Irish goddess of the Tuatha Dé Dannan, in their own use. And while Cerridwen, the Welsh Mother Goddess, is not precisely called a deity of herbs, she nonetheless kept the Cauldron of Knowledge and Inspiration and knew what to brew in it. Whatever the herbs, they hatched the wisdom and talents of Britain's greatest ancient bard, Taliesin. Today, there are nine Midsummer herbs named in Britain. Mugwort—believed to cure blindness—is the queen of them all.

The list of herb deities is infinite, with infinite numbers of plants figuring in infinite myths and named for the gods in infinite languages.

The Middle Ages introduced the first "household" book, written by a middle-aged Parisian bourgeois to train his child wife. *What the Young Bride Should Know about Managing a Home* featured myriad uses for herbs. And it gave rise to instructional texts for women, mostly written by men or with men's well-being firmly in mind.

I have a bookshelf made by Uncle O'Hara, in which I store books passed down through my family. Here I keep a collection of writings by women gardeners that are, in their way, descendants of the household book—with one foot out the door! Among my favorites are Clarkson's *Magic Gardens* and *The Heart of a Garden,* by Rosamund Marriott Watson, written in 1907. Watson was an English noblewoman, presiding over a huge estate, whose lavish book provides gilded description of her gardens, excoriations of her gardener, and long lyrical passages full of phrases that are unattributed to their originators, poets such as Alexander Pope and John Keats. Lady Watson addresses her rhapsodic prose to various ancient Greek deities—who are both inspiration and nemesis—and peppers chapters with her own sonnets. She lacks the hearty instructions; she simply, well, *waxes,* entirely devoted to her garden.

One of the household books I inherited that sits on Uncle O'Hara's shelf is inscribed "Christmas 1905," to my paternal grandmother from Aunt Eunice, our "kitchen witch."

What Can a Woman Do? Or Her Position in the Business and Literary World, by Mrs. M. L. Rayne, seems to have been an encouragement by Eunice—whose life was relegated to quilting—to my grandmother to find a vocation. She never did, but seemed bored and self-centered all her life and thus was a boring grandma, too.

In 1898, the emancipated, intrepid Mrs. Rayne—writing to

women across class lines—set out possible employment in such female-unfriendly fields as "the profession[s] of literature, journalism, law, medicine, music, telegraphy . . ." There were also possibilities for jobs as government clerks, stenographers, typists, photographers, wood engravers, or dressmakers. Included, of course, is advice on "How a Working Girl Lives," her personal appearance, proper acquaintances, and so on.

The chapter on gardening calls it an occupation "well-adapted to women as it offers healthy employment in which delicacy of touch, judgment, calculation, and expectation are all realized without an undue amount of bodily labor." Mrs. Rayne cites several young women "who appeared to be fatally ill with consumption," who recovered by gardening. She expresses surprise that "so few American women attempt to earn a living [gardening] and that a work that is both pleasant and profitable should be left almost entirely to the foreign born population."

Strawberry and flower farms, Mrs. Rayne informs her readers, are "excellent avenues to money-making for women." Then she ups the ante by describing the successes of several pioneer women who started farms in the American West singlehandedly, implying that any woman with gumption could follow suit. With that challenge, Mrs. Rayne moves on to a chapter about the profitability of poultry farming.

A favorite of my grandmother and Aunt Mil was *Facts for Ladies*, by Mrs. Amy Ayer Kinsley, with Dr. Robert A. Gunn, apparently self-published in 1890.

Facts for Ladies is a surprisingly thorough and forthright work, which discusses everything from how to decorate a "model gentleman's den" to "displacements of the womb." There are beauty tips—such as homemade toilet water made of barley meal—and the insistence that "beauty cannot be maintained without daily bathing, preferably two or three times a day." Featured are inspirational portraits of "queens of beauty," such as the actresses Ellen Terry and Lillie Langtry (who, like Cleopatra, is said to have bathed in milk).

By the time Mrs. Kinsley hit the presses, the vast store of women's herbal knowledge had long been assumed by men and given over to "scientific" notions and patent concoctions, many of which were, of course, plant medicines. By 1890, Old Wives' common sense had become the property of physicians. Dr. Gunn tells Mrs. Kinsley's audience what to every peasant was obvious and un-questionable. For example, he insists that breast-feeding is *de rigueur* for the health of the child (although by the 1940s, doctors discour-aged nursing as hopelessly outdated). Yet he also advises the expec-tant mother to chug shots of whiskey against headaches.

Books like these preserved for women only a smidgen of their previously held information, by no means revealing the whole story. *Facts for Ladies* is admirably frank and revolutionary for its Victorian times and probably genuinely helped women of the middle and upper classes sort through events in their lives that were not consid-ered proper to discuss.

Yet this, like most household books, directed women toward pleasing men, and left illiterate women—who until the twentieth century were much of the world's population—completely out of the loop. The few European women who understood herbs—through oral transmissions—were more often than not painted as scary, wicked witches or nasty stepmothers in folk and fairy tales.

According to the Grimm Brothers—who were recording the popular, rather sanitized German lore making the rounds in the early nineteenth century—old age, herbs, and wickedness go hand-in-hand. Elsewhere, herbalists had less malevolent reputations, like, say, the Buschfrauen, bush women of central Europe, who had hol-low backs (dowager's humps?), lived in hollow trees (in splendor, one hopes), and revealed the secrets of herbs and healing to mortal women, supplying the knitters among them with magic balls of never-ending yarn.

The Dziwonzony, Polish wild women of the woods, who live in underground burrows ferreting out the secrets of nature and herbal medicine, are attractive role models, too.

Italian folktales featuring herbs dispense with witches in favor of tales about parsley girls, marjoram brides, or rosemary maidens, like this one in a story collected by, among others, Italo Calvino:

> *A queen of Italy is delivered not of a human infant, but a rose-mary bush.*

She places her precious child in a beautiful pot and waters it three times a day with the milk of her own breasts. The little bush grows and grows.

A young Spanish king, the queen's nephew, comes to visit.

"Aunt," he inquires, "what plant is this?"

"This is my daughter and I water her three times daily with my milk."

The Spanish king is fascinated by the rosemary. When he leaves Italy, he steals the bush, buys a nanny goat with which to feed it on the voyage and returns home. He has the rosemary planted in his garden, and orders the gardener to feed it three times a day with goat's milk. And every day, he visits the garden, plays his flute, and dances around the rosemary bush.

Until one day, a maiden steps forward to dance with him.

"Where did you come from?" he asks.

"From the rosemary," she answers and disappears back into the bush when the dance is done.

Each afternoon, the king rushes to the garden to play his flute for Rosemary and dance with her. And when the dance is over, when they have conversed, held hands, and kissed, she retreats into the spiky, fragrant foliage.

The king must leave on official business. He tells Rosemary to wait for him in her bush, and says he will alert her to his return with three notes on his flute, but until then, she mustn't emerge. He warns the gardener who waters her with milk that if he comes home to find Rosemary withered in the least, the gardener will be beheaded.

The king's three sisters are curious maidens, much entranced by their brother's afternoon visits to the garden with his flute. Visits that last well into evening. Now that he's gone, they enter his bedchamber, find his flute, and carry it to the garden.

The first sister toots a note. The second sister toots a second note. The third sister toots a third note. Out pops Rosemary. The sisters grab her by her long hair, and beat her unmercifully. She flees back into her rosemary bush and the bush begins to wither.

The gardener is frightened. Nothing he does, no buckets of the sweetest goat's milk, seem to revive the rosemary bush. He runs for his life.

In the woods, he hears two dragons gossiping about the king's rosemary bush. "Is there no way to save it?" the she-dragon asks the he-dragon.

"Keep this a secret," the he-dragon says and bends low to whisper. A dragon's whisper projects for miles around. The gardener listens.

After dark, the frightened gardener climbs the dragon tree, and sneaks through the dragon's horrid snoring. He draws blood from the he-dragon's windpipe and scrapes fat from the she-dragon's scruff. He runs home as fast as he can. He boils them in a pot and greases the whole rosemary bush twig by twig. The bush dries completely. The girl emerges, healthy and whole. The gardener takes her into his house. His wife cares for her.

When the king returns, he wastes not a minute getting to the garden. He blows his flute three times, but no one appears. He tries again. Again no one appears. The rosemary bush is withered, not a leaf left.

The king is furious. He screams at the gardener. "Your head will roll this day!"

"Come in," the gardener replies. "There is something wonderful within."

And there is Rosemary.

The king punishes his sisters. He sends a messenger to the King and Queen of Italy to tell them of his marriage to their daughter, Rosemary. Those two, who had despaired, are overcome with joy and soon their ship sails into the Spanish port. Rosemary awaits them on the dock. They all rejoice and at the feast the foods and wine are flavored all with rosemary.

My mother didn't grow herbs. I wonder which ones my Irish grandmother may have been familiar with? What herbs might my great-grandmother have remembered as vital to people's lives back on the "auld sod"? Saint John's wort was much valued in Ireland and Britain, celebrated as one of the nine at Midsummer, at the vigil for Saint John the Baptist, and associated with the Sun.

The Greeks placed Saint John's wort around religious icons to ward off evil spirits. Throughout Europe, it guarded against witchcraft and prevented lightning strikes to the house. Rural African

Americans called it Saint John the Conqueror, and it is considered effective in dressing wounds, easing sciatica, neuralgia, gout, arthritis, burns, depression, and gastric troubles. It was thought to promote hair growth and could be used to foretell the future. A well-rounded herb indeed.

Saint John's wort is the first in my medicinal garden to demand trimming. I stuff the flowers gently into Mason jars, pour grain alcohol over the fetching yellow petals, and cap them to cure for two weeks, before straining the tincture into little bottles.

The Inquisition and subsequent missionaries for "progress" never entirely succeeded in wiping out the "good healer," the herb doctor, the wise woman, the medicine man, the *curandera,* the shaman, those who make a conscious practice of communicating with the Earth, listening to her wisdom, and utilizing her gifts with care.

> The obligation to endure gives us the right to know.
> —Rachel Carson, *Silent Spring,* 1962

Saving Grace

July is a difficult month, demanding much from garden and gardener. All the lovely plants are holding on for dear life through the heat and increasing dryness. Constant attention is required to prevent them from giving up the ghost. Even the weeds have slowed. My mother called July the "high noon of the season." It's also the hour of the annual, when the borders thrive with Shirley poppies, nasturtiums, sweet peas. The larkspur cheers the poppy garden, where the roses are fading. The marigolds are on their way to turning this yard into a sun palace, but they'll not hit their peak until August.

Plums, nectarines, and peaches are flooding the grocery stores and beginning to show up at our farmer's market. Mine are hard as rocks, with at least a month to go before they're ready for harvest. Then it'll be a battle between me and the squirrels and raccoons over who gets the choicest fruit.

I water early in the morning and in the evening, a few minutes every day, with long soakings for thirstier perennials. The auxiliary "rains" I simulated for the plants in spring, the hardy downpours I'll give them in fall, are wasteful. Sprinklers send most of the water to evaporate in the hot air. I wish Nell were here to help me keep up with this, but she's gone to summer camp and I'm on my own.

Susie Next Door sits on a lawn chair in her front yard every night after dark, drinking a beer, aiming a hose at her joyful stands of wildflowers and sunflowers.

The Faux Forest is dark green, a respite from the heat that pounds the rest of the garden. The sumac, which grows over the patio, the musk rose wrapping its trunk, offers some shade. An umbrella over the table helps, as does a red nylon cloth, yards and yards long, used for a performance based on text from James Joyce's *Finnegans Wake* and strung from two trees.

The white carnations are reaching their prime. They bloom in the Poetry Garden and as a border to the kitchen herbs. The low-lying dianthus are in need of a trim to revive their fluted, coin-size flowers. The lilies are full. I worry about the midsummer perennials—red-hot poker, shasta daisies, a reprise of mountain bluet and cranes-bill geranium, sea lavender beginning, true lavender as overpowering as granny's hanky drawer, fat globe thistles—and grasshoppers.

Before this garden was full of plants, it was full of grasshoppers—much to the delight of the cats, who bounced after them, caught them, ate them, and threw them up in the house. Grasshoppers eschew moist greenery and thrive where it's arid.

Pa Ch'a was the Chinese patron god of grasshoppers and patron of the crops, whose job was to prevent pests from destroying the fields. Depicted in human form, his mouth is a bird's beak and his feet claws. I need such a "scarehopper" in the front yard, where they're most prolific, probably breeding in the xeric hellstrip, which dries fast, surrounded as it is by sidewalk cement and the glare of macadam.

I conduct my daily July census armed with a pair of scissors. Susie turns sickly green at the sight of my brutal grasshopper beheadings. Clip. Snip. Crunch.

And that's about all I do for pesticides.

Except ladybugs.

* * *

The time has arrived for the Annual Ladybug Rescue Mission, visits to the nurseries to buy the last of the bug bags, at sale prices. Half the bagged bugs are dead. The others escape into my garden.

> *Ladybug! Ladybug! fly away home,*
> *Your house is on fire, your children alone,*
> *Excepting the youngest, and her name is Ann,*
> *And she has crept under the drippings pan.*

There's no question a ladybug will fly away home when you chant the rhyme. Anyone who's tried it knows it's so. We were taught that if we watched where she went, we'd see the direction from which our true loves would arrive. Mine seemed to be destined to come from all points on the map. Predictions of multiple marriages?

It was forbidden for us to kill ladybugs for fear of misfortune. Some say if a ladybug lands on your hands, you'll receive new gloves. If on your dress, a new frock.

Ladybugs are especially enthusiastic aphid gourmets and thus maintain the balance. Aphids are carefully herded by ants, whom I consider far more conscientious farmers than most humans. The roses and peonies on which the aphids graze return each year in full health, whereas we've rendered countless acres hardpacked and infertile. When the aphids get too out of hand, I spray them off with a hose. It takes them a day or two to find their way back, or to be rounded up like dogies by the ants.

As for the ants, when they're building their cities too near a place I prize, I begin working to discourage them with continuous plantings over their metropolis. Practices such as pouring boiling water down their holes are barbaric and needlessly cruel.

I do some companion planting, but not with much conviction. Ultimately, I'm more interested in my mythological garden felicities than in botany. At places like Perelandra in West Virginia, Scotland's Findhorn, or Rodale's farm in Pennsylvania, companion planting is an art and a science. At my house, it's blindman's buff.

Ladybugs adore tansy. Who wouldn't? Its scent is magnificent. A smattering of its feathery leaves minced onto pancakes or waffles (an old German custom) starts the day in Heaven. When tansy is grown next to roses, the ladybugs also have a convenient neighborhood grocery, a feast of aphids.

Tansy will survive almost anything. It made sense to plant it in the rose garden against aphids, as well as the poppy frenzy. In fact, tansy, with its big, yellow, button-cluster flower is almost as unruly and prolific as the poppies and takes over their cages in late summer. I've hardly got a friend who hasn't received a pot of it from me (along with ubiquitous lemon balm, oregano, and comfrey, neatly packaged in baskets as "starter" herb gardens!). This is as dirty a trick as giving puppies as door prizes at children's parties. It's a wonder I have friends at all.

My grandmother smeared cabbage stalks with oil and soot against the slugs. A friend goes after the cabbage moths with a tennis racket, whacking them to death and improving her game. My late Aunt Anya, a native Russian, married to my mother's brother O'Shea, started cabbages in bottomless tin cans. When the seedlings were ready to be planted outdoors, Anya stuck the whole thing in the ground to protect against larvae.

Mothballs around squash hills are said to inhibit raccoons. It seemed to work the one time I tried it. Mothballs dug in with carrots will prevent carrot fly. I don't have carrot flies . . . that I know of. Or, the Old Wives advise, hang mothball rings on fruit trees. I'm not convinced that whatever's in those mothballs won't leach into and poison the soil.

Old Wives recommend marigolds and garlic practically everywhere as pesticides and I'm happy to oblige. Beer in bottle caps placed temptingly around the garden will drown booze-craving slugs. Horsehair ropes laid on the ground fencing the cauliflower bed will stop slugs dead. Black thread tied around fruit trees will deter the birds (or strangle them).

My mother paid us a penny apiece or a dollar a jar for collecting Japanese beetles, that scourge of rosarians. My brother made loads of money. He has the Midas touch. I, however, was constantly distracted, watching them. A scarab beetle, the grub of *Popillia japonica* arrived in this country in the roots of imported nursery stock and landed first in Riverton, New Jersey. It damaged millions of dollars' worth of commercial fruits and vegetables. What did I care? I was fascinated with the beetles' stout taupe-colored back, lovely iridescent green head, and tarsal claws that wriggled in protest when we picked them off the shrubs. I've rarely met an insect I didn't like.

An English gardener advised that "if it moves slowly enough, step on it. If it doesn't, leave it—it'll probably kill something else."

Or, as a pragmatic pal says, when confronted with almost any gardening challenge, "It's the soil, stupid!" Among others things, turning it over before winter and leaving it lumpy will freeze larvae.

The surest pesticide as the Old Wives advise, is to sow seeds generously:

> *One for the rook,*
> *one for the crow,*
> *one to die and one to grow.*

It seems absurd—pretentious—to claim that my garden is almost pest-free and that I do virtually nothing to make it that way. Nonetheless, it's true. My garden is healthy and without notable predators. I don't know why. Not witchery. Not saving grace from the gardening gods. Not magic.

One reason may be that I'm not conscious of pests. I pay almost no attention to the *idea* of pests. Here's where denial comes in handy. Except for the grasshoppers—and mosquitoes—I don't think of insects as pests.

True, there are fewer garden pests in Colorado than in more humid zones. However, as we introduce new, hybridized, hardier plants to the area, we're bound to bring along the insects that thrive on them. Many of these adjust to the new environment, as many animals have to urban living, learning to survive on human garbage. Picture the pimpled, overweight raccoon and coyote, suffering heart congestion from living off fast-food scraps. Some, like starlings and cowbirds, shove out the indigenous or milder creatures, a game of lose-lose as the natural world shrinks in ever-decreasing concentric circles.

If we must develop the habitats of other creatures, if we must pave Paradise, then as gardeners, on big or little land, we should try to re-create a bit of what's been destroyed. It will never be adequate, but a garden that welcomes birds, butterflies, insects of all kinds, and doesn't prey or spray against the "bad" ones—thereby inadvertently murdering the "good" ones—is vital.

A garden is *not* a garden, but a sterile, short-lived museum, if it doesn't welcome all the sentient beings who can thrive in it.

The response to the introduction of new insect pests has been to develop tougher, stronger poisons. Rachel Carson launched the modern environmental movement with her book *Silent Spring*, in which she exposed the use of DDT and its awful results. She warned that we must be aware—and have a right to be *informed*—of the toxins, from nuclear and industrial waste to household products, polluting every atom on Earth. We should be made aware not just of the contents but also the larger consequences of using artificial herbicides and pesticides (and artificial fertilizers that seep into the water table). The old slogan that encouraged the postwar American boom, "Better Living Through Chemistry," is one of the worst lies ever perpetrated. We are still asked to believe it, and we do.

Here's what I fear:

I fear that the real reason my garden is nearly pest-free may be because of the use of chemicals for miles around me to make blooms bigger, lawns greener, aphids disappear.

And yet . . . I surely have "bad" insects in my garden. I must. Because I have "good" ones.

> Pink poppies wave
> behind barbed fence
> white butterfly glides through
> —Tree Bernstein

The Souls' Return

The lack of flowers in June profusions is more than made up for in July by the flutter and flash of butterflies, who gather for nectar in the garden, emerging daily from caterpillars fattened on milkweed and other delicacies. The dill stalks are decorated with yellow and black striped caterpillars. Across the years, I've planted buddleia, trumpet vine, echinacea, monarda, sweet rocket, lavender, ice plant, and more to attract and feed them. They draw the hummingbirds, too.

The butterflies arrived with spring. Swallowtails. Red Admirals. Mourning Cloaks, Skippers, Painted Ladies. A few at a time, like the flowers, then as the nectaring plants bloom, as the eggs turn to caterpillars, then pupa, the garden fills with them. Susie's wildflowers have sealed the deal and attract all the more.

Throughout summer I watch for Monarchs, trying in my desultory way to keep track of the numbers. Monarchs are disappearing from the world. Pesticides, herbicides, and genetic tampering of crops are partly to blame—as they are for the extinction of countless other butterflies and insects. Ironically, in the case of Monarchs, poverty is also a culprit. In winter the butterflies swarm across miles of land and sea to roost in the oyamel forests of south-central Mexico. These trees are necessary to the Monarchs' survival, yet are being deforested at a frightening rate, thanks to the immense destitution of the people living there. To the desperately impoverished, "protected" lands mean nothing in the face of cold and starvation. The migrating Monarchs are bookended by dangers: from indigenous peoples to the south who themselves are nearly extinct and by rich loggers in the north.

Some Old Wives are Old Dolts. To wit: the belief among American settlers of German descent that caterpillars were made by witches with the devil's help. They were called *teufelskatze,* devil's cats. Another example of the damage done when Pan was demonized.

By July, the dominant butterflies are the Cabbage Whites, sometimes called "cabbage moths" but which aren't moths at all. They swarm in flighty tunnels. When I'm ready to harvest, I hose the cabbages and cauliflower to dislodge the worms. Whatever's left I'll pick off at the kitchen sink and any I missed will simply have to be supplementary protein.

> *The caterpillar on the leaf*
> *Repeats to thee thy mother's grief.*
> *Kill not the moth nor butterfly*
> *For the Last Judgment draweth nigh.*

The poet and visionary William Blake's verse expresses a worldwide belief that butterflies are souls reincarnated. In the Celtic story of Etain, a girl is turned to a butterfly, then swallowed by a queen and reborn. In a famous Japanese story, the long-dead love of a dying octogenarian comes in the shape of a white butterfly to claim him, and in another legend, they represent filial piety. In ancient Greece, the words *psyche*, *soul*, and *butterfly* were virtually interchangeable. Indeed, the girl Psyche in the Greek romance metamorphosed into a goddess through her trials for love of Eros.

Dragon- and damselflies float over the sunny Nilus, rest on the laundry, glistening turquoise, iridescent green, sparkling black. The Fiesta Dinner Theatre cottage garden bristles with cosmos, sweet pea climbing the hot-pink fence—a portion of scavenged picket. Hollyhocks, sunflowers, zinnias, marigolds, shastas, and pots of coral geranium. Coral is too subtle for the Dinner Theatre. Next year, red, orange, and pink in these painted Mexican pots.

A letter arrives. An answer to my question about Celinda's garden and what flowers she might have grown in the early twentieth century, when Kate, born in 1908, was a child:

> *Ask and ye shall receive . . . We never had a formal garden, just patches here and there. My mother grew sweet peas by the wellhouse, driving stakes, usually hoehandle seconds, into the ground, then stretching strong string between the poles for supports.*
>
> *She also had peonies and iris in that patch. There's still a spindly peony and an iris or two, shaded by a large maple, which has grown there in the 66 years since my mother's death.*
>
> *Along the barn, she had dahlias. I never liked them—they had no pleasant odor.*
>
> *West of the barn, along the road and also by the back porch, she had cosmos. And she grew zinnias, asters and bachelor's buttons. She had lilies of the valley, which still exist, as do the white English violets and myrtle. The hollyhocks by the house are gone, as are the phlox. There may be a few straggly Golden Glow still beside the back shed. The orange day lilies along the walk still bloom everywhere.*
>
> *And a spirea still blooms by the porch, but the mock orange is gone as is the large flowering almond. She always had a pansy bed and also liked petunias. She had grape hyacinths and snowdrops and*

some of them have survived, too. And she liked roses . . . I much pre-
fer carnations or snaps or stock.

We had a bed of cannas in the yard. My father liked them. I never
thought they were pretty. When they became scarce, we had a gera-
nium bed I liked much better. My mother grew nasturtiums, but I be-
came violently allergic to them, so she grew no more . . .

The letter continues in spellbinding detail. "That'll teach you to
ask questions!" Kate knows how happy it makes me to learn the
minutiae of the past and is glad to accommodate me with stories,
some of which I've heard—asked for—again and again. One day, sitting in Kate's parlor, chatting and playing cribbage, it occurred to
me that old folk are compelled to tell their stories repeatedly, because we are supposed to get them by heart, remember, and pass the
wisdom on. This is the core of oral tradition, far older and more natural than writing, and it is the most effective way to transmit all the
vital knowledge of the tribe, from survival skills to cosmology, ge-
nealogy to the techniques and tricks of successful gardening.

Celinda was mild, unflappable, dignified—a lady in the best sense of
the word—who staged a hunger strike and locked herself in her bedroom when her parents refused to let her marry Amos. Too low class,
they said. Too wild, too impetuous and quick-tempered. Never mind
that he was a teacher and later became an influential attorney and judge.

Celinda's parents relented. "They decided they'd rather have a
married daughter than a dead one," Kate said. "She would have gone
through with it, and they knew it. She didn't make idle threats."

I see Celinda in her boots, long skirts, hair piled on her head, a
muslin apron, with puffy sleeves like an overdress, and thick gloves,
puttering around the garden. I feel her pleasure, away from worka-
day drudgeries. I hear her good-natured laughter, when, as Kate tells
it, Amos—who forswore drink for Celinda's sake once a month for
a few days or a week—came home late one night deep in his cups.
Kate and Celinda confronted and scolded him. To prove he was
sober, he rolled up his sleeves, stepped out of doors, and began watering the cosmos and impatiens off the back porch.

"He didn't notice," Kate chuckles, "that it was pouring down
rain."

AUTUMN

August

SEASON'S THRESHOLD

great bounty of Earth,
great bounty of Sea,
great bounty of Heaven
be yours,
and your life be hale,
your life be fruitful.

—Celtic prayer, variation

The Bread Month

Lughnasadh. First harvest.

The tomatoes in the new *beltane*-blessed bed are outrageously abundant. I've never had such a crop. One for the basket, one for me. I bite through polished red skin. The juice dribbles down my chin and neck. In the heat, seeds dry fast on my shirt.

Elizabethans called tomatoes "love apples" and thought they were aphrodisiacs. They satisfy every libidinous molecule in my body. Not until the trussed, upright Victorians were tomatoes eaten as regular fare, for along with being lusty, they were considered, as members of the nightshade family, to be poisonous. The Victorians needed all the sensuality they could muster, so it's not surprising that this was also when fairy lore was at its height in English painting, literature, and theater, and that the fairies were popping up in every corner of the garden, manifesting all the emotional, sexual, and spiritual passions the Victorians repressed.

This too was the era when, despite its rigidity, or more likely because of it, William Robinson, and then Gertrude Jekyll and Edwin Luytens were designing the "natural" garden.

From my bedroom perch, I watch as a young bluejay scours the tomatoes for worms. Each time he lands, the plants pitch toward the ground, then jerk upright as the bird carries his prize to the apple tree.

Carrots, leeks, beets, peppers, chilies, squash . . . everything's ripening so quickly, it's hard to keep up. The raccoons, birds, and squirrels are helping as best they can. Here we are at *lughnasadh,* first harvest. And here is my kitchen garden, feeding us.

In the beginning, as I began cultivating this garden, I had the notion that if I planted zucchini whenever I dug a new bed, the squash would choke out the weeds and nourish and tenderize the soil for the following season, when I could plant flowers or anything else I chose. The technique worked well. One year, I planted too many and the zucchini threatened to choke *us* out of house and home. After zucchini bread, cookies, cakes, pickles—1001 recipes for zucchini—we called the food editor of the local newspaper and asked him to publicize our Zucchini Adoption Agency. Free zucchini to anyone who wanted it, with free delivery to old folk. The phone rang off the hook. Many of the callers were elderly, housebound, or apartment dwellers who missed garden-fresh produce—even if it was zucchini.

A vegetable garden without zucchini seems somehow off-kilter. If all else failed, it's one food we can be assured of.

My metaphysician friend grew up in inner-city Chicago, without, she says, so much as a houseplant. Almost nothing gives her such unalloyed pleasure as her garden. This year, she's grown amaranth "to honor the ancient grain," and calls to announce, "It's a thug! An absolute thug!" A thug, whether amaranth or zucchini, that will grow almost anywhere under almost any conditions, we agree, is essential when it comes to filling many bellies.

In Britain and Ireland the first harvest was celebrated on the first and second days of the month, as *lughnasadh,* originally the festival of the ancient Celtic Sun god Lugh in honor either of his foster mother Tailtu, or of his marriage, depending on what you read. Wife or mother, she was the Earth Goddess. In August, the Sun plunges into the Earth and the heat they generate brings all things to maturity.

The moon hangs low and fleshy, as if giving birth to this cornucopia.

Lugh the Longhanded (for the Sun's digits stretched immeasurable distances) had three fathers. His body was marked by red lines around his neck and belly, delineating the portions each father had begotten. Agni, Vedic god of fire, had three bodies and three births and supported the sky. In August in Colorado, Agni and Lugh gang up on the ground and beat it until it splits, now and then provoking prairie fires.

These dog days "officially" begin in July, when the Dog Star Sirius is ascendant. In humid climates, the sticky air was thought to carry illness. It was the time of year when dogs were believed to develop rabies and venomous snakes came out in force to spread plague and fever. In Colorado, the threat is desiccation.

My skin is sandpaper. There's not enough sunblock in the world to keep me from "photo-aging." My big hands, occupied in dirt for months, are rough as tree bark. My feet are so hard I could walk across hot coals. The sidewalks and stone paths feel like hot coals. At night, to prevent them from cracking, I rub my feet with Hoof-Alive, a formula for horses I buy at a tack store. My family suggests it might be easier to wear shoes, but I can't. I need the sensation of dirt and grass and stone while I garden, my bare feet absorbing the full experience of being with and in the Earth.

Feet, my yoga teacher likes to say, aren't as intelligent as hands. I know what she means. Feet have their own "animal" genius, savvy I don't want to harness with shoes.

The Anglo-Saxon *lughnasadh* was *hlaf-mass,* "loaf mass," when the corn was harvested and the Corn King killed and transformed into bread.

On *lughnasadh,* I bake bread stuffed with garden vegetables and herbs for dinner. A yellow cloth on the patio table and yellow citronella candles. We make pass-around poems on a yellow legal pad while we eat.

Heart
Of
My
Existence.

Flycatchers skim from the phone lines into whirlwinds of gnats. My husband sits through dinner wearing his binoculars, watching the aerial dance and keeping a telescopic eye out for other visitors looking for seeds. When the meal is finished, we read our poems aloud and pick plums off the trees for dessert. The apples and peaches—trapped after all these years of growth under a canopy of branches from larger trees—are coming along gradually. I've hung the trees with streamers of aluminum foil and bells to discourage birds and squirrels. They're not fooled for long.

At *lughnasadh,* the Brigit-chums gather again in one of our gardens for tea and sherry and an embarrassment of breads. Sweet and savory, round and flat. The rings originally represented the cycle of the year; rolls symbolized the rounded and complete year.

Lughnasadh was Christianized as Lammas, when new corn was taken to the church to be blessed. But here again, the Church discouraged earthly rites and so, along with other factors, the journey away from Nature—and gratitude for her generosity—began. By the Industrial Revolution, the divorce was complete. That there are gardeners of any sort—from religious to romantic, culinary to ornamental—is a continued affirmation of Nature's munificence. At *lughnasadh,* chariot races and sword play, games of strength and chance were enacted in mourning for the corn. Until the early twentieth century, *lughnasadh* was kept as a day of remembrance of dead kinfolk, a custom that reaches as far back as—perhaps farther than—Egyptian harvest rites (which took place in March, April, and May), when the gardener/ farmer chanted laments over the first-cut sheaf, which felled the spirit of the kern. Then prayers were made to Isis, who grieved for her husband-brother Osiris as he embarked on his return to the House of the Dead.

Lughnasadh was another ribald holy day, full of revels, meant to assure the last harvest would be plenty, food enough to get through an adverse winter, and to ensure fertility in the next season. In Ireland, there were processions. Young men carried hooped wreaths for catching brides, with whom trial marriages were made for a year and a day. Sex and death entwined, when throughout Europe, men and women—Sun and Earth—copulated in the fields, as the Greek Corn Mother, Demeter, was said to have done with Iasus the Healer.

In Russia, women cut the first grain and enshrined it in the house through winter. In ancient Palestine, the Feast of Weeks marked the wheat harvest, when two "wave loaves" made of finely ground flour and baked with leaven were offered to Yahweh as the first fruit.

Eating the first fruits of the season was observed throughout the world with reverence and ceremony. An act of eucharist, communion with the divine provider.

Long ago, as now, August was the month of fairs. Today, these are frequently arranged by Chambers of Commerce. In antiquity, the *lughnasadh* or other annual harvest fairs featured trade in animals, food, seeds, and preserves, arts and crafts, and sporting games. Here, too, the handing down of legal judgments was made. Folk came from miles around—to Tara in Ireland, to the Althing in Iceland.

The first harvest, as it intensifies into many across the next two months, offers community, sharing, solidarity, mutual labor, mutually earnest and joyful application of work and creativity. It's evident in my neighborhood with the smells of roasting corn, barbecues, and laughter breezing over fences. Evident in the weekend traffic heading east to the prairie, where city folk line up at roadside stands to buy corn and squash. Evident with the crowds at farmer's markets, where local gardeners—urban farmers—sell their excess.

As the garden begins to proffer its ready fruits, an indescribable connectedness and continuity occurs, a harmonious exchange of energy between gardener and garden manifested in full. Ful*fill*ment. The rewards of our labors.

There are sunflowers in vases in every room. Yellow dominates outdoors, too. Blooms untouched by heat and drought, as if making up for the Sun's decline—and final fury—with expansiveness and sociability. For all the vividness of the garden, the glittering coffers of gladiola, phlox, Jupiter's beard, or balloonflower, there's a sweet somberness in the air. The beginning of the end is now.

For the first time, I've tried growing artichokes. Not for food, but because ecologist/gardener Jim Nollman, whose books I admire tremendously, once wrote that he considers the artichoke one of, if not *the* most beautiful flower in the world.

Now *that,* I thought, is a challenge.

The artichoke is one of the oldest cultivated vegetables in the world, beloved of Greeks and Romans and thought by the seventeenth-century astrologer/physician Nicolas Culpeper to provoke lust. (Making a meal of tomatoes and artichokes, though apparently Spartan, may have its rewards after all.)

Artichoke is also a thistle and those, of course, attract birds. So there was every reason to give artichokes a chance. I put in six trial plants. My daughter, however, doesn't see "flower" when she looks at an artichoke—she sees lunch.

I'm in the kitchen puttering. My daughter trots by juggling three fine, fat artichokes.

"My flowers!" I shriek. "The most beautiful flowers in the world! What *have* you done?"

"They're *artichokes,* Mom," she says calmly, reasonably, filling a pot with water. "They're a little old. We better get right on them."

I explain, with just the slightest edge of falsetto in my voice, that I wasn't planning to harvest them. I was waiting to see what they look like as flowers, because I'd read that they are among the most beautiful flowers in the world.

She whips butter with lemon. "You've got three left, Mom."

> Beautiful John, Beautiful John.
> Our tears drop so the rain
> will fill the ditches and water the grass.
> Beautiful John, Beautiful John.
> Your mother's searing tears
> water the woodlands and the glades.
>
> —Rumanian, traditional

Stifling Nights

Hot. Dreamless. The swamp cooler hums full blast.

I wish it would rain. Every dog day, I soak the flower and vegetable beds, trying not to let water stand too long and evaporate. I
feel guilty using water at all. I should have planted an entirely xeric
garden, ignored my woodland fantasies. I should have created something altogether indigenous, not so utterly indulgent. In so many
parts of the world, this is the hunger season, when drought brings
horrifying famine. Those two percent of us who consume eighty-
five percent of the world's wealth take for granted the availability of
food in any season. And here I am, wasting water, wasting land, feeling a terrible guilt that I'll forget by the next rainfall.

Agni the Fire God's brother, Vivasat, is the god of the Sun and
rides through the sky on a chariot drawn by seven ruddy horses.
He is called upon for success in the garden and the fields. Sun/
Viva/Life. Whenever Vivasat is unhappy, he creates the oppressive
heat that causes the plants to wither and the rivers to dry. Vritra is
the Serpent of Drought. Indra, God of Rain and Thunder, is his arch
enemy and defeats him in every battle. The battles, described in the
Hindu *Mahabarata,* can be long, victory illusive for months and
months.

For all their fortitude and my desperate watering, some flowers
are simply collapsing under the weight of Vivasat's distemper. But
the hollyhocks rise above it all in their beds near the alley against
the backdrop of grapes, and in the hellstrip, where they thrive in
lousy soil and pitiless sunshine surrounded by the grisly platinum of
rabbit brush, wormwood, horehound, and yarrow. They look their
best at evening. In this weather, who doesn't? In daylight, they resemble shabby cinder wenches, with holes in their leaves where the
grasshoppers chew on them. At dusk they shine forth, dressed in
brand-new finery. The twilight catches in their blood-crimson,
peach, pink, ivory, and amethyst cups.

Both ponds seem to need constant replenishing. After a fitful
sleep in the heat, I trek to the Nilus's edge, stick my feet in the
water, and watch the waterlilies as they open. They're like clock
hands, impossible to catch moving, and each lily lasts only a day or

two. According to herbalists, waterlilies are governed by the moon. In ancient Egypt, however, they were associated with the Sun god Re. Their pink-yellow centers and succulent white petals are exquisite as stars.

My daughter joins me. She peers into the water and sees baby fish. Gray "feeders"—hundreds of them.

My grandmother taught my mother to mulch the garden with the outer leaves of lettuce and cabbage. I also use corn husks, spent Oriental poppy leaves (first carefully removing the seed heads to avoid a poppy epidemic). I cut the tired, browning iris and day lily leaves and lay them in cross hatches on newly watered ground to hold the moisture. I work alongside the robins, who've returned to take up residence in the Enchanted Garden, until they've pecked away all the grapes. And the flickers are back, too, no longer especially interested in aerating the grass for ants, but hunting out berries. I watch them through the den window as they climb the bricks on Susie's house, picking off woodbine.

The downy woodpeckers work the mullein for bugs. The woodpecker's scientific name, *Picoides pubescens*, comes from the Latin for "puberty." The down resembles the first signs of a young man's beard. The woodpecker's red head indicates its ability to find fire by boring into wood. The blaze on its crown seems to underscore its industriousness, as well as this fiery weather.

The hellstrip plantings are mostly xeric. I've given up watering there entirely, except for a spot where last week I had the notion— probably a touch of heat stroke—to plant all the cherry seeds from a pound or so we bought at the farmer's market. I dug a hole, emptied the seeds into it and covered it again with a dollop of manure. If the little peach could suddenly appear from a pit, why not a cherry tree? I water it, knowing full well that nothing will happen while I watch it, and nothing may happen for years to come.

> *A sweet well for those who thirst in the desert;*
> *it is closed to those who speak,*
> *but it is open to those who are silent.*
> *When the silent come, they find the well.*

In many parts of the world, prayers like this one from ancient Egypt are spoken when newly drawn water is sprinkled on the ground. Water is revitalization, purification. It washes away impurities of the soul. In Buddhism, it is an embodiment of the principle of enlightenment. Baptisms of diverse forms, including baptismals of the garden, take place everywhere—fertility *poured* over land or talisman or person, effusions of divine grace.

In most of Europe and the United States, turn the faucet and there it is. We assume our right to water and are often indignant when droughts threaten or actually occur. We're unprepared to think of water as anything but a perpetual entitlement.

My front yard, with its cooler microsystem and massive swards of vinca and ivy—old enough to do without much water—is an oasis, an island of green that engulfs the front porch and makes it one of the most pleasant places to inhabit these days. Oases were the first gardens, providing nomadic humans with rest, shade trees, and water. Water for drinking, for nurturing plants, and for ablutions before prayer.

Lake Titicaca is called the Womb of Humankind. Millions of pilgrims visit the Holy Waters of the Kami at the Shinto Ise Shrine and the Arike Pond in Japan. For the aboriginal peoples of Australia, Lake Wabby is holy. In New Zealand, the emerald lakes below Mounts Tongariro and Ngauruhoe were sacred to the Maori. A marriage ceremony is not complete among the Yaqui of Mexico until the bride fetches water from the nearest well or river and the couple shares the drink from the same gourd.

To share water is to establish an unbreakable bond. To withhold or steal water is an act of absolute hostility, guaranteeing an instant, everlasting enemy.

The nomads of the Sahara and the steppes of central Asia carry rugs with traditional Persian garden motifs and roll them out on the ground when they make camp. There they take meals and tea "in the garden." In the same spirit, Muslims who are not near water at prayer times wash with sand.

In August, in ancient Egypt, the irrigation canals were opened to enable the rising waters of the Nile to pass into the interior. This was the union of Osiris and Isis, so vital for prosperity that the cutting of the dams had to be done at the most auspicious moment. The growth of the crops was secured by the sacrifice of a "bride" to the water and later by casting gold into the Nile to fructify it.

Today, there is a truncated cone of earth in front of the dam on the side of the river near Cairo called *aroos el Nil,* "Bride of the Nile." In August, ceremonial boats still traverse the Nile, one carrying a "princess," the bride, who these days is rather more like a county-fair queen than a sacrificial maiden. She floats in her boat, in a ritual older than history, but thanks to modern dams, the annual flooding—the marriage of the gods—no longer occurs; new sediment is no longer drawn into the land, while the mouth of the Nile is becoming plugged with silt.

At the inundation, ancient Egyptians drank ceremoniously from the Nile "upon the swirl of new water."

The city of Ur on the Euphrates flooded annually. Houses were built high on stilts and gardens were ziggurats, like the Tower of Babylon, terraced temples with shade trees planted at every level. The Greek goddess Io was the Moon as Rainbringer. Her priestesses in Argive performed heifer dances as if they were cows driven mad by flies. While they danced, they called on the goddess for relief.

Elaborate irrigation systems were invented with the first gardens in the Near East and Central Asia. Some ancient irrigation systems are still in use and frequently serve far better—and are less environmentally harmful—than newfangled systems and dams introduced to "underdeveloped" nations by First World aid organizations.

Figs and grapes ripened in ancient Palestine despite the long, rainless summer. Serious drought was exceptional, but devastating when it happened. The ongoing terror of drought is illustrated in such Old Testament tales as that of Elijah, who in a contest of miracles, defeated the idolatrous priests of Baal by causing a three-year drought. Not even dew fell.

It is so hot we're all faint, when an artist friend stops by to donate a ceramic mermaid to the Nilus. She is to be a talisman against drought, Bringer of Rain, guardian of Sparky and Butch. We name her Aine—She of the Bright Stars and Waters—a goddess who lives beneath Ireland's Lough Gur and who rises from the lake in the darkest dark of the moon each month to comb her hair. Every seven years, she causes the lake to dry and a tree to rise from its bed. She sits beneath the tree and knits until she is satisfied with the gifts people bring her. Then she fills the lake again with water.

We secure Aine on the Nilus island and burn a candle in her crown labeled MAKE RAIN from a local "magick" shop. She grins and grins, but the rain still doesn't fall.

I catch the dishwater in a pan (rinse water, good only if "natural" dishwashing soap is used) to pour on my least drought-resistant plants, especially the azaleas. When I clean the compost bucket, I fill it with water for the vegetable gardens. Some people keep rain barrels and I'm seriously considering it.

Rainmaking customs are known all over the world, the most contemporary being cloud seeding. One may as well swing a hazel branch in the air, twirling three times right, three times left. My mother said she once saw her grandmother, long settled in Fresno, California, doing just that. If not a hazel branch—the dowsers' favorite tool and a wand wood of long-standing—then burning ferns would open the clouds.

The Water Cross of Uiste was raised in the Hebrides when rain was needed and lowered again when there was enough. My favorite rainbringing ritual occurs in certain Chinese provinces, where people shout for rain. If no rain comes, shouting at the cloudless sky is at least cathartic.

Watering for water is another magic formula, and I've subscribed to it inadvertently. More than once, I've finally surrendered, given the plants a long drink only to have rain or snow fall the very next day.

Some aboriginal people of Australia had a rain stone whose striations, according to anthropologists, looked like rain. After ceremonies, the stone was buried in the sand and the wait for water began.

When at last the sky can't seem to stand another minute of rising heat, it bursts with a sparse sprinkle, welcome but short-lived, which evaporates when it hits the hot ground. Through it all, the sun keeps shining.

First the humm
of the wings then
kutch-tcha-tu!
kutch-tcha-tu!
as the
blue green & gold
morning light
beams on
the hummingbird
as it floats
blurringly
in front of the azalea bush
& in between
calls
it dips
into the deep
red recess
of the blossoms
for
sweetness

—Ed Sanders

Bird of the Palpitating Sun

Tiny as they are, hummingbirds are powerful agents of creation—or deities themselves—in myths throughout the Americas. To the Arawak Indians, the hummingbird was the procurer of sacred tobacco seeds; to Hopi and Zuni peoples, the hummer brings rain, so that dances and ceremonies are made invoking the bird to intercede with the god of rain; to the Aztec, the hummingbird—*huitzilopochitli*—was a god of Sun and war; and the Mayans believed that the hummer taught the other birds to make strong nests. In Mexican folk medicinal lore, the bird's strong heart—which beats fifty to seventy-five times a second—is a cure for many illnesses, physical and spiritual.

This extraordinary heart sustains the diminutive creatures on annual migrations clear across the Gulf of Mexico.

At my sister-in-law's high mountain cabin, broadtails and the bully rufous hummers surround the cabin so thickly they barricade the door.

I like to believe that the broadtail hummingbirds are at last visiting my garden because of the flowers I've planted to attract them. These are largely the same ones that attract butterflies.

The truth is they come because their mountain territories are being eaten away for housing developments.

There aren't many in my yard. One visitor the first year, then two and still no more than four, always in August. The "hum" is the sound of rapidly beating wings. My husband can hear their *kutch-tcha-tu,* even when he's rustling papers, but my ears aren't trained. I have to stop everything to listen.

In late afternoon or early morning, I sit on the back steps and wait for hummers, hoping to catch a glimpse as they dive in*outinout* of blossoms, then flirt a second with the feeders full of sugar water that bring more ants than birds. How can any creature move so quickly and still know where it's going? How can any heart beat so fast?

On Hiroshima and Nagasaki Days groups of townspeople meet at a spot on the creek near our city library, at a Peace Garden. A Buddhist monk, who walks the city chanting and drumming, round and round, neighborhood to neighborhood—and seems to weave the community together—leads a procession. In the twenty years since my father's death on Hiroshima Day, I've attended this ceremony. His passing is still a source of pain and I can barely speak or think of it.

I hang behind the peacemakers and drop flowers in the stream, as the Japanese did with spent bouquets and as my mother, brother, son, and I did when we buried my father's ashes near the stream behind the Virginia house, in the dogwood grove. A haiku from the seventeenth-century Japanese master, Basho—perhaps the greatest haiku poet in the world, whose work my father loved—thrums through my head like an old, familiar song:

my life
haphazard
separated from my friend.

On the August new moon, I plant the fall leaf vegetable crop, a bit late, but it's iffy, regardless, in this climate.

Every gardener has moments, some more than others, when an absolutely perfect tableau appears, a calendar shot, a postcard, the kind of picture we usually see only in gardening catalogues: orange marigolds against the wide blue of morning glories climbing the laundry line; the red-orange of the French Cinderella pumpkins peeking through the yellow marigolds; blue bachelor's buttons and peachy hollyhocks in the alley against the hardening green of the grape leaves; the voluptuous maroon tassels of love-lies-bleeding draped over a bed of pink and blue pincushion flowers; the "black" nasturtiums debonair under the second shy growth of delph-blue delphinia; a shimmering hummer darting in*out* of the brassy trumpet-vine flowers.

The daisies in shady spots are still flourishing. They are sometimes thought to be the spirits of stillborn infants. The Scots call daisies "bairnwort," because of the chains children make. Daisies are thought to be a pesticide: the bitter taste repels insects. And daisies are faithful flowers.

A sunflower in Susie Next Door's yard leans over the fence, peers into my yard. In back, Susie has fashioned a sunflower shield against the alley traffic and the Dumpster. Those she planted in the hellstrip next to the busy street are the talk of the town. People pull over in their cars just to gaze at these delirious beauties—some lemon-colored; some field sunflowers eight to ten inches in diameter started from a handful of commercial birdseed; some velvety, rusty-red designer sunflowers, plush as curtains. Their bold health suggests Susie has a sunflower-growing gene. Indeed, her father is a sun-flower farmer in the Midwest.

The yarrow, too, is robust. I used to make a yarrow mouthwash tincture for my mother, which she swore eased her gingivitis. I offered a yarrow infusion to my father against baldness, but he declined. It was way too late.

I cut asters daily to prevent them from going to seed and spreading all over the garden. It's an exercise in futility—they're like dandelion puffs—but it would be worse if I didn't. I display them in buckets around the house with cosmos and sunflowers. When they're spent, I toss them in the wildflower beds, where they promptly set to work propagating.

In the August stalemate, stones, stone paths, rock gardens, and rock walls keep me busy. Where the Faux Forest thins and tapers away, I'm planting a shade garden among free-standing rock walls, reminiscent to me of old fields in New England, Ireland, Bolivia, or Sardinia, wherever the terrain is stony. I play with the rocks, stacking and restacking them, stuffing the gaps with dirt mixed with clay and water, and planting those with moss or any crawler whose roots are shallow.

It's significant to me that these rock walls are no more than two feet high, that they're fragmented, and that these three- to four-feet-long fragments stand in asymmetrical proximity to one another, curved, like arms inviting an embrace, yet tumbling as if they'd once functioned as a deterrent no longer necessary.

"Stones touch human beings because they suggest immortality," Lucy Lippard writes in *Overlay*, "because they have so patently *survived* . . . Earth and stone are two forms of the same material, symbolizing the same force. Virtually every culture we know has attributed to pebbles and stones, rocks and boulders, magical powers of intense energy, luck, fertility and healing."

Years ago, Lippard's "Stones" chapter gave me my first glimmer of understanding about the continuum of stones/Earth/stars/cosmos and why stones are the bones of the ritual art I make in my garden, the spines of the tales told in my landscapes.

She notes that "gardeners, quarriers, stonemasons, builders and sculptors are among the rare few to remain in touch with stone, the most basic and most mythic of materials."

The meaning of stone in cosmologies—where many a creation myth depends on stone to open the world to its beginning and/or discharge human life onto the Earth—and the meanings of stones in horticulture, agriculture and to artists, occupy volumes. Beyond the metaphysical, there are tomes about the practical uses of stone for buildings, hearths, gateposts, thresholds, roads and such mythopractical uses as gravestones, tombs, ley lines, and prehistoric stone formations that appear to be laid out in imitation of constellations.

I have no access to big boulders. Fancy garden megaliths are too costly to import into my garden, without the aid of giants like those who purportedly transported the megaliths of Stonehenge across the Irish Sea. Phallic stones, like those in Greece, Mesoamerica, the Celtic world, Japan, and so on around the world, were often placed at the edges of fields to ensure fertility. Somewhere, I found a long, cylindrical pink stone, which I anchored between the vegetable garden and the Nilus. And there is the ivory, gold-flecked tubular stone in the Moon Garden behind the white peony. White stones were called "godstones," which could bring prosperity, should a gardener turn one up.

My kids and I used to keep a basket of "angry stones," mostly grumpy, gray pebbles. We took them to the creek, where we sat on the bank reciting our complaints into them, then tossed them into the flowing water to wash away hurt feelings. If this wasn't entirely effective or kosher psychology, at least it was something to do besides stew and argue.

The stones we've collected across years of walks and journeys fill many bowls, catching dust, so that when I built the Nilus, I had enough to line one shallow end of the pond.

Shinto shrines are built to honor stone. Cairns in Nepal are called *obos*, ritual rocks stacked stone by stone by passersby, each stone a prayer, one prayer mounting another toward Heaven. Casual cairns often appear on hiking trails. Everyone's lives are travelogues of stones.

Zen gardens of raked gravel set with boulders frightened me when I was a kid in Japan. They seemed a picture of the end of the world, stripping it to its skeleton (boiling life down to its bare form *is,* I think, the idea). Austerity has always scared me a bit. On the other hand, I loved the romance of the Futami Rocks, *meota iwa,* Husband and Wife or Married Rocks, which lie in the sacred waters near Ise City. The two rocks are symbolically joined in matrimony by an ornately braided rice-straw rope and are incarnations of

Izanagi and Izanami, the Creators. The *torii* gate atop Izanagi indicates that the spirits, the *kami,* keep watch over the shrine. Once a year, the rope is ritually renewed.

The dolly appears again as stone and clay effigies of the goddess buried in garden beds and fields, or offered like Saraswati to water. On a hike in Arizona, near Canyon de Chelly, I found a Mother Rock, a stone shaped so like a Paleolithic female figurine, I brought her home. She stands a foot high in a bed of blue pincushions, anemone, ajuga, and coral bells, appropriately lowly flowers for an Earth Goddess, and she's not too far from the sublime salmon azaleas.

My favorite stone was carved by a friend into the shape of an otter. It currently occupies a niche within the Castle Wall.

And I have standing stones, albeit short ones. A garden catalogue I recently received offers a mail-away, cast-stone obelisk, resembling a dwarfed Washington Monument or Cleopatra's Needle. Another offers a cast-stone Celtic cross for the garden and a cast-concrete straddle stone, a miniversion of Stonehenge. After a millennium's pause, the spiritual power of standing stones again commands attention, thanks in large measure to the Druid revival and Celtic Renaissance, which in the late nineteenth and early twentieth centuries began exploring a largely neglected history, and bringing folklore and myth previously ignored to public attention. These movements certainly stoked the Victorian fascination with fairies.

Most gardeners, however, aren't especially nostalgic about rocks. Laboring against them one has the sense they're breeding. Indeed, it was once commonly held that garden and field stones grew from a "motherstone" or "quickrock" and spawned underground like potatoes. But once out of the ground, the stone loses its potency, which explains the relative stability of paving stones.

When I was busy colonizing the Colony, I built a wall of sandstone bricks and clay—two to three feet high, ten feet long, and more like a planter. It crumbles and careens like ruins, vinca and succulents sprouting from the cracks, embedded in an old, white ceramic vase and a cobalt blue teapot I loved, broke, and couldn't throw out.

One friend divides her vegetable and flower beds with big, broken, colorfully glazed platters. Kids skipping down the alley stop to ask why she grows plates. We have a pile—between lambs ears and pink valerian—of crockery shards, which we dedicate "to the future of archaeology."

This tumbling and careening of stones in my garden reflects a sentiment for archaic wreckage and my fervent dislike—and fear—of walls.

Fences and walls were first raised to deter animals or halt winds. With the rise of social classes, walls served to discourage enemies as well as hoi polloi, just as the gardens within displayed social status. (Happily, neither gardens nor hierarchies are stable over time. Both require constant alertness and curtailment.)

The fairy tale "Rapunzel" is all about walls. And ladders. It begins when the pregnant wife can't stop herself desiring the rampions in her neighbor's garden. The wall is high and daunting, the neighbor distinctly unfriendly. Intimidated by overbearing yearning on the one hand and belligerence on the other, the husband is unable to ask outright for what his wife wants. Instead, he climbs his ladder on a moonless night, then scales down the wall on the other side.

He's caught red-handed. He trades his unborn child for an onion. The baby girl Rapunzel is given over, then reared behind walls, imprisoned in a tower by the witch-neighbor.

Oddly, for a Grimm Brothers' tale, Rapunzel finds solace, safety, and maturity in the forest, eventually freed by the ladder woven from her hair, which has never been cut. (Could the interminably trailing hair be an emblem of Rapunzel's raw, unsocialized wolf-girl adolescence? Could shearing that hair be symbolic murder by the witch, who understands she no longer has a pretty, pliable girl to adore, but a woman with a mind—and a garden—of her own to tend?)

In the Grimms' tales, fences and garden walls usually guard against the forest, the wilderness, the terrifying Other. But here, Nature is Rapunzel's asylum from the cruel possessiveness that stone walls represent.

Each person has a right to privacy. Landscape designer Gertrude Jekyll always created secret enclaves in house and garden for retreat, like our Enchanted Garden, Nilus terrace, or Fiesta Dinner Theatre.

Breezy cottage garden fences are welcoming and largely decorative. Plants are meant to spill from the garden, through the pickets, inviting the neighborhood to admire and enjoy. But walls and stockade fences send an unpleasant message of ownership and isolation.

Magical "walls" were created through various rites such as Roman Lupercalia, when in spring, naked youths carrying strips of goat and dog hides ran twice around the boundaries of the old Palatine settlement, tracing an invisible, protective circle around the city to shut out all things harmful.

In Christian theology, the Virgin Mary was identified by the church with the *hortus conclusus* or enclosed garden. Outside, lay a deadly "wall of thorn"—the unclean world.

I was reared in countries—not unlike the United States is becoming—where the distinction between rich and poor is drastic. The privileged classes live behind compound walls topped with menacing broken glass and impenetrable, curled barbed wire, war zones overlooking peaceful, carefully manicured gardens.

Beyond the barricades is extreme poverty, which, from the time I was little, terrified and shamed me. When I was very young, I knew—as do all the children of the privileged, though we may not want to think it—that poverty was the *real* life, the *real* home to which our servants, our gardener, my beloved nannies returned every night or once a week. In adolescence, this separation by walls from the world at large—from the pulp and piquancy outside— often made me feel as lonely and trapped as Rapunzel. Those walls were yet another thing that shaped my propensity to escape into fantasy. I lived in a fortressed Otherworld, never-never land for most people.

Certainly, there are necessary precautions. But we should distinguish between the demands of the garden—to protect it from wind or unleashed dogs—and our paranoia, our loathing, cynicism, and xenophobia. The first symptoms of this malady in any culture are the walls we build around our gardens, which can put us in danger of becoming as corrupt and stunted as Rapunzel's witch.

*   *   *

During the dog days of August, the Dog Star guides the gardener. There are meteor showers every night. The shooting stars are sometimes reflected in our Nilus.

When I was a child in Latin America, I watched the Southern Cross through my bedroom window. My Quechua nurse, Mariluz, called the constellation Star Woman:

> *For many evenings Star Woman watches a lonely man lying in a meadow watching her.*
>
> *At last, she slides from the sky to lie beside him and on the fifth night, she agrees to leave the sky and marry him.*
>
> *"For my wedding gift," she says, "you must make me a garden."*
>
> *The man is befuddled. The people hunt and gather, eat wild animals and wild fruits. To show him what she wants, Star Woman floats to the sky and returns with potatoes.*
>
> *The man will not eat them. He will not touch the strange starchy things with his tongue. Star Woman grips his hair, and pushes a piece of potato into his mouth.*
>
> *The man chews, swallows, and smiles. He digs the garden plot as Star Woman directs.*
>
> *Star Woman rises back into the sky and returns with corn, rice, yams, beans, and peanuts. All these good foods they grow in their garden. They live well and one by one their neighbors dig garden plots, too.*
>
> *The man who had been ugly and lonely before he married Star Woman has become bold and beautiful by the love and well-being she brings. He falls in love with another, human woman, and leaves Star Woman.*
>
> *Star Woman weeps. She cries and cries and when she runs out of tears, she climbs back into the sky.*

"If that man had been true to her," Mariluz said, "she might have brought more gifts. Because of him, we do not have all the things that Heaven can offer."

The act of gardening makes the world whole and is therefore an act of higher purpose. Our faithlessness to Nature deprives us of everything the cosmos might provide. We shortchange ourselves.

*   *   *

In this new rock garden, I've so far planted bleeding heart, fox-glove, hosta, and annual New Guinea impatiens, shocking magenta to pull and titillate the eye. The naturalism I strive for can't over-come my vanity. Where things blend too well, they disappear from undiscerning eyes. The theater of gardening demands I draw extra attention to certain areas. Magenta does the trick and then some.

The glade violets march on into this rock garden and will have to be restrained if anything else is to live. If I can keep them in check, I might at last have primroses.

My stone walls, like the coyote fence, aren't meant to deter peo-ple, but to attract the devas and Nature spirits. Only the Castle Wall is supposed to keep people out . . . of the shed. It was built where the barnlike doors were falling apart to prevent prowling youngsters from camping, as they have, inside the shed. I wanted the Castle Wall, piles of artfully fitted granite, to fill my eyes with legends and fairy tales. I wanted more stone crevices for succulents and drippy things to sneak through chinks, the way I imagine Medieval abbey walls to have been. Inside, the rocks jut into a seat, anticipating the day I figure out how and can afford to turn the shed into an out-door house. I wanted the *tectonics* for my summer house.

Built into the dense wall are glass tiles and bottles that catch the starlight flickering on granite. Mother stones and lodestars. Stars and stones stretching toward each other. And back to Earth's nativity.

September

If all our eyes had the clarity of apples
In a world as altered
As if by the wood betony
And all kinds of basil were the only rulers of the land
It would be good to be together
Both under and above the ground
To be sane as the madwort,
Ripe as corn, safe as sage,
Various as dusty miller and hens & chickens,
In politics as kindly fierce and dragonlike as tarragon,
Revolutionary as the lily.
   —Bernadette Mayer, "The Garden (for Adam Purple),"
   Avant Gardening

The Generous Month

The work is hardy, but the soft weather makes it easy and pleasant. The harvests go on. Planting and transplanting to be done, then roots carefully mulched to preserve moisture and fend off the coming cold.

Morning glories and scarlet runner beans—Susie Next Door's and mine—cascade along the laundry line, up the coyote fence. They mingle with the silverlace above the pond, weave in and out of gaps in the shed wall. The silverlace blossoms, fine and frothy in the air, turn instantly to muck when they land in the pond. Their drifting is hypnotic.

Lo and behold, here are the three remaining artichokes, blooming purple from that icky, hairy stuff at the heart that scrubs your tongue. They *are* beautiful. What a shame we can't have our artichoke flowers and eat them, too.

Gray September mornings. Wonderful silence as we head toward Keats's "season of mists and mellow fruitfulness."

The zinnias feel the pinch, they gleam in the afternoon sun, but when I look closely at the petals' tapered ends, I see the slightest withering at the tips, hinting at the increasing night chill. Still, they're spectacular in the van Gogh vase Kate gave me for foxgloves. In the cottage garden, zinnias make a motley mosaic with aster, marguerite, shasta daisies, cosmos, larkspur . . .

Susie's sunflowers on the hellstrip are towering and top-heavy. One has taken against Art the Mailman. It bops him upside the head every afternoon, as he jaunts by with his cart, dodging left, dodging right.

The squirrels climb the heavy stalks, tear furiously at the seeds.

Goldenrod. Chrysanthemums. Betony. Baby's breath. Coneflower. A marmalade ocean of orange marigolds I unleashed everywhere this year, taking full advantage of the hundreds of needle seeds each dried flower offers.

Now and again, leaves flutter to the ground like moths. Some trees show just the barest change in color. In Colorado, we'll not get the feverish fall blaze. For that I'll visit Kate in Ohio in early October, my annual birthday pilgrimage.

Rusty keys hang heavy from the ash trees. The rowan berries are molten scarlet. The rowan, or mountain ash, is a thoroughly magic tree. My grandmother hung its branches and berries in her house for luck—and although she never said so, they would have kept witches away, too. It was customary to tie red ribbons on the branches before the berries were ripe, but what self-respecting witch would fall for such a lame trick?

Bewitched horses can only be controlled with rowan rods. Rowan rods deter lightning and were used for divining metal. Although I've never heard of their culinary use in North America, rowan berries are edible and make tasty pies, jellies, jams and wines. Like the apple, they're considered a Food of the Gods. It is the "quickbeam," an oracular Tree of Life, Candlemas Tree of Fire.

September blow soft
'til the fruit's in the loft.

Trees were once considered Earth phalluses, but fruit trees were always associated with the goddess, the feminine principle.

In the Enchanted Garden, there's another picture-perfect tableau: two yellow pears surrounded by bunches of purple grapes and the vine wrapped around the trunk. A Dutch painting. The first tree I planted in this garden was the rowan; one of the latest is this pear, which leaped up in what seemed like a matter of minutes. In fact, it took at least five years to show any maturity. The garden is time's trompe l'oeil. Caught blissfully in the cycles of seasons, it's easy for the gardener to lose track of the years.

To ornament trees with talismans brought luck, love, or healing. When my rowan was a bareroot sprout, I hooked a little locket with pictures of my children into its skinny whip trunk. The locket disappeared into the bark.

There are wishing trees and trees that bring us health or babies or marriages. How we behave toward trees and shrubs helps determine our fortune. In Ireland, one never disturbs a lone bush or transplants "fairy thorns," whitethorns, hawthorns. These lonesome shrubs don't belong to mortals. Only loss results from removing them. The custom of nailing coins or crosses and other charms to "lucky" trees sometimes led to the trees' demise.

When I planted the pear, I wrapped a silver snake bracelet around its trunk, loosely, leaving plenty of room for the tree to grow within it. It did. And then it consumed the snake. Silvery snake bits are still visible.

Of the fortunate trees, the apple is luckiest of all among Europeans. The pear is a close second.

These days, at Kate's house, in the cool shed off the kitchen, the fruit gallery houses household cleaning products. Seventy and more years ago, Celinda packed apples and pears in straw and stuffed them into this loft. They were picked before they were entirely ripe, so they didn't turn to mush in their winter burrow.

The pears came from Kate's father Amos's deserted farm outside town. There was a pear orchard on the farm, and during the Great Depression, Kate told me, Amos put ads in the newspaper offering pears to anyone who cared to go out and pick them. FREE OF CHARGE was printed in capital letters and boldface.

There were hundreds and hundreds of pears, more than Kate and Amos could possibly eat. Celinda had died not long before and neither Kate nor Amos had any inclination to pick and store them. Amos's notion, Kate said, was that the pears might fill a hungry belly, or that a truly enterprising soul, like Amos himself, might pick enough to sell for desperately needed cash.

No one, absolutely no one, took Amos up on his offer. He ran the ad daily for a week or two, and still no takers. He was outraged. Whatever the reason for the lack of interest, it only further convinced him of folks' fundamental laziness, no matter their need. Amos had proudly and ruthlessly pulled himself up by his bootstraps, allowing nothing to get in his way. If he could, so could others. (Wasn't it odd that, in the 1980s, our city zucchini was snapped up like candy, but in the 1930s, Amos couldn't give away his farm pears?)

When Kate sold the farm, I was grown and out of touch. The pear trees, the green mossy creek, the splintered buildings are affixed to my memory like cobwebs.

The apple crop everywhere is excellent. On the east side, where a much larger tree than my dwarf has dropped its fruit wantonly on the lawn, the curses and shouts of the latest property manager—raking them, hating them—lobs through the Faux Forest into my garden. His antagonism depresses me. The violence is painful, up close and bending my ears, hurtful to realize that Nature doesn't necessarily make all people happy, isn't a source of spiritual contentment for everyone, but an annoyance, a stumbling block, or an enemy to be defeated.

Had I known those apples would be the source of such a rage knifing the quiet air, I might have offered to clean them up myself and then juiced them. I remember cider pressing in Ohio, when we stuffed the trunk and backseat of Kate's car with bushel baskets full of apples and drove to Uncle Willie's farm. He rendered the fruit into tawny juice and poured it into gray glazed jugs. Some we drank right away and some was put into small wooden barrels to harden in the storm cellar.

Apples aren't grown or enjoyed as readily in countries beyond

Europe and North America, where they are loved and revered like no other fruit. Whenever my mother found apples at the embassy commissary, it was a grand day for her and my father, an Ohio boy who loved apple pie and apple fritters above all foods.

The squirrels are having a field day on my tree. (Do the raccoons climb it at night to pick apples, too? Likely.) Every morning, it's a race to see which of us can get the fruit first. The squirrels are ahead, about ten to two! But there's one apple hanging from the very tip of a thin branch, where they can't balance or reach. I grin sadistically at the frustrated creature barking and shaking its tail, flipping, trying to get that ruby reward.

The crab apple branches nearly drag the ground. But the squirrels don't care for straight crab apples much more than we do. They're strictly for the birds.

In September, my mother-in-law hiked up a mountain to her favorite crab apple tree, picked a big backpack's worth, and marched back down again to make jelly. In her late eighties, she could no longer make it up the mountain and so she came to my house to gather them. Still later, we picked the crab apples for her, until she could no longer make jelly.

Much of the myriad folklore about apples is concerned with romance, prettifications of the apple's original bawdy reputation as a symbol of fertility. An apple hidden under a girl's pillow will cause her to dream of her sweetheart. The peel of an apple, cut in one long strip then thrown over the shoulder, will form the initial of a maiden's future husband. Flicking the pip in the air indicates the future lover's home.

> *Pippin, pippin, paradise*
> *Tell me where my true love lies.*
> *North, south, east, west,*
> *Tell me where my love does rest.*

That apples are related to roses is an added romantic bonus.
It wasn't all good news. In Hessen, Germany, to eat an apple on

New Year's Day meant you would be plagued with sores and itches, doubtless a reference to Eve's illicit apple consumption in the Garden of Eden, the original Judeo-Christian sin that got all the other sins rolling and introduced pestilence of every kind.

In Celtic mythology, the Apple Woman was another version of the destroyer goddess. She meted out life and death like the Indian Kali Ma. The Apple Woman was a goddess of the land, and where she walked, flames ignited her footsteps. Apples, like rowan berries, were seen as flames, the tree's vitality that invigorated the partaker . . . an apple a day keeps the doctor (or illness or witches or evil spirits) away.

The Welsh goddess Olwen, whom Robert Graves calls the "laughing Aphrodite," was also associated with the apple. Her tracks are the white flower of the trefoil, the clover, which blossomed wherever she stepped. (It's disturbing to note that the Greek goddesses so seldom seemed to laugh. By the time the tales we know were told, they'd lost their authority and independence, no laughing matter.)

According to Graves, apples are "chieftain trees," rowans are "peasant trees." Oranges, which appear far later in European folk and fairy lore, are good as gold. Many fairy tales begin with orange trees: *There once was a king, who had an orange grove/tree . . .* The action begins when the oranges are stolen or enchanted.

My peaches are finally ripe. They're old trees and don't bear well anymore. We've got just four or five good ones. The spontaneous young peach on the east side was so laden I propped it up with crutches.

It's rare that a fruit tree takes the role of a World Tree. In China, however, the Taoist philosopher Lao-tzu told of a peach tree so tall Paradise rested on its apex. The tree stood at the top of the highest peak in the Kwun-lun Mountains. Hsi Wang Mu, Goddess of the West and Empress of Immortals, lived in a Jade Palace in the peach tree's branches. Her hair was tangled and messy as leaves. Her teeth were like tigers' and she had a panther's tail. Sparrows brought her food as she patrolled the garden and looked over Earth.

My favorite Japanese story was about Peach Boy. My mother had a ceramic Momotaro doll, complete with sword and peach and tiny penis. In this scene, Peach Boy was newborn without his pants, but wearing a gorgeous peach-blossom brocade jacket. He resided in a glass box on a shelf next to similar Japanese dolls representing other wondrous legends, all associated with Nature and the garden.

There is an old, old couple, childless and so poor they haven't enough to eat. One day the old woman is washing clothes in the stream, when she sees an enormous peach floating and bobbing on the water. She has never seen such a big fruit. She thinks of supper. What a hearty meal this peach will make. She has no stick to draw it in. She sings it a song instead:

> *Distant water is bitter*
> *Nearby water sweet.*
> *Leave the distant water*
> *And come into the sweet.*

The peach drifts nearer and nearer as the old woman sings. It stops at her feet.

Her husband comes home, tired and hungry. They sit on either side of the peach. The old man raises a knife to carve the fruit, when suddenly it splits open and out tumbles a pretty baby boy. The baby is laughing and can speak.

"Don't be afraid," he says. "The gods know how much you wanted a child. They have sent me to comfort you in your old age."

The couple is overcome with joy. They caress the little boy, they sing to him, they call him Momotaro, Son of a Peach.

When he is fifteen, Momotaro tells his father he must take a long journey to an island where the oni live. The oni are demon spirits with three eyes on each head, three fingers on each hand, and three toes on each foot. Oni have gaping mouths and horrible horns. They carry diseases and inflict people with death. If not with death with kidnapping. If not with kidnapping with stealing. If not with stealing with taunting.

Momotaro promises to kill the oni. His father knows Peach Boy is supernatural and gives him permission to go. All the devils in the world cannot harm one who is sent from Heaven in a peach.

The old woman gives Momotaro three rice cakes to sustain him on his journey. Along the way, he meets a monkey, a dog, and a pheasant, who agree to accompany him, each in return for a rice cake. Momotaro and his three trusty companions defeat the demons and free a group of imprisoned maidens. They go home triumphant to the old man and the old woman and the people of the village, to whom they return treasures pillaged by the oni.

In many cultures, there's a Fruit of Death. The feminine principle of give and take at work again. In ancient Greece, the death—and love—fruit was the pomegranate, which Hades fed to Persephone so that she was obliged to return to him. The apple signaled the death of innocence for Adam and Eve.

I know a Tibetan refugee, whose uncle, she told me, was obliged to hide from the Chinese. She was a little girl in 1957, when the Chinese invaded Tibet, young enough, her family judged, to be beyond suspicion, and so she was chosen to take food to the uncle in his hiding place in a cave. One day, she picked peaches, put them in a basket, and carried them to her uncle. She couldn't know that she was being followed. Perhaps, she now thinks, it started because the soldiers craved those ripe and juicy peaches. But soon they noticed that there was more to this harvest. They caught her uncle and killed him before her eyes. She dropped her basket of peaches and ran away screaming.

This woman would never again eat a peach. They had become fatal fruits.

> In the beginning, wisdom and knowledge were with
> the animals. The One Above showed himself through
> beasts so that man should learn from animals.
>
> —Pawnee proverb

Wild Life

More evident now than ever. Squirrels and raccoons and the occasional skunk. At night, the raccoons knock on my study window and peer at me while I type. The young ones tilt their heads, curious. The old ones nudge them on.

Everyone's preparing nests and stoking up. When the cold comes to stay, the raccoons will vanish. The squirrels' coats are bushy and their tails widening, another signal of a hard winter.

Native American Pawnee and other primal peoples understood us all to be animals together on this Earth—the human animal often the last and least. It was animals who "named" humans, not the other way around. There was mutual understanding between our worlds, and there were rituals of permission and renewal when human hunters killed.

The animals in our gardens and homes are nearer to us than our human neighbors, backyard beasts exotic as zoo animals once we get to know them: birds, 'coons, mice, squirrels, and skunks; fleas, spiders, ladybugs, earwigs, houseflies, even cockroaches, and mosquitoes. Whether we "like" spiders or "hate" moles is irrelevant.

Mythologies worldwide testify that animals are responsible for our spiritual awakening and frequently for our creation. A mark of holiness from ancient Greece to Saint Francis was the ability to charm the ferocious beast. In the Christian era, saints and hermits associated themselves with the concept of peace among all animals. "Peaceable kingdom" paintings, such as those of Jan Bruegel the Elder, Henri Rousseau, and Edward Hicks (who made no fewer than a hundred variations on his original painting), depict an ideal world where all sentient beings lie down together. Sadly, and strangely, in the Middle Ages, animals were usually excluded from paintings of Eden or Paradise.

Watching animals in and around the garden, it's hard to fathom that these often comical, entertaining creatures could have the kind of serious dignity we often imagine is necessary to qualify as "cosmological." Even without our anthropomorphizing, these animals reflect back to us our own actions: our greed and frenzy, our hard work, how we protect and teach our young, playfulness, lust, and goodness. They can be tricksters, like coyote in the Apache tales or like foxes, crows, and ravens in other stories worldwide.

Hunters, non-agrarian peoples, revered and identified with animals in intricate and complex ways. Generally, early horticultural peoples looked upon animals not simply as competitors, but as com-

panions, *other people,* gods, ancestors, and/or kin. Mass murder leading to extinction of species was almost unheard of, a crime perhaps
as heinous as killing your siblings. Shamans, prophets, visionaries of
all sorts, including gardeners, understand the delicate web of psychic
and physical interdependency among all animals. We are a society. A
collective.

The squirrels make us laugh. *And* they are inseparable from the
garden or our daily lives. They live here. They need us. They are not
pets, not pets-once-removed. In a very practical sense, we need animals, in the garden and in the wild. Animals have always been,
among other things, auguries for human beings. From the start,
we've watched them for advice and signs from the weather to
whether herbs, berries, fungi, and fruit were edible or could heal.

The Greek Aesop's Fables tend to put a human morality spin on
animals and their doings; nonetheless, they demonstrate how other
animals have always taught humans how to behave, survive, and
thrive.

Raccoons have moved into one of our chimneys, closed off
where it was attached to a kitchen coal stove. The cubs scratch,
squeal, and squabble all night long. I wonder if, before the next crop
of young ones, I should seal the chimney. But I can't see what harm
they're doing. I grow fruits and vegetables. My husband feeds the
birds. We attract these animals. Aren't we responsible for them, too?

A decade ago, there was a squirrel we named Maeve after the
great Celtic queen, who carried a squirrel familiar on her shoulder.
At meals in the garden, Maeve the Squirrel stood by my feet and
scratched my leg, then waited politely, holding her hand to her
heart, until I tossed her a bite. If I ignored her, she reminded me she
was there with another light scratch. The next summer, she was
gone. We imagined she'd taught her children to be friendly, but none
of Maeve's descendants has ever again been so trusting.

European farmers—and today's old-fashioned gardeners—realized that in order for there to be harmony and thus fertility, there
had to be enough planted for everyone: *one for the rook, one for the
crow . . .* the saying goes. Garden fences keep no one out. Scarecrows
work, more or less, but their presence is mostly symbolic. Poisons
and guns have miserable repercussions, bad karma, which severely

undermines the sanctity of the garden. (And pity the poor gardener in ancient Egypt, who had to contend with hippos!)

A garden that isn't partly given over to birds, bees, insects, and small mammals and that does not provide elements to attract them is incomplete and sterile. Seed by seed, creature by creature, the garden gives us a way to comprehend Nature. Not all of Nature or Nature as a whole, but to the extent that it concerns human experience, the garden can offer us empathy for other living, growing beings.

In September, mule deer begin edging out of the mountains, gradually leaving their summer browsing spots and coming to town. They'll winter over in people's backyards, leaving poop pellets and indentations in grass and groundcover. Most old-timers don't mind. Most welcome the deer as friends and plant ornamentals the deer don't care for, build high fences around vegetables, or simply give the garden over to the animals. One family I know has surrendered entirely, puts salt licks out for the deer and corn for the squirrels and raccoons. They keep bird feeders everywhere. Theirs is an animal garden. The deer, they say, mow the lawn and clip the evergreens into topiaries at far less cost than a professional landscaper. For a while in summer, most but not all of the deer meander back up the mountain, giving the vegetation a chance to recoup.

Newcomers are often highly indignant about the deer. Nonetheless, they build homes higher and higher in the foothills, farther and farther into deer, bear, and mountain lions' territory. The outrage when a mountain lion makes off with someone's gourmet toy poodle is laughable to the old-timers. They were not amused, however, when not long ago, a woman ran screaming out of her house with a rifle and killed a deer grazing her petunias. There was idle talk about forming a lynch mob to avenge the deer and a flurry of letters to the local newspaper.

> I watch the green field growing
> For reaping folk and sowing,
> For harvest-time and mowing,
>   A sleepy world of streams. . . .

Pale, beyond porch and portal,
  Crowned with calm leaves, she stands
Who gathers all things mortal
  With cold immortal hands.
—Charles Swinburne, "The Garden of Proserpine"

The Mysterious Flowering of Daughters

In the tender, cool breath of almost-fall, roses are returning.

The coil and knot of vines and thorns recall Sleeping Beauty's impenetrable palace, hidden for a century behind skeins of verdure. The wrathful vine guarding a snoozing princess. The garden gone wild, when the "civilizing" virgin collapses into a snoring heap. Did the seasons change while the Sleeping Beauty lay comatose? Was winter suspended along with her age?

It is a story quite opposite from that of Demeter and Persephone. When the princess falls asleep, the garden becomes increasingly disordered. The prince arrives to awaken her and life reverts to well-bred formality. When Persephone goes away—falls asleep in her underworld realm—the garden, that is, the world, dries up. Only when she leaves her "prince" does the garden bloom again unfettered.

My daughter goes back to school. Summer is really over.

After hugs, kisses, and call-the-minute-you-get-theres, I retreat to the garden and wander, unable to settle on any task. Letting the children go—whether to summer camp when they were small or back into their own adult lives—is difficult and never gets easier.

The bond between mothers and daughters is thought to have been the focal point of the ancient Greek Lesser Mysteries in February, when Persephone is on her way up from underground. Her mother Demeter awaits her in anxious anticipation. The barest signs of spring indicate the Mother's excitement. Persephone leaves her home, her duties, her womanhood in order to become a girl again at her mother's side (and don't we all revert to childhood in the presence of our mothers?).

Persephone is New Crop, bud and blossom.

She arrives and in the Homeric poem, "Hymn to Demeter," all that first day long, the sun shines as Mother and Daughter

> *bask in each other's presence . . .*
> *receive joy*
> *and give joy*
> *one to the other.*

Is it the Daughter's first returning footsteps or the Mother's joyful anticipation that vaults the dream of Spring into reality?

In September, the Greater Mysteries were celebrated at the Autumnal Equinox in the city of Eleusis, where Demeter sought rest during her search for Persephone. In September, the girl who's been abducted by Hades, Ruler of Death, must now return to the underworld. That's the deal: she visits her mother and the Earth turns to spring; she leaves and fall sets in toward winter.

Return she truly *must*. Daughters *must* be set free to build their own queendoms, to fully occupy and run them. I say this to myself repeatedly. There are times I wonder if I'm trying to talk myself into it. Letting go can be as painful and debilitating as chopping off fingers.

The daughter sprouts in her mother's garden, but she flowers elsewhere. Vacations are well and good, but the young woman had to get back to another job in September. Persephone seems to have ruled equally with her husband Hades, pale King of Shades, a shady, shadowy character indeed. While Hades was virtually ignored in worship, and rarely appears in myth, the Greeks raised temples to Persephone, as comforter to the dying, guide to the dead, and guardian of midwives. Her name was never to be revealed to those uninitiated at the Mystery celebrations; she was "the unspeakable girl," spoken of in euphemisms (much as the name of God could not be spoken by Jews). She was sometimes called "Murder." She was sometimes referred to as "Dread." She was "Mighty."

The myth of Demeter and Persephone has offered the Western world ample interpretations about the relationship between mothers and daughters. The myth's meanings seem unlimited, its significance to the exaltation of Nature and Earth by humankind almost unparalleled. Persephone's liberation from her mother creates the ground in which the seasons can flourish. Life, therefore, is stimulated and made potent.

Although the rituals were celebrated at Eleusis annually for thousands of years, their most profound contents are one of history's best-kept secrets. Various rites are described, but the "mystery" of the Mysteries is unknown. "No one," it was written, "may describe the essential gifts of the ceremonies."

These "essential gifts" were, I think, exactly as Mara Lynn Keller writes in *Reweaving the World—The Emergence of Ecofeminism:* "The central experience of the initiation was never revealed . . . because the mystical insight itself was beyond naming, ineffable."

It is known that the festival—which could be attended by anyone who had not taken a human life—was one of gratitude to the Mother for teaching humankind the art of cultivation and for decanting from her body the cornucopia at this time of year. The celebration to honor Demeter certainly included rites corresponding with her various names: Barley Mother, Corn Mother, Pig Mother, Green Demeter, Giver of Gifts, Fruit Bearer, Warmth, Healer, Lightbearer, Wrathful, Gentle. Besides the pig, Demeter's animals included the horse, the dolphin, and the dove, around which rituals were also conducted.

Her sacred plants were wheat and barley, the staples. Pomegranate, the fruit signifying sex and death. Poppy, flower of sleep. In September, this sleep is gradually embracing the Earth and our gardens. It is simultaneously the sleep of the maiden in her unawareness before she was taken from her mother and the sleep that overcomes the mother when the daughter departs.

When Persephone leaves her, year in, year out, Demeter does not smite the world with winter out of vengeance. Nor does she wallow in sorrow. She withdraws out of generosity, giving a gift to the ground itself. Without this in-gathering, plants, animals, and soil can't maintain fertility. (Once upon a time, farmers were well aware that crops had to be rotated and that each field needed to rest without planting for a season, lest the soil's nutrients be sapped for good. This was the expedient side of Pan's—or the devil's—acre.)

The maiden leaves her mother in September, because there's no choice. Only corruption comes of prolonged infancy. The witch in Rapunzel, for instance, tries to keep the "daughter" captive right up to the point where she is threatened with psychic deformity. If spring and summer never ended, the vibration of the world, its resonance, would resemble a broken record stuck on the same note, trapped in a single groove. Even tropical countries, or those billed in tourist brochures as enjoying "eternal spring," have seasons. No plant can bloom—nothing can function—without a breather.

The snake, the fifth of Demeter's animals, slips underground, protects grain against rodents, and regenerates by shedding its skin, like the seasons, like the Earth, life to death to life to death. In Earth-based spiritual practices—where gardens are the hub of a wheel that reaches into the wilderness and is as eternal as infinity and as round as time—joy in life and hope in death become possible.

In all faiths, there are levels of obeisance for Nature—sometimes buried, sometimes, as with Shinto, the absolute core. They might be in writings such as those of Saint Francis. They might be found in the names and tasks of the gods themselves. They might be animal deities or enlightenment found under a ficus tree. The clue might be in the afterlife spent in a garden called Paradise. The greatest spiritual fulfillment, whatever our worldviews, is first to be found in the Earth.

And yet, Demeter herself raged that we mortals "know not good from evil when it approaches," a warning we must learn to heed. The garden is the manageable manifestation of Nature, where we can learn everything we need to know, including good from evil. The "ineffable . . . mystical insight" can be recreated daily in our gardens and in the wilderness.

It's believed that at the Greater Mysteries, the story of Persephone's abduction by Hades, and Demeter's nine-day search for her, was dramatized for participants and initiates (called *mystai,* who began their initiations at the February festival). It was the time for purification, renewal, and resurrection. Among the rituals, as always, were dances, all night *panegyreis* at the Well of Fair Dances, where participants bathed in sacred water. There were star, sun, moon, and sea dances and dances in the eddies of streams.

*   *   *

Each time my daughter leaves this home, which is no longer her place, I think about how Persephone must leave Demeter to flower. If daughters leave their mothers in love, rather than anger, they leave a great harvest, the great comfort of bounty and beauty, the likes of which stand before me right now in my garden.

When my daughter was six, seven, and eight years old, the story of Demeter and Persephone was her favorite: the maiden's abduction and descent to the Underworld and her role as its queen. Her mother's wrath, her return to the Upperworld for two-thirds of the year. My daughter demanded the story constantly. When she was nine or ten, I tried her on the Homeric poem, but by then she was losing interest. Her own "descent" was beginning, the scene being set for her departure.

Did I tell my daughter the tale of Demeter and Persephone so often and so fervently, because I wanted her to be able to design her own life? Because my mother had refused to let me go? I married young. I had to be abducted or I would never have left nor been permitted to control my own life. It's the ill fate of every princess that she has almost no autonomy. Individuality is almost alien to those who grow up in tight-knit tribes. My family were travelers, and we lived our lives as if sealed together inside our suitcases. To leave betrayed the clan.

At sleepovers, I told the story to my daughter and her best friend. We sat in the garden, two little girls and me. My daughter's friend insisted the story had to end with Persephone returned to her mother, where she would stay forever and ever and never, *ever* leave. Cerberus could no longer be a snarling three-headed dog guarding the gates of Hell, but was to be replaced by a good-natured four-headed kitten.

One night, a few years ago, my daughter called from school to tell me her friend had taken her own life. The reasons were complex and probably unknowable. The "why" of it will always be a mystery. No blame, no clinging mothers, no abuse, no lack of love and support, and certainly no cheap and easy analysis can be applied to this tragedy. Yet somehow, the minute I heard the news, my memory flew back to the sleepovers and the revised version of the Demeter and Persephone myth, which she'd demanded. She had loved the story, but she wanted the teeth taken out of it. She loved the story, but wanted a different outcome.

This Persephone-Daughter will never return to her mother. At the same time, she will chose never to leave, for she would never grow up, never take her mother's place as we all must (whether or not we have children). Though Persephone and Demeter, basking in each other's presence, gaze always toward autumn, this Demeter-Mother is left alone in never-ending winter.

As daughters have an obligation to go and mothers an obligation to let them go, so daughters are enjoined to return in order for the circle, the cycle, the wheel, the seasons to remain unbroken.

The daughter is the flower. The mother the fruit. In the garden, I find my center, sigh, and resign myself to my daughter's absence until Christmas break. Indoors, on my mirror, where we leave notes to each other, she's hung a woodcut, a gift she made for me—knowing I was writing this book. On a Post-it, she's scrawled, "So long, Mama-bean. I love you. *Back soon.*"

October

Of all the endemic beauties of the eastern continent the sycamores are paramount . . .

They evoke cool streambottoms . . . their pale, soft-
palette reflections awrinkle in the deep smallmouth
pools; in October their fallen leathery leaves shoal and
drift on sleepy creeks and rivers.

> —Merrill Gilfillan, *Burnt House to*
> *Paw Paw: Appalachian Notes*

Unbroken Circle

There are a few fall plantings of spinach and lettuce yet to pick,
enough for one last salad. I haul half a bushel of green tomatoes in
from the cold and admire the tenacious, muscular roots as I pull
tomato trunks out of the ground, chop them with a hatchet, and
turn them under.

The green tomatoes that haven't been pickled or made into
chutneys and pies or fried in cornmeal are put to ripen in brown
paper bags. When they're finally red, they taste like wet cardboard
in salads, but they make adequate sauce with plenty of herbs and
garlic.

Winter squash is harvested when the skin can't be punctured by
a thumbnail. A basket and an old crock in the kitchen hold my annual crop. I pile straw on the rows of root vegetables.

Fresh manure and compost are settling into the turned beds. Bat guano and mushroom fertilizer I've tried for the past two years are expensive but wonderfully potent, so "hot," they have to winter over. I mix it all with juniper, pine, and spruce branches to balance the alkaline. I water the acid-loving plants one last time with pots of strong, cheap coffee.

The drizzly days are gloomy and cozy. The woodstove is back in gear.

These are the days for chores. Good days for dumping dirt from clay pots and cleaning them, for seeing to it that the terra-cotta bird-bath platters are turned over so they don't catch water, freeze, and crack. For cutting back the mint and breathing its strong scent one last time, for trimming the lambs ears that are turning to goo, for leveling sunflowers, covering the garden furniture, arranging final bouquets of gaillardia and the rough flowerheads of rabbit brush, the final, feathery cleome flowers, the Russian sage. For picking the last roses to dry from the ceiling in the Upside Down Garden in our kitchen.

Wet droves of snow. I walk into the bathroom to shut the window. There's a little mountain bluebird shivering on the sill. On the outside sill, the male waits, bluer and colder. I turn, rush out, slamming the door behind me against the cat. I run downstairs hollering for my husband, who lumbers up with no idea what this shrieking's all about. He sees the bird, grabs a towel, grabs the bird, and gently shoves her out the window to her mate.

A warm week. My husband spots a blue grosbeak and a crested flycatcher in the garden.

A box of tulips arrive. Last spring's lavish lilacs so pleased me, I had a notion to plant the color along the ground. And here they are, though I'd forgotten the impulse—as usual. I dig bulbs into the hell-strip, where their amethyst, purple, and lavender will form a weird convergence, like smeared paint, below the lilacs. The garden is over, the season calls for new activities. Here is one final gesture, a planting that reminds me of this summer's joys and that spring is not really so very far away. If I was beginning to feel downcast by the onset of gray, it's cheering to press these bulbs into ground that is not yet frozen.

*   *   *

Rumbling, abnormal vibrations seep from the east-side house. I pay little attention. In a few hours, I'll be on a plane to Ohio.

Susie Next Door and I meet on the sidewalk. She's excited. The east-side house has been sold, after years of on-again-off-again attempts. My heart catches. What will this mean for the old rugosa? What about my grapevines sprawled so luxuriously over the dead trees? What of the dead trees, now part of this environment? *My* environment. What about the Faux Forest? Will my woodland be thinned and castrated? Will a stockade fence, so popular here, be raised to impinge on light and spaciousness?

Sides. Your side my side. The landlords annoy me, so I bestow my contempt on them. But their absence and obliviousness has given me the freedom to spread out.

Now what? What will become of the young peach? Will this new owner cut it down? Its leaves are going. Will he or she even recognize it as a tree? Should I post a sign on it?

The airport limo arrives. I hug Susie and turn my thoughts to Kate and Bridie waiting for me at the dear old house, where I'll settle like a child again, into warmth and goodness and familiarity.

There's not the vaguest public transportation from Cleveland to Kate's village. It's dark when I get there in a rental car I've wheeled around several wrong turns into other towns and an empty drive-in movie theater.

At Kate's house, I sleep like a log, as if I were under a spell. Rain thumps all night on the slate roof and thunder drives me burrowing under the covers. Kate refuses to believe I'm not a late sleeper. There are mornings snuggled under homespun blankets in my late Aunt Marion's four-poster when I snooze till noon.

Three days into my visit, I'm awakened by a screechy tootle. Bridie—dressed to the nines—and Kate—leaning on her walker, blowing a miniature harmonica—croak the "Happy Birthday" song outside my door. Then a hearty Ohio breakfast and Pootsie from down the road, whose birthday it is today, too, drops by and we exchange chocolate bars.

I take my annual walk to the cemetery, past Kate's woods, past new houses, and across a highway, picking leaves tinted vermilion, claret, maroon, chartreuse, and foxy cinnamon, until my arms are full of fall colors. In the cemetery, the hydrangea trees are blooming.

I find the family plot, a kind of neighborhood, definitely a community, way at the back of the grounds, in mossy shade. I tidy the impatiens and geraniums Kate planted on Memorial Day. I go from stone to stone composing leaf arrangements on each grave, anchoring them with acorns.

October afternoons are sunny. Kate and I wander the garden, all my rush and busyness sedated by Kate's crippling arthritis. She shows me the places she described in her letter, where Celinda planted flowers and many still grow. Their longevity is astonishing. And magnanimous. Tomorrow, I'll climb the ladder to prune the lilac and cut back the roses on the wellhouse. Ted has come by several times a week to do odd jobs and handyman chores since I was a child and he was in his late teens. Strong as he still is, there are some tasks that simply don't get done anymore.

That night, Bridie and I take a few turns around the living room to Kate's old jazz on pristine 78s. In Bridie's octogenarian heart, there's a flapper eternally kicking her heels through a blackbottom.

Kate loves to drive, she learned when she was nine. No licenses were required, and it wasn't unusual for children in rural areas to be behind the wheel. Cars weren't as fast and dangerous, highways and freeways didn't exist, the roads were mostly dirt, the traffic mostly horses, carriages, and wagons.

"You had to be careful of stray animals and young Amishmen racing their carriages at breakneck speed down the road. They were a handsome bunch. An accident to look forward to," Kate said.

When she was ten, her father needed an important legal document delivered seventy miles to Cleveland. No one was available to take it, so little Kate hopped into the family Model T, made the delivery, and arrived back home at sunset. Celinda was not pleased. Amos, however, was overjoyed and threatened to hire Kate as his courier from then on. Celinda glowered, but she knew it was only a joke. Or did she?

Amos was bigger than life, a cup that ran over. I love to hear stories about him and the enthusiasms that got the better of him, like the day Kate was born and the nurse presented the twenty-minute-old bundle to her proud new papa. He skipped out the door clutching infant Kate and headed uptown to show her off to his cronies.

Kate eyes the sporty red rental car and says she wishes she could maneuver herself into the bucket seat to give it a test spin.

Instead, we go riding in her old Chevy every day of my visit. Kate and I alternate driving. Bridie's in the front passenger seat, nodding off. The countryside is littered with roadside stands, piles and piles of the season's truck-garden crop. I'm especially taken with the Hubbard squash and once had a collection drying on my kitchen shelf, like a colony of miniature barnacle whales. Eventually, I handed them out as rattles and noisemakers at a music party and the next day lined their lumpy, broken carcasses into a bed of nasturtiums—textures recalling an undersea garden—before I composted them at summer's end.

Kate knows the best roadside stands. Berries, apples, peaches, pears, potatoes, peppers, watermelons and cantaloupes, buttercup and delicata squashes, leeks and onions spill out of pickup beds or are neatly arranged on jury-rigged counters made from crates. Pies and breads, eggs, and gallon jugs of fresh milk. Oak and sycamore, maple and sassafras trees with their mitten leaves, blurred gold, pink, copper, and crimson line the route.

We pass Amish buggies and Amish kids on Rollerblades. We chug up a rise Kate calls Pumpkin Bump. Pumpkins are high on the hit parade of American place names. There are two Pumpkin Hills in Maine alone and at one of them, the farmer was also immortalized in verse:

> *Jabez Benson raised the pumpkins,*
> *Hannah baked the pie.*
> *Jabez ate so many,*
> *He thought to God he'd die.*

Early supper on the road, then home, where Bridie and Kate play cribbage, while I attack the mending I save all year to bring on this trip.

"Honey," Kate teases, "you mend rags I'd be ashamed to give to charity."

Bridie, sipping a beer, offers to buy me a new wardrobe or at the very least, a new lace tablecloth. "I'm sick of seeing this one turn up every year with new rips and holes in it."

"But it was my grandmother's," I sputter. Bridie's unmoved.

The year I brought a friend's quilt to rebuild, I made an impression at last. Every evening, I laid it out on the floor for inspection. That year, Kate gave me Celinda's lovely sewing kit for a birthday gift. Diminutive silver scissors, sharpie needles, and a petite thimble that barely fit my pinkie.

The stone fireplace Amos built as a distraction when Celinda died, roars behind me. Kate and Bridie on the davenport, playing cards printed large, the newspaper all over the floor, me in the overstuffed chair. Once here, I never want to leave. Folks drop by, but not as many as used to, when this town where my father and Kate grew up had a population of about eight hundred and everyone knew everyone and all their business, too. Each time we came back, when I was a kid, we were front-page news in the local Gazette: HOME TOWN BOY NOW DIPLOMAT BACK ON LEAVE WITH FAMILY.

The village has burgeoned to three thousand, a Cleveland bedroom community with new housing developments and plenty of mobile homes stuck onto old farmland. Hot shots buying up the old Victorian houses and turning them, Kate says, into "circuses. Why would people want to live in houses dolled up like restaurants?"

The houses here have vast lawns and stately trees, but almost no one has a garden, even in the small nearby cities devastated by poverty and unemployment since the industries went belly-up or moved away.

There's a Stop & Shop and a Walgreen's where the Wilsons had their grocery and the Sheldons had a drugstore and ice cream parlor. The movie theater has become a dry cleaning establishment. There are two or three video rental stores.

The droves of visitors who popped in and out of Kate's house at random—the door was never locked—have died or fled the cold Ohio winters for retirement villages in sunnier, drier climes. Kate winters awhile each year with Bridie in California, but she will not leave home, this house and land, her place. Meanwhile, all around her, all over the country, people pull stakes constantly, a constant shuffle of real estate and jobs and half-formed friendships and communities. Houses no longer homes but commodities.

"I was reading my mother's diary the other day," Kate says. "They'd just bought the house, and she wrote that she hoped they'd be able to live here for ten years. Here it is, almost a century later."

This village is not my community, nor was it when Kate's house was lively with friends. We were guests, and the proof was in my father's local fame as a hometown-boy-made-good. And gone for good. We didn't participate in the doings of the village nor offer opinions on its political or social life. My father's parents and their parents and their parents were as much a part of this village as its sidewalks and fairground. My father chafed at the confinement and couldn't wait to leave. Except for his father, a civil engineer, his was the first generation to attend college, he and his cousins were the first to spread their dreams into the far-reaching wide world. All that are left here of my immediate family are the gravestones and a few memorial placards, including my father's name on a list of local boys the town sent to World War II. The wars cracked old communities open, younger generations fled, while outside ideas, once unable to penetrate, sneaked in: "How you gonna keep 'em down on the farm, after they've seen Paree?"

I've gardened as if I would live in Boulder forever.

And I've lived in my Boulder house with one foot out the door for more than twenty years.

When my mother's household goods were shipped from Virginia, they sat in my front hall for a long, long time in their packing crates.

"Why," my husband asked at last, "aren't we unpacking these boxes?"

It wasn't grief that kept me from opening and emptying them, it was comfort. I am never more *at home* than when I'm surrounded by the trappings of transience. The garden—unlike the house—provides diversity and movement.

Kate's house, with Kate in it, is my place, but it will not be and never was my home. At Kate's I expect everything to be just as it always was from my childhood. And I'm quick to notice any small thing that's shifted.

When I was a young woman, Kate was my Hekate—the Greek goddess with three heads of lion, dog, and mare. She of the Three Forms, full Moon, dark Moon, and Earth. In the tale of Demeter and Persephone, it is Hekate who negotiated the emergence of Persephone from the underworld and mediated her freedom as an adult woman. Kate did this for me.

Bridie and Kate nap in the den. I try to read under the big white oak. But I'm thinking about how Kate is also my Hestia. My hearth. *Kate* is my place.

I watch the Ohio topography from the plane's porthole. This land was originally thick with woods. Now there are smatterings of trees, mostly windbreaks between fields. And the irony is that, while these trees were cut for farms, today farming is becoming extinct.

A few hours later, the plane begins its slow descent. Below, the vast topography of the American West is laid out in blocks of aridity and dots of drought interrupted by great rounds of unseasonal green, where massive irrigation sprinklers snake in slow, twirling dances. The terrain is altered, the unbalance vividly evident. This misuse and overuse of one resource and desertion of another makes no sense. And it's heartbreaking.

> O if we but knew what we do
> When we delve or hew—
> Hack and rack the growing green!
> Since country is so tender
> To touch, her being so slender,
> That, like this sleek and seeing ball
> But a prick will make no eye at all,
> Where we, even where we mean
> To mend her we end her,
> When we hew or delve:
> After-comers cannot guess the beauty been.
> —Gerard Manley Hopkins, "Binsey Poplars"

Steve Next Door

The For Sale sign is gone and there are builders and painters and roofers and carpenters swarming the east-side house. Susie was right. It finally did sell.

I stalk my garden, glaring suspiciously at this brigade of workers, seeking out . . . who? Which of these people might be the new owner?

A young man—younger than my son—strides into my yard and shakes my hand. "I'm Steve," he says. "I'm your new neighbor."

Before I tell him my name, I blurt, "You know, this rugosa is very *very* old, and therefore probably very *very* valuable." *Valuable,* I decide, is a word that'll hit any landlord in the soul!

This one smiles indulgently, disarming and adorable.

"And *that's* a tiny baby peach!" I continue. "It just grew here spontaneously. It was a gift, you understand. A *gift* from the garden, and this year it provided the tastiest fruit . . ."

"I have my own peach tree?" He's excited. My defenses drop a notch.

Next day, he comes by to chat again. He'll live here and build an office in the carriage house. Where other landlords were decidedly absent, this one will be positively present. His dad, Steve says with intense pride, is a gardener and he'd like to garden a bit, too. Maybe vegetables. Probably roses like his father. Definitely a lawn. "I'm a grass kinda guy." And for once I don't scowl at the mention of turf.

Soon we're discussing the dead pines. Next, we're agreeing to split the cost of raising more lattice in place of the pines along the old chicken-wire fence. Not a stockade, but an airy thing that'll give us each some privacy, and also be open and friendly. Everything I say, he seems to agree with.

Here is Susie's male counterpart—Steve Next Door. I'm galvanized. Here's something new to think about. And I'll no longer be isolated, bookended between strangers. This injection of fresh neighborliness perks me up.

The mid-October weather's holding. I saw down the dead pines—a surprisingly gratifying ritual—and rake both our sides. Steve Next Door apparently doesn't mind what I do. He'll follow along pulling stumps. Shared labor is delicious.

"Jenny, you're a master of disaster," he says about the piles and piles of branches and trunks in my wake. His good cheer is already transforming the place.

I leave two plum saplings on Steve's side. How these youngsters, gasping for who knows how long under the gnarled rubble, managed to sprout at all is a miracle. In the bliss of the work, I realize I've been waiting a long time to get my hands on this stuff. The dead pines pinned us in and pinched the possibilities. But even I wouldn't have gone so far in my trespassing as to take them down without permission.

I shape plum branches to cascade onto Steve's side, so he'll have a flow of blossoms and fruit and the Faux Forest won't seem ravaged. What will we decide to plant in the new, shared light that's pouring in? Trumpet, to attract more hummers? Hops vine? Clematis? More climbing roses?

The Faux Forest is thinner now, but in spring some of the plums will bloom again after many years. What's been lost in the lovely woodland density will be more than made up for with vines along the lattice fence and whatever Steve plants in his long-dormant, newly revealed bed. I stare from my favorite bedroom perch onto the trimmed forest and imagine how it would look with, say, another dwarf bloodleaf maple for more color in the depths. Mahonia. Shrubs for autumn color and winter shape . . . a forest tapestry of varying greens and points of other subtle colors.

Now there are three-way conversations between Susie Next Door, Steve Next Door, and me. The old rugosa is safe. The peach tree is prized. My fairy godmother, my little red calf is working overtime.

Pray to catch a single ray of thought of the Unmanifest
Contemplate the order of Nature animate and inanimate

Such epitaphs were common in ancient Egypt, when October brought the realization of Horus to Isis—She Who Is Parent of All Things—called Mother of Time, Space, and Elements and the Mistress of the Gods.

With the sinking of the Nile, her husband Osiris, god of vegetation, was murdered by his brother Set, who tore his green body to pieces. In grief, Isis cut her hair and went out to find him. Her journey mirrors Demeter's search for Persephone.

Among other similarities, their attempts to bestow immortality on a human child were thwarted, leaving the child only partially initiated, "semi-immortal," as it were, emblematic of the human belief in our reincarnation or resurrection, our belief that death is as impermanent for us as it is for vegetation. As if in mimicry of flora, humans conceived of transmigration.

It is said that the women of Egypt gave the women of Greece the art of gardening. Isis taught planting to her people, while Demeter rewarded the shepherd Triptolemus with barley seed, a plough, a beehive, and a chariot drawn by serpents to travel the world teaching the honeyed art of horticulture.

Isis found her husband, not once, but twice, a process reminiscent of the dicey stop-and-go beginnings of Spring. Piece by piece she reassembled him, just as bud by bud, seed by seed the growing season returns after a period of dormancy.

She pieced Osiris together, but she could not find his penis. In certain versions she substituted a shaft of gold—that is, a sheaf of wheat—and Osiris revived long enough to implant Horus, the hawk-faced Sun god, into the womb of the goddess.

His conception marked the time of ploughing, as the vegetation god ploughs the womb of the goddess, and for planting, the realization of the seed in the womb. Then Osiris retreated to the Underworld to await the next enactment of the annual drama.

Where does the green go and how does it come back, if not through the grace of unutterable mysteries? The Mysteries of Isis were celebrated in ancient Egypt in October. Her quest takes a year, a full turn of the calendar: of river rising and sinking, of ploughing and planting, growth and decay, plenty and scarcity, Chaos and unity, spun in perfect pattern and perfectly orchestrated to Nature.

Among Nature's—and the garden's—greatest mysteries is her resilience. In the stories of Isis and Demeter it is their—however reluctant—resilience, as well as persistence, that bring the green back to life.

A Cooper's hawk lands on the tree outside my study, not five feet away. He waits a few seconds, long enough for me to admire his sublime insignia and dignified bearing, then skims after a house finch. A king of the underworld come to shroud us in winter.

There is a harvest moon tonight. Red. Saffron. The color of harvest festivals.

> In a silver lake, what's the rush?
>
> —Reed Bye

November Eve

A few days of summer, followed by cold, followed by more summer, then cold and back and forth. A rapacious wind turns up one night and smashes the bottles on the spirit tree. I crawl around the roof outside my daughter's room picking up cobalt and emerald shards.

Day by day, the garden's disappearing. A deserted stage. Plaster saints and virgins, ceramic donkey, birdcage, old furniture, benches, iron fences and bedsteads, stone walls, the Gray Guardian of the Woods, Aine the Mermaid . . . ghostly set pieces.

The "scaregown" is shredded and drooping. The nightie's cotton is wafer-thin, dissolving from months of water and sunlight. Her straw hat was chewed away by raccoons. I situate a plastic human skull on her empty shoulders and light a tiki torch behind her. She'll be a ghastly, gleaming spectacle, a thrilling phantasm for trick-or-treaters scurrying along the alley. Tomorrow I'll pull her apart and bury her in the compost.

I remember one November Eve in Boston, we opened the door to find no Little Mermaid or Batman, but a full-grown calico cat. She stepped lightly over the threshold, arched her back, marched into the living room and stayed. We named her—what else?—Halloween. Everyone loved her. Everyone but me.

I was suspicious. I kept my distance. Witches are renowned for trading their bodies for those of animal familiars. Hadn't my granny told me so? Hadn't the stories I'd read all through childhood proven it?

This cat was not to be trusted. Exactly how, I asked my husband, had he known to answer the door right then? Had he heard a ring or a knock? I sure hadn't. I interrogated the entire family. They loved Halloween. They felt lucky and flattered she'd chosen us. She knew just where to come for sustenance and affection.

"You see there?" I said. "She *knew*. She *chose*. Doesn't that tell you something?"

One May night, as I lay sleeping in my white cotton nightgown, pregnant and big as an igloo lying in bed on my back, I saw my new baby in my dreams and then I heard her, piping and squealing, squeaking like a little bird. I shook my husband.

"She's born! Wake up!"

He blasted out of bed like a firecracker. Leaning toward me, a look of solicitous fear on his face, he saw Halloween giving birth to a litter of seven between my legs.

"Don't move," he whispered. "You'll kill them."

"Kill who?"

"The kittens. Halloween's having kittens."

I heard licking and soft mewing.

"You're her nest, Jenny."

I tried to raise my head to see, but my belly was in the way. I went back to sleep. I was no threat. I was too big to toss and turn.

In the morning, I slipped out of bed as carefully as I could without disrupting Halloween's family. We got a box for the kittens, filled it with soft rags and she carried them into it by their scruffs.

A week later, I gave birth to my daughter. Until the kittens were grown, every time Halloween and I heard a squeal or a squeak, we ran to see which was calling—kittens or baby. We passed each other in the hallway or gave each other inquiring glances in the kitchen before bolting side by side up the stairs.

We were inseparable from then on.

It will snow on Halloween. It always does. The veil between the worlds will be visible, the ancestors will visit.

Susie and I greet each other across the corridor from our porches. We're both setting out jack-o'-lanterns. We joke that we're "fair-weather friends," that this is our last meeting before the planting season strikes up again.

In the dusk, I pace around and around the garden, remembering its summer glory, taking my final census.

The lamium suffered too much heat and soil that dries too quickly. In spring, I'll move it to a cooler, wetter spot. The hops vine needs more room. It may prefer climbing the new lattice fence to living scrunched in the medicinal garden. The evening primrose seed never germinated.

Most of the fruit was terrific this year. Maybe it's time to plant a new peach tree . . . but *where*?

I look over the fence at Susie's garden. I can hardly believe the miracles she's produced.

I forgot to clip the spent lilac flowers and must do so soon, if they're to bloom with any vigor next spring. A new rose, "Golden Showers," didn't make it. Another case of forgetfulness. But the peonies and tulips, the poppies, even the crazy larkspur were unspeakably gorgeous. The liatrus and salvia, the scabiosa and that slow, slow yellow geum have finally come fully into their own.

The sawfly, which hit green ash trees this year, didn't get mine. On the other hand, there are signs of fire blight on two of the crab apples. . . .

Round and round. I try never to think of the garden in terms of "success" or "failure." No gardener I know really does. It seems inappropriate to bring the spirit of competition into this sacred place whose function is to mediate for the divine.

Gardens are completely personal, not up for judgment. There's no right or wrong in Nature. There are gardening flubs, miscalculations, and so on, but none of it matters much. The garden is always in flux, forgiving, ready and able to teach, ready and able to change on its own, as well as with our interventions. We bring our sorrows here to let our sorrows go; we bring our joy here to share our joy with birds and bees and flowers and trees. Paradise is precisely here, in the oldest, strongest, most majestic oak and in the thinnest, weakest, most anemic window plant. What counts is how we give ourselves to it.

Success or failure, triumphs or troubles, whenever I look over the garden from my bedroom perch, I can see nothing but perfection, simply the Nature of it all. Everything in the garden coexists in constant, active relation. *I am.*

Here, linear time ceases, so that history and myth blend seamlessly with this day, this moment, this breath. In the garden we are entirely of the cycle: in summer we sense its retreat; in winter we hear the echoing green.

I suck the cold October air into my throat, sitting on the back stoop, watching the sunset, the spectral elm, twisting kern dollies from twigs, grasses, and the last of the chrysanthemums.

ACKNOWLEDGMENTS

This book would never have happened without photographer Valari Jack, who a few years ago took photos of my garden for her own project. Her pictures fertilized my imagination and got me going. I thank her for her goodness in allowing me to use a few of them here and for her immense patience with me.

For this book's broader conception, her wonderful editorial skills, and her many kindnesses, I thank Rosemary Ahern.

The drawing of the abduction of Persephone in the chapter for September, was created for me as a woodcut by my daughter, Sarah C. Bell, an artist who's often been my collaborator. I am infinitely grateful for her love, her gifts, and her devotion.

I'm indebted to the contemporary poets and writers who gave me permission to reprint their breathtaking work: Tree Bernstein, Reed Bye, Merrill Gilfillan, Lucy R. Lippard, Bernadette Mayer, Edward Sanders, Jane Wodening, and John Wright. Some of their extraordinary books are listed in the bibliography.

To the dear poets of the past with whom I grew up and whose work I've included here, I pay obeisance and send gratitude across the ages.

I can't begin to list all those who've galvanized, supported, and inspired me as a writer and/or gardener, let alone thank them all here. Some include Lani Abbott, LaVon Alt, Elizabeth Bell, Rick

Breese, Julie Carpenter, Christopher Collom, Sierra Collom, Molly Davies, Greg D'Avis, Ellen Geiger, Lisa Gesner, J Gluckstern, Bobbie Louise Hawkins, Nita Morrow Hill, Caroline Hinkley, Ellen Klaver, Marilyn Krysl, the Leggetts one and all, Timothy Lange, Mary Jane Makepeace, Marilynne Mason, Patricia McFerran, Polly Motley, Max Regan, Karen Ripley, Randy Roark, Suzy Roesler, Mabeth Sanderson, Kristine Smock, Diana Velasquez, Peter Warshall, Karen Wilding, and Peter Lamborn Wilson.

And, of course, there are Susan Chandler and Stephen Remmert, key players in my current gardening life. Bless you.

Mostly, I thank my husband, Jack Collom, for his remarkable generosity. He has opened and enriched my life immeasurably, not the least with his love of Nature and poetry.

My beloved son, Matthew Heath, brought charm and wildness to my garden and makes my life ferociously wonderful and scary. I'm truly grateful, though still a little shaky when I think back on superhero stunts, broken limbs, and other hair-raising antics.

I give this book as well to my grandson Cameron Heath and my stepgrandson Joshua Lerman, new and amazing people in the world, who are causing me to rethink the garden once again. Years ago, it was entirely available to my children: I'm still stepping on and digging up Matthew's Legos, marbles, and toy soldiers and Sarah's autopsied doll parts and toy trucks. Today, my garden accommodates my own childlike fancies. Soon, it may provide the next generation with joy, imagination, peace, and place.

A SELECTED BIBLIOGRAPHY

Anderson, William. *Green Man: The Archetype of Our Oneness with the Earth*. New York: HarperCollins, 1990.

Baker, Margaret. *Folklore and Customs of Rural England*. Newton Abbot, London: David & Charles, 1974.

Beardsley, John. *Gardens of Revelation: Environments by Visionary Artists*. New York: Abbeville Press, 1995.

Berger, John. *And our faces, my heart, brief as photos*. New York: Pantheon, 1984.

Bernstein, Tree. *On the Way Here*. Boulder, Co.: Baksun Books, 1997.

Bownas, Geoffrey. *Japanese Rainmaking and Other Folk Practices*. London: George Allen & Unwin, 1963.

Briggs, Katherine. *An Encyclopedia of Fairies, Hobgoblins, Brownies, Bogies and Other Supernatural Creatures*. New York: Pantheon, 1976.

Bye, Reed. *Passing Freaks and Graces*. Boulder, Co.: Rodent Press/Erudite Fangs, 1996.

Calvino, Italo. *Italian Folktales, Selected and Retold*. New York: Harcourt, Brace, Jovanovich, 1980.

Campbell, Joseph. *The Masks of God: Primitive Mythology*. New York: Penguin, 1987.

Carmichael, Alexander. *Carmina Gadelica, Hymns & Incantations Collected in the Highlands and Islands of Scotland in the Last Century*. Edinburgh: Floris Books, 1992.

Cerny, Charlene and Seriff, Suzanne, eds. *Recycled/Re-Seen: Folk Art from the Global Scrap Heap*. New York: Harry N. Abrams, 1996.

Christian, Roy. *Old English Customs.* London: Hastings House, 1966.

Clarkson, Rosetta E. *Magic Gardens.* New York: Collier Books, 1992.

Collins, Marie, and Davis, Virginia. *A Medieval Book of Seasons.* New York: HarperCollins, 1992.

Collom, Jack. *Arguing with Something Plato Said.* Boulder, Co.: Rocky Ledge Cottage Editions, 1990.

————. *Dog Sonnets.* Hoboken, N.J.: Jensen/Daniels, Talisman House, 1998.

Crossley, Kevin. *The Norse Myths.* New York: Pantheon, 1980.

Crowell, Robert L. *The Lore & Legends of Flowers.* Illustrated by Anne Ophelia Dowden. New York: Thomas Y. Crowell, 1982.

D'Andrea, Jeanne. *Ancient Herbs in the J. Paul Getty Museum Gardens.* Malibu, Calif.: J. Paul Getty Museum, 1982.

Diamond, Irene, and Orenstein, Gloria Femen, eds. *Reweaving the World: The Emergence of Ecofeminism.* San Francisco: Sierra Club Books, 1990.

Ehrenreich, Barbara, and English, Deirdre. *Witches, Midwives and Nurses: A History of Women Healers.* New York: Feminist Press, 1973.

Eliade, Mircea. *Myths, Dreams and Mysteries.* Translated by Philip Mairet. New York: Harper & Row, 1960.

Emrich, Duncan. *Folklore on the American Land.* Boston: Little, Brown, 1974.

Evans-Wentz, W. Y. *The Fairy Faith in Celtic Countries.* New York: Citadel Press, 1990.

Francis, Mark, and Hester, Randolph T. Jr., eds. *The Meaning of Gardens: Idea, Place and Action.* Boston: MIT Press, 1990.

Freeman, Margaret. *Herbs for the Medieval Household for Cooking, Healing and Divers Uses.* New York: The Metropolitan Museum of Art, 1979.

Galeano, Eduardo. *Memory of Fire, A Trilogy,* New York: Pantheon, 1985.

Gantz, Jeffrey, trans. *The Mabinogion.* New York: Penguin, 1976.

García Lorca, Federico. *The Gypsy Ballads of García Lorca.* Translated by Rolfe Humphries. Bloomington, Ind.: University Press, 1953.

Gaster, Theodor. *New Year: Its History, Customs and Superstitions.* New York: Abelard-Schuman, 1955.

Geismar, Maxwell, ed. *The Whitman Reader.* New York: Pocket Books.

Gilfillan, Merrill. *Burnt House to Paw Paw: Appalachian Notes.* West Stockbridge, Mass.: Hard Press, 1997.

Grace, Eric C. *The World of the Monarch Butterfly.* San Francisco: Sierra Club Books, 1997.

Graves, Robert. *The White Goddess.* New York: Farrar, Straus and Giroux, 1948.

———. *The Greek Myths.* Volume 1 and 2. New York: Penguin, 1955.

Heath, Jennifer. *A House White with Sorrow: Ballad for Afghanistan.* Boulder, Co.: Rodent Press, 1996.

———. *On the Edge of Dream: The Women of Celtic Myth and Legend.* New York: Plume, 1998.

Hill, Nita Morrow. *Your Essential Nature: A Guidebook of Essential Oils for Energy Workers.* Boulder, Co.: Baksun Books, 1998.

Hobhouse, Penelope. *Plants in Garden History.* London: Pavilion, 1992.

Jackson, Kenneth Hurlstone. *A Celtic Miscellany: Translations from the Celtic Literatures.* New York: Penguin, 1971.

James, E. O. *Seasonal Feasts and Festivals.* New York: Barnes & Noble, 1961.

Kees, Hermann. *Ancient Egypt: A Cultural Typography.* Edited by T. G. H. James. Chicago: University of Chicago Press, 1961.

Kellaway, Deborah, ed. *The Virago Book of Women Gardeners.* London: Virago, 1996.

Kerényi, C. *Eleusis: Archetypal Image of Mother and Daughter.* Translated by Ralph Manheim. New York: Schocken, 1977.

Kowalchick, Claire, and Hylton, William, eds. *Rodale's Illustrated Encyclopedia of Herbs,* Emmaus, Penn.: Rodale Press, 1987.

Kramer, Samuel Noah. *History Begins at Sumer: Thirty-nine Firsts in Man's Recorded History.* Philadelphia: University of Pennsylvania Press, 1981.

Lai, T. C. *Noble Fragrance, Chinese Flowers and Trees.* Swindon, 1977.

Lane, Beldon C. *Landscapes of the Sacred: Geography and Narrative in American Spirituality.* New York: Paulist Press, 1988.

Levi-Strauss, Claude. *The Raw and the Cooked, Introduction to the Science of Mythology.* Vol. 1. Translated by John and Doreen Weightman. New York: Harper Torchbooks, 1969.

Lippard, Lucy R. *Overlay: Contemporary Art and the Art of Prehistory.* New York: The New Press, 1983.

———. *The Lure of the Local: Senses of Place in a Multicultural Society.* New York: The New Press, 1997.

Mabey, Richard, ed. *The New Age Herbalist.* New York: Collier Books, 1988.

Mars, Brigitte. *Natural First Aid.* Pownal, Vt.: Storey Publishers, 1999.

———. *Dandelion Medicine.* Pownal, Vt.: Storey Publishers, 1999.

Martin, Laura C. *The Folklore of Birds.* Old Saybrook, Conn.: The Globe Pequot Press, 1993.

Mayer, Bernadette. *Another Smashed Pinecone.* New York: United Artists Books, 1998.

Mazzanti, Anna, ed. *Niki de Saint Phalle: The Tarot Garden.* Milan: Edizioni Charta, 1998.

Merivale, Patricia. *Pan the Goat-God: His Myth in Modern Times.* Boston: Harvard University Press, 1969.

Monaghan, Patricia. *The Book of Goddesses and Heroines.* St. Paul, Minn.: Llewellan, 1993.

Moore, Charles; Mitchell, William; and Turnbull, William Jr. *The Poetics of Gardens.* Boston: MIT Press, 1997.

Nicholson, Philippa, ed. *V. Sackville-West's Garden Book.* New York: Atheneum, 1969.

Nollman, Jim. *Why We Garden: Cultivating a Sense of Place.* New York: Henry Holt, 1994.

Nordh, Katarina. *Aspects of Ancient Egyptian Curses and Blessings: Conceptual Background and Transmission.* Uppsala, Sweden: Uppsala University, 1996.

O'Donohue, John. *Anam Cara: A Book of Celtic Wisdom.* New York: HarperCollins, 1997.

O'Flaherty, Wendy Doniger. *Other People's Myths: The Cave of Echoes.* Chicago: University of Chicago Press, 1988.

Opie, Iona and Peter. *The Lore and Language of Schoolchildren.* Oxford, England: Clarendon Press, 1959.

———. *The Classic Fairy Tales.* Oxford, England: Oxford University Press, 1974.

Petrie, Flinders. *Religious Life in Ancient Egypt.* London: Constable, 1924.

Prest, John. *The Garden of Eden: The Botanic Garden and the Re-Creation of Paradise.* New Haven: Yale University Press, 1981.

Pulleyn, Simon. *Prayer in Greek Religion.* Oxford, England: Oxford University Press, 1997.

Rieu, E.V., *Virgil, The Pastoral Poems.* Edited and translated by E.V. Rieu. London: Penguin Books, 1949.

Rodale, J. I. and Staff. *The Complete Book of Composting.* Emmaus, Penn.: J. I. Rodale Press, 1971.

Rosenthal, M. L., ed. *Poetry in English, An Anthology.* Oxford, England: Oxford University Press, 1987.

Rothenberg, Jerome, ed. *Technicians of the Sacred: A Range of Poetries from Africa, America, Asia, Europe and Oceania.* Berkeley: University of California Press, 1985.

Sanders, Edward. *1968: A History of Verse*. Santa Rosa, Calif.: Black Sparrow, 1997.

Sanders, Miriam. *The Nature Writing of Miriam Sanders*. Woodstock, N.Y.: Woodstock Journal Publications, 1997.

Sechrist, Elizabeth Hough, ed. *One Thousand Poems for Children: Based on the Selections of Roger Ingpen*. Philadelphia: Macrae-Smith, 1946.

Shakir, M. H., trans. *The Qur'an*. Elmhurst, N.Y.: Tahrike Tarsile Qur'an, 1990.

Sheldrake, Rupert. *The Rebirth of Nature: The Greening of Science and God*. New York: Bantam, 1991.

Sholapurkar, G. R. *Religious Rites and Festivals of India*. Delhi: Bharatiya Vidya Prakashan.

Shuttle, Penelope, and Redgrove, Peter. *The Wise Wound: Myths, Realities and Meaning of Menstruation*. New York: Bantam, 1990.

Singh, Gopal. *The Religion of the Sikhs*. Delhi: Asia Publishing House, 1971.

Springer, Lauren. *The Undaunted Garden*. Golden, Co.: Fulcrum, 1994.

Sproul, Barbara C. *Primal Myths: Creation Myths Around the World*. New York: HarperCollins, 1991.

Toor, Frances. *Mexican Folkways*. New York: Crown, 1950.

Tyldesley, Joyce. *Daughters of Isis: Women of Ancient Egypt*. New York: Penguin, 1994.

Vickery, Roy. *Oxford Dictionary of Plant Lore*. Oxford, England: Oxford University Press, 1995.

Wilson, Peter Lamborn, and Weinberg, Bill. *Avant Gardening: Ecological Struggle in the City and the World*. New York: Autonomedia, 1999.

Wodening, Jane. *The Inside Story*. Boulder, Co.: Baksun Books/Rodent Press, 1996.

———. *Mountain Woman Tales*. Boulder, Co.: Baksun Books, 1996.